Praise for

SEX IN PUBLIC

"*Sex in Public* cogently dispels the myth that certain expressions of sexuality are 'correct' and 'normal,' while others are 'incorrect' or 'abnormal.' Drawing from the sociological literature, interviews with people across diverse sexual identities and communities, and their own personal experiences, Angela Jones makes a powerful case that sex is multidimensional, ever-shifting, and deeply social."

—Julia Serano, author of *Whipping Girl*

"An exquisite blend of research-based insights and real-world examples about the unpredictable realm of sexual behavior, *Sex in Public* is a juicy read! Never coy, Angela Jones confronts what is both deliciously creative and stiflingly constrained about sex. They show us that it is precisely the act of trying to understand those repressive forces that frees our sexual imaginations, making sex a vital pathway toward a better collective future."

—Jane Ward, author of *The Tragedy of Heterosexuality*

"*Sex in Public* dares to explore sexual sociology without defanging the erotic. Angela Jones writes fearlessly about their own sexual subcultures while remaining curious about the lives and identities of others. Rigorously deep, gleefully vulgar, accessibly welcoming. A new classic!"

—Tina Horn, author of *Why Are People into That?*

"Angela Jones has offered a timely Black feminist primer on erotic empowerment. Jones rightly insists that empowerment isn't just about individual autonomy, it's about actively crafting a social world that prioritizes sex education, sexual literacy, joy, and a fierce commitment to dismantling intersecting structures of domination. Fearless, candid, and bold, *Sex in Public* is necessary reading for anyone interested in imagining a different kind of world, one that approaches eroticism and freedom as fundamentally linked."

—Jennifer C. Nash, author of *Black Feminism Reimagined*

SEX IN PUBLIC

SEX IN PUBLIC

The Transformative Social Power of Our Erotic Lives

ANGELA JONES

SEAL PRESS
New York

Seal Press
Hachette Book Group
1290 Avenue of the Americas, New York, NY 10104
www.sealpress.com

Printed in the United States of America

First Edition: June 2026

Published by Seal Press, an imprint of Hachette Book Group, Inc. The Seal Press name and logo is a registered trademark of the Hachette Book Group.

The Hachette Speakers Bureau provides a wide range of authors for speaking events. To find out more, go to www.hachettespeakersbureau.com or email HachetteSpeakers@hbgusa.com.

Seal books may be purchased in bulk for business, educational, or promotional use. For more information, please contact your local bookseller or the Hachette Book Group Special Markets Department at special.markets@hbgusa.com.

The publisher is not responsible for websites (or their content) that are not owned by the publisher.

Print book interior design by Amy Quinn.

Library of Congress Control Number: 2025046087

ISBNs: 9781541605435 (hardcover), 9781541605459 (ebook)

LSC-C

Printing 1, 2026

CONTENTS

AUTHOR'S NOTE

This book contains research on and personal accounts of sexual abuse, sexual violence, systemic trauma, and discrimination. I never describe sexual assault in detail. Still, some readers will want to know that discussions of sexual violence appear throughout the book. Please read with care.

INTRODUCTION

Humans have been thinking about fucking, talking about fucking, drawing, filming, and simulating fucking in art, and telling others how they should or should not be fucking since the beginning of recorded history. Artifacts, from art to writing to fertility totems, date back to when the first *Homo sapiens* evolved from their hominid predecessors some two to three hundred thousand years ago.

Our ancestors were just as obsessed with eroticism as we are today. Unfortunately for us, advanced economies, technologies, and systems of governance and surveillance have complicated contemporary sexuality. As new advances introduce new opportunities for human connection, corporeal pleasures, and empowerment, erotic change also presents new dangers and reinforces existing systems of inequality, thwarting sexual liberation on a grand scale.

Sex is everywhere, and yet so many of us lack the foundational knowledge to understand it. To improve our sexual literacy, we must first and foremost recognize sex as a public matter, not a private one. Sex is never solitary. It is just as much a social ritual as it is an individual quest for pleasure. Yet, so many books about sex and sexuality leave the social part out, giving their readers the misguided idea that their sexual problems are only personal ones.

Social messaging is clear—sex and sexuality are personal. Our bodies, what's going on inside them, and our desires, behaviors, and identities—especially non-normative ones—are private. What happens in relationships and any sexual subcultures we might belong to is a private matter. All of this is a lie.

Our sexualities are political, and without a deep understanding of their complexities and how the world around us shapes them, our capacity to make healthy and empowering decisions surrounding our sexuality is hampered. When we acknowledge that sexuality is necessarily communal, we open up new avenues for individual empowerment and social changes that allow for more human freedom.

Social systems set the stage for all the sexual theater in our lives, but you'd never know it from the individualistic ways that most people talk about sex. The public understanding of sex thus far has been shaped by psychologists, evolutionary biologists, and sexologists, who have failed to grasp that sex is always political and enacted within systems of power. This book flips this tired script!

We can't truly make sense of sexuality without also understanding its economic, political, and social roots. Over the past few decades, the work of feminist thinkers and sociologists has provided us a set of tools for seeing these dimensions of social life in a more dynamic relationship with one another. Only by equipping ourselves with these insights can we see sex and sexuality in all of its multifaceted dynamism. By understanding sexuality in these more holistic terms, we can *all* live our best sex lives and rethink how we, within global cultures, can regulate and grapple with social issues related to sex in ways that acknowledge dangers but simultaneously prioritize bodily autonomy, sexual justice, and pleasure.

The time to recognize sexuality as a political force, and to stop seeing sex as a private matter, is now! Understanding sexuality fully and the power of the erotic requires us to recognize and call out the social systems and political mechanisms that constrain human sexuality like an eighteenth-century corset. This book is an invitation to loosen those ties, or maybe even to burn that torture device entirely.

I was about seven the first time I asked what, for some parents, is *the* dreaded question: "What's sex?" I remember sitting on the edge of the yellow bathtub in our oh-so-1970s bathroom as my mother, the free-love hippie activist, looked at me, smiled, and carefully answered. The precise details are lost to time, but I know she gave me an age-appropriate, clinically informed, albeit heteronormative response. In some ways, I was lucky not to be subjected to nonsensical stories about storks or heavenly miracles. In other ways, I wish I could go back and deliver to my younger self the sexual education that I needed.

To her credit, my public school teacher mother responded to my sexual precociousness with affirmation, warmth, and reassurance. Curiosity about my body and sex was normal, she told me. Pulling out our *World Book* encyclopedias, we flipped through the human anatomy overlays as she taught me about my body and the bodies of boys and men. When I was about eleven, she bought me a *Playgirl* magazine, so that I could see *real* men's naked bodies—a choice she may have regretted later on.

My younger pervert-self cut out smaller images of naked men and kept them in one of those little shiny gold cardboard jewelry boxes. Dripping in the excitement of a concupiscent preteen, I wiped my brow and showed the jewels to my friends at school. Two kids told their parents about my old-school dick pics, and they were no longer allowed to be friends with me. This was one of the first times that I can vividly recall beginning to realize that the sex education I was receiving was vastly different from that of my peers—and that for some, sex and the human body were the sites of shame and secrecy.

Nakedness was not taboo in our house, and I have an inordinate number of naked early childhood pictures to prove it. We never used euphemisms—favoring vulva, labia, clitoris, penis, testes, scrotum, and so on. But my friends had "privates," "flowers," "monkeys," "things," and "pee-pees." As I got older, it was clear how important it was to my mother that I did not feel shame about my body, and that I understood my body's capacity for pleasure—that I knew what and where my clitoris was, and that masturbation was normal and natural. Still, as well-intentioned as my mother was, we can never fully escape the broader social structures that insidiously socialize us.

When I was around twelve, my best friend, Aiyana, and I used to make out frequently. She'd pretend to be the man, and we'd couch our exploration in the heteronormative scripts that were available to us. At this age, I was a so-called tomboy who felt attracted to girls and boys. Still, I had no language to understand my desires, just the messaging around me—Disney princesses and princes, Ken and Barbie, Clair and Cliff Huxtable, and, as if in big flashing lights, the message that being gay or anywhere outside of expected gender and sexual norms was shameful.

My mother did not hide queerness from me, per se, but LGBTQ sexuality was not a part of the curriculum she had in mind. My uncle was gay and lived with his partner in San Francisco in the 1980s. His partner was his *friend*, and when my uncle died at thirty-three from AIDS in 1985, I was not told what he died from—a decision my family felt shielded me from the collateral damage of HIV and AIDS stigma and gay bigotry.

Part of me now understands that it was a different time. But the absence of honesty about my uncle's sexuality and his death taught me that being gay was something you hid, and something society punished you for. His death and the revelation of the whole truth, years later, were both pivotal moments in my sexual socialization.

I wish I could have received a far more honest and straightforward story, not just about my uncle's sexuality, but about all the other parts of our sexualities—our erotic desires, behaviors, identities, relationships, and communities. I wish my education regarding consent had not begun and ended with warnings never to speak to or take rides from strange men that I did not know. After all, all the men who sexually assaulted me over the years were people I knew.

Sometimes I think about all the missed educational opportunities in my childhood and beyond, speculating that if they had been handled differently, it would have saved me a world of hurt and harm. This book was inspired by all the things I wish I had been taught, my hard-earned lessons, and the years of research that have led me to know there are better ways to understand sexuality—ways that lead us to erotic empowerment and sexual liberation.

Sexuality is messy. To the extent that sociologists have written about sexuality, most have focused on the three primary dimensions of sexuality—what feminist sociologists have termed the *sexuality prism* of sexual desires, sexual behavior, and sexual identities.[1] As the sociological formula goes, the absence or presence of what we want (desire) motivates what we do (behavior) and the labels we assign to ourselves because of our actions (identity).

But our desires do not always align with how we move through the world and describe ourselves. Sociologists have aptly named this misalignment *sexual discordance*. This discordance often drives individuals to endlessly search the bookstore's self-help aisle for a cure for their sexual blues. People have desires they choose to never act on. For example, a man might secretly want his wife to strap on a dildo and fuck or "peg" him in the ass.[2] Still, he would sooner turn to celibacy than utter a word of his desires to anyone—including his wife, who is his best friend and life companion.

Folks may also engage in sexual behaviors that are seemingly out of step with how others understand their sexual labels. For example, feminist sociologists have studied straight-identified college girls who frequently hook up with other women at college parties; some insist they are not bisexual or lesbian but are having fun and building *sexual capital*.[3] Many of them feel that public displays of sex acts with other women excite men and increase their marketability among men, whom they see as potential sexual partners in what sociologists call *hookup culture*.[4]

The fact is that sexuality is far more fluid than meets the eye, and the social categories and labels we rely on often obscure this reality. Still, people need cultural and community spaces where they feel safe in order to reconcile their desires with their behaviors and identities. The social scripts of these milieux shape how we understand and enact

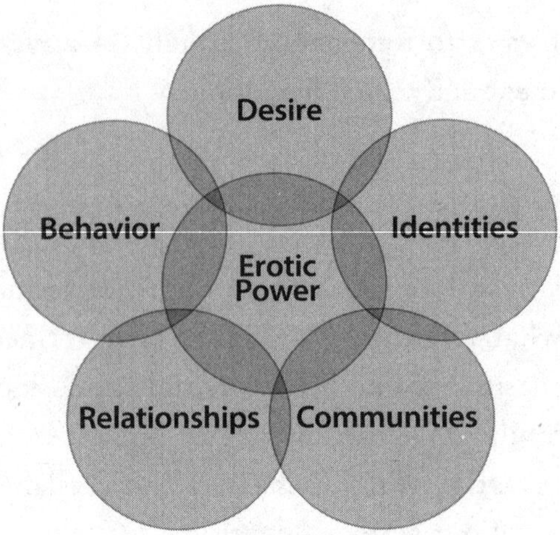

The erotic power model of sexuality.

our own desires. This is why it is so critical to study the connections between our personal sexuality and the social contexts that shape and, hopefully, support it. If our communities do not affirm and support our sexualities, it leads to shame and sanctions.

Sexuality lives in the world through five interconnected dimensions: desire, behavior, identities, relationships, and communities. What this helps us understand is that our sexuality has a social life.

Sexuality organizes societies, shapes their regulation, and vice versa. The day's sexual mores govern political ideas and policy—in ways that we see playing out around the world, from the policing of people's uteruses to anti-trans legislation to the criminalization of sex work. Sexuality shapes our access to social institutions and experiences at the community and interpersonal levels. It drives where people live, their social circles, dress, and the rituals and events they attend. As we move through these environments, we internalize rules and norms, which, if we violate them, can be a source of undue shame. However, suppose we recognize the cultural and political underpinnings of shame. When shame shows up, we know this part of our personality has arrived to ask us to think more about the social rule we are breaking, and who needs to change—us or society?

Relationships and community are central aspects of sexuality. They are also sites where people produce erotic power. People form intimate relationships in various ways, with varying organizational structures, and, increasingly, in ways that disrupt *mononormativity*: the pervasive idea that monogamy and dyadic relationships are the ideals. Whether intimate relationships take the form of a one-night stand, swinger couples hooking up at a sex party, or a polycule of three or more people, these unions are the site of eroticism. People find erotic empowerment and joy when they explore their desires and identity-specific erotic needs within supporting relationships and communities. When this happens en masse, it expands sexual and relational norms for everyone.

Sexuality also has a cultural life. One of my favorite examples plays out in feminist Jane Ward's phenomenal book *Not Gay*. Ward explores the lives of straight white men who have sex with other straight white men. These men post on Craigslist to get a quick blow job and watch sports with other dudes, all while insisting that this sexual behavior does not make them gay. Before judging, listen to their rationale: For these men, attending the occasional circle jerk or engaging in oral sex with other men does not make them gay because they do not participate in gay culture of any sort. No Pride parades. No bathhouses. No rainbows. No posh flats in the gayborhood. No desire for a romantic relationship with a man. No LGBTQIA+ activism. No gay pubs—not gay!

Zooming out, we can see that sexualities have a cultural life, with their own language, norms, values, symbols, and material culture. Leather (gay BDSM) communities developed the hanky code, using a system of different colored handkerchiefs to signal interests in various forms of erotic play.[5] Today, while at the popular Oasis Aqualounge social club in Toronto, people can use different colored plastic bracelets to signal their sexual tastes and provide nonverbal consent. An upside-down pineapple in the proper context will let other swinger couples know you and yours are on the same team. These subcultures create spaces for affirmation, support, dignity, play, and pleasure.

Belonging is another source of gratification and is integral to combating sexual shame.

Drawing inspiration from the Black feminist poet Audre Lorde, who wrote about the *uses of the erotic* as a source of power and strength for women, this book explores the erotic empowerment that we can find when we are connected to our bodies and know our sexuality fully, as well as human-produced erotic power that changes the world.

Black feminists have reshaped conceptualizations of the erotic for decades, freeing eroticism from its conflation with sex. We broaden the understanding of *eroticism*, defining it as an embodied human desire for connection and intimacy. As Lorde reminds us, "the erotic is not a question only of what we do; it is a question of how acutely and fully we can feel in the doing. . . . The need for sharing deep feeling is a human need."[6]

Thus, this book is about eroticism, not just sex. And, when all is said and done, you will come away with an understanding of how erotic desires operate within our bodies, how the world around us shapes our sexuality, and how, despite social and political regulation, people harness deep pleasures by living authentic sex lives in like-minded relationships and supportive communities.

When we expand our thinking about sexuality by connecting it to social forces and systems and when we appreciate the multidimensional nature of sexuality, we know our sexuality fully. This allows us to powerfully assert our desires and govern our sex lives better, with less external regulation. These transformations can ward off bad sex, increase pleasure, expand public ideas, and promote social change—that is, erotic power in action.

Empowerment has become a depoliticized buzzword. I believe erotic empowerment is a somatic experience, profoundly shaped by the practices and behaviors of others, our cultural milieux, and the systems of power that govern our lives. As I'll argue about the concepts of consent and sex, too, there is no one-size-fits-all definition if we understand these terms through the lenses of embodiment and power. What empowerment feels like and the specific conditions needed to have the experience vary from person to person.

Still, in its most general sense, I define *erotic empowerment* as a set of corporeal sensations produced when eroticism is rooted in bodily autonomy, consent, open communication, and respect for boundaries. It is facilitated when we recognize that risk and power are present in all erotic encounters, leading to intentional practices of care. Personally, because power shapes all sex, I have also felt profoundly empowered when eroticism defies norms and challenges ideas about appropriate sexuality.

I also use the term *erotic empowerment*, as opposed to *sexual empowerment*, to encompass a broader range of intimate encounters and to ensure we do not foreclose empowerment for those who, for myriad reasons, don't desire or engage in what people traditionally define as sex.

Erotic empowerment is a somatic experience, not simply a mindset. It flows like lava in our tissues. Popular empowerment discourses are often predicated on what philosophers refer to as mind–body dualism. For some, empowerment is an attitude, and once a person has acquired new knowledge and mastered specific skills, this empowered person can use their body to access more pleasurable sex. But no such division exists—our mind is but one part of our body, and there is no "I" separate from the body.

Put simply, I want our collective thinking about empowerment, of which our mindset and thought processes are but one networked part, to center the body. Empowerment reflects not just a way of thinking, but embodied practices. Thus, I want to shift our expression of this process from "I did *X* to become an empowered person" to "I experience empowerment when *X* happens" and "This is what empowerment feels like in my body."

Empowerment is often portrayed as a solitary journey of discovering the self, building self-confidence, and cultivating self-love. I am so down with this and agree that experiencing erotic empowerment requires us to understand our sexual socialization and to nurture and sustain shame-free relationships with our desires and bodies. However, this definition and thinking still fall short.

The logic of empowerment as a mindset neglects that bodily shame is also a structural problem, that the social forces and industries around us are what make us feel shame, and that, as a result, shame is deeply rooted in so many people's bodies.[7] Frankly, we need to stop pretending that anyone can fully escape the *body-shame industrial complex* without the destruction of the capitalist industries that function to make us feel like we are broken and that their endless, costly products will fix us.

As Sonya Renee Taylor showcases in *The Body Is Not an Apology*, when we understand the economic, social, and political forces that produce self-loathing of our bodies, we can advocate for and self-actualize radical self-love to heal the harms of socially imposed bodily shame.[8] Readers, I so hope that aspects of this book will help advance this goal for you.

Empowerment is a political and embodied experience, not an object to be acquired. As Koa Beck argues in *White Feminism*, "sanitizing 'empowerment' away from radical, deeply historic activism was pivotal for fourth-wave white feminism because it had to become transactional—something you could buy, obtain, and experience as a product rather than an amorphous feeling that rushed in from challenging power."[9]

So, no matter what snake-oil salespeople tell you, you cannot buy empowerment. It requires introspection, self-work, and action to create new embodied practices. Erotic empowerment is also not a fixed or permanent state of being, a synonym for pleasure, or the equivalent of sexual conquest, nor is it magically unlocked when someone's so-called body count reaches 100—I assure you, when I did, no balloons fell from the ceiling. Nobody brought me an oversized empowerment check.

I want to prompt everyone to consider what erotic empowerment *feels* like in their bodies—what do we need to know about ourselves, and what forms of social nourishment do we need from others to have the experience? Once we understand the Social Life of Sexuality, it will demand that we ask new questions about erotic empowerment. What do our bodies need to feel it? What social conditions? What forms of care? How do I need others to show up and support my sexuality? What external restrictions has culture placed on my sexuality, and does it feel empowering when I reject them? And how does that experience feel throughout the body?

Erotic empowerment requires that we not only think about what we need to do for ourselves, but also what we need from our partners, communities, and social systems around us. The world around us also needs to change!

And this is precisely where erotic power comes in!

Erotic power is a social force that results from the collective expression of human sexuality. Human eroticism is a powerful social force that motivates people to change the world through what feminist artist-scholar Gigi Otálvaro-Hormillosa calls *erotic resistance.*[10] When people, like the ones I'll soon introduce, make their sexualities publicly visible, it causes social change. Erotic power prompts cultural change, introducing new language and terms, values, beliefs, norms, and aspects of material cultures and technologies.

Consider sexual subcultures that once hid in the dark. As more people openly practice polyamory and BDSM and as asexual people, swingers, sex partygoers, those working in sexual economies, and other societal rule breakers come out of the shadows and proudly stand erect in the mainstream, it pushes the boundaries of acceptable sexual behavior and identities. The erotic power that people produce expands the realm of what's readily available for all.

So, for scholars, thinkers, policymakers, scientists, and armchair theorists, I offer *erotic power* as a framework that enables us to examine how eroticism shapes social life and reshapes systems of power, as well as how the collective expression of sexuality brings about change. Centering *erotic dialectics* allows us to name and study the ongoing tug-of-war between the institutions that work to control and regulate human desire, sexuality, and bodies and the people who resist those regulations.

No institution is untouched by human eroticism. Our expansive sexualities—our desires, behaviors, identities, relationships, and communities—affect law, medicine, economies, families, media, and so much more. We must talk about how institutions and people have responded to *erotic change* over time. For example, political leaders' responses to erotic change are too often rooted in their quests for naked power, as well as fear and bigotry, leading to harmful and repressive policymaking rooted in prohibitionist logics, which the sex rabble then continue to resist—rinse and repeat. Still, I also want to complicate the simplicity of this metanarrative of historical and cultural change.

Erotic change is constant, but it is also not a cut-and-dried linear story. When people's collective production of erotic power fosters cultural changes, these effects are not inherently politically progressive or supportive of all forms of justice. Instead, what we observe is that most of the time, as sexualities become more public, they are commodified and often reproduce and reinforce systems of inequity and forms of injustice, even as they open up pockets for pleasure and resistance and spaces for affirmation, joy, and erotic empowerment.

In erotic spaces of transgression, yet another erotic dialectic becomes visible. As you will find over and over again in this book, while the places and communities that people create for their collective eroticism can challenge systems that regulate and control sexuality, they are also often sites where racism, classism, ableism, and cissexism show up, excluding and harming people. On the ground, people's individual and community-level journeys for pleasure and empowerment often stifle sexual liberation on a grander scale, which requires dismantling systems of oppression.

Yet, I have also traveled to and explored spaces that provide blueprints for sexual liberation beyond individual pleasure and empowerment. I center people's experiences of individual and community-level eroticism and empowerment because they are the incubators of and playgrounds for what is possible on a grander scale. If these spaces of resistance, affirmation, and pleasure are enticing, I hope they will also serve as an invitation to everyone to join the sex rabble and resist.

I was not given the sex education I deserved, and I say that knowing I had it better than most in my generation. None of the institutions that socialize us—schools, family, media, religion, government, and so on—provided me with the necessary tools to comprehend my sexuality fully, navigate sexual violence, understand consent, demand pleasure and bodily autonomy, and ward off societal shame and stigma.

In the absence of an inclusive, shame-free, empirically and clinically informed, trauma-informed, and pleasure-centered sex-positive education that recognized the social life of sexuality and the political origins of sexual shame and stigma, I, like many sexual rule breakers, had to learn these things myself, much of it by trial and error.

Through lots of sex—solo, partnered, and in groups—I have learned much about my desires, my relationship to my own body, and how past trauma and existing systems of power shape how I do or don't communicate my desires, needs, and consent. Those of us who are sexually adventurous by societal standards often shy away from talking about experiences with sexual trauma and violence. We know all too well the ways that political pundits and others weaponize our experiences of sexual trauma to dismiss our sexualities as rooted in pathology, call us deviants, and drum up support for repressive policies and actions. Still, for so many of us, these experiences have shaped our sexuality and our relationship with sex and our bodies.

To be clear, I don't believe we can necessarily fuck our way to freedom because sexual liberation requires transforming social institutions and systems of inequality, but, for me, being a whore, both literally and figuratively, has been a critical tool for developing self-awareness. And some of the most vital lessons I have learned have been through failing at sex. Talk about kissing frogs. I have had some really bad and unenjoyable sex, but even those encounters have helped me come to know precisely what I desire, want, and need, and how to communicate all that to partners.

I have also learned so much through sexual adventure and play in non-normative sexual subcultures and by hanging out with other freaky people. Sex workers, queer and trans people, kink and leather folk, nonmonogamous people, and an entire cast of sexual rule breakers are the people who have deepened my understanding of my sexuality's relationship to the communities, cultures, and systems of power around me. These communities have shown me that bodily autonomy is the linchpin of sexual freedom. From these people, I first learned to expand my thinking about what counts as sex and to not get so caught up in a destination that I forget to enjoy all the forms of eroticism that come before I climax, if I even do. It is through the affirmation, care, and joys I've experienced in these communities that I've come to reject societally imposed shame.

My personal experiences have shaped my career as a sex researcher and writer. My desire to understand my sexuality better, in more profound and nuanced ways, led me to the science of sexuality and a wealth of published research across disciplines, which have helped me to understand sexuality as a physiological, psychological, and political phenomenon. This research has helped me to realize that sex and sexuality are not synonymous, and that understanding sexuality fully requires us to know our embodied desires, what we like in erotic behaviors (if we like them at all), our sexual identities, and how these individual aspects of our sexualities are also connected to relationships and communities. Having a complete understanding of our sexuality and how systems of power shape it allows us to make choices in our erotic lives that are consensual, more autonomous, empowering, and pleasurable.

But the personal is also political, and my voice is a sharp tongue speaking truth to power. Audre Lorde tells us that the time for marginalized people to talk about our experiences with our full chests is now because we were never meant to survive.[11] Shouldn't those experiences include the erotic? In a world that would rather see us gagged, speaking publicly about our desires, joys, sexual yearnings, pleasures, pains, and power is itself a political act.

As a Black feminist sociologist, I refuse to squander what I consider the gifts of Black feminism—the methodological, conceptual, and intellectual innovations that lead us to what I call the *Black Feminist Erotic Imagination*, a framework for studying and analyzing the complexities of human eroticism and its imbrication with systems of power and pleasure.[12] It reflects the feminist principles and values that guide my research and writing.

My work is rooted in long-standing Black feminist traditions and practices. As Brittney Cooper writes in *Eloquent Rage*, "I'm not merely a feminist who happens to be Black. I'm a Black Feminist, *capital B, capital F.* That means I learned my feminism from Black women, and my feminist theory and praxis is situated in the particular ways Black women have understood, thought about, and written about the problems of racism and sexism across space and time."[13]

Applying the Black Feminist Erotic Imagination entails focusing on and centering eroticism, power, marginality, pleasure, and embodiment, as these are critical lenses through which to analyze sexuality. My Black feminist approach to research and writing is intersectional and interdisciplinary, incorporating experiential knowledge—knowledge gained from personal experience. Brittney Miles notes, "Black feminist tools and frameworks cannot be separated from narrative and storytelling; they are intertwined."[14] The Black feminist tradition shows us that testifying allows for witnessing and sharing stories, with so much to teach everyone.

The purpose of this book is to undo what has been done to us. By looking to the example of marginalized sexualities worldwide, I seek to explain and explore each component of our sexualities, drawing on cutting-edge research with diverse people and communities to highlight how the world around us—institutions, systems of power, and cultural norms—shapes each facet of our sexualities *and* how our sexualities shape them.

After discussing the social life of sexuality and the history of the science of sex in the first chapter, in each one thereafter, I display one component of our sexualities to showcase its social life and help you relate it to your life. However, each piece is so deeply connected to the others that, even if I am discussing desire, for example, discussions of behavior, identities, relationships, and communities still appear. These slippages point to how intertwined desire, behavior, identities, relationships, and communities are as parts of our sexuality.

You'll meet asexual (ace) sex workers and other people on the ace spectrum who help demystify desire. I'll introduce you to the newest sexual technologies, and we'll see just what sex dolls can teach us about the relationship between systems of power and contemporary sexual behavior. I'll take you with me to sex clubs and introduce you to swingers of various stripes to highlight how our overlapping identities shape our erotic lives. Polyamorous people from around the world, foregrounding the voices of Black polyamorous educators and community leaders, demonstrate the central role that relationships play in our sexualities and how relational norms are changing every day. Together, we will explore BDSM erotic community spaces online and in Berlin and organizations such as the Lesbian Sex Mafia to understand the critical function of communities, which, when supportive and affirming, are vital to our sexual well-being.

Unlike other books that have told the stories of organized political movements concerned with sexual liberation, this book centers people's resistance in everyday life. Focusing on views "from the bottom" allows us to witness resistance. Like feminist philosopher and activist María Cristina Lugones, I believe that resistance isn't a political endgame, but a beginning and ongoing part of political struggle, reflecting human adaptivity and creativity.[15]

The perspectives of people who resist sexual norms and regulation animate this book. This means that, for some readers, the people and communities we'll meet may be unfamiliar; other readers may find themselves represented. Whether you are learning about particular desires, behaviors, identities, relationship styles, or communities for the first time or you are so familiar with these concepts you could write a book on them, there is always so much to learn from marginalized people who resist constraining social norms.

Throughout the book, I use these discussions to show how the erotic acts as a profound source of power from which humans exercise agency and draw pleasure. At times, as we will see, the erotic also acts as a catalyst for liberatory changes in the world. Through a politics of perversion, members of the sex rabble challenge respectability politics and generate change—changes that everyone can benefit from.

My sincerest hope is that this not remain a purely academic discussion—that the reader can use the erotic power model of sexuality as a framework to understand sexuality anew. Even as I focus on non-normative sexualities, this model and all the lessons in this book are open to everyone, regardless of their identities. Otherwise, sexuality is doomed to remain a biological, private, and personal matter.

So, with that—I invite you to *feel* the erotic power in these pages.

Chapter 1

THE SOCIAL LIFE OF SEXUALITY

Sexuality has been celebrated, regulated, revered, and punished for as long as humans have been human.[1] But it wasn't until the late nineteenth century that it became the subject of scientific study. And as soon as scientists started to fit sex and sexuality into a set of terminologies and systems, by classifying and evaluating consensual human desires and behaviors, they also pathologized them—marking some desires and behaviors as abnormal. Much of the intellectual history of the science of sex is marred by conflict over labeling, categorizing, and establishing normative and hierarchical systems of sexuality.

Never mind that countless historical artifacts and works of art and literature on the human experience celebrated ecstasies and freedoms of eroticism of all kinds. Instead, nineteenth-century scientists and their twentieth- and twenty-first-century followers set about cataloging what I'll call the three D's: deviance, disease, and dysfunction.

In some ways, this may not be so shocking—the eggheads with clipboards somehow managed to make sex boring! But there is a more sinister edge to the science of sexuality. As writer, sex educator, and sex worker Tina Horn argues in *Why Are People into That?*, the scientific impulse to pathologize people's ethical and consensual desires is no different in its goals and effects than that of the religions that label them sinful.[2] How different is it, really, if sexual rule breakers are being condemned on religious grounds, criminalized by vice laws, or monstered with medical terminology?

Yet, before we dismiss the whole body of scholarship that today's understanding of sexuality is built on, we can still learn something from the work of the past 140 or so years. The history of sexual science can not only help us understand where contemporary insights are coming from, but it also offers us a vantage point for seeing the socially constructed nature of ideas about sexuality *as* they are being broken down and remade.

Now, as interesting as I hope you find the upcoming brief history of sexual science, you might wonder what such an account has to do with your sexuality. Ideas born in the realms of science and academia do not live and die there. The people who create these ideas about sex and the sexual hierarchies they've imagined inform how the public understands sexuality. This understanding filters into the worlds of medicine, family life, the law, education, and media. So, even if you have never attended a research conference or read any of the books and articles by sexual scientists, their ideas show up in mainstream culture, institutions, and politics, from pop culture articles and social media reels to information at your doctor's office to governmental policy and hearings.

The history of the science of sex is also plagued by what I call *scientific sexism*—the willful rejection of feminist writing and theorizing as not scientific enough or too political. Because feminists draw from humanistic methods such as participant observation, conversational-style interviews, and other qualitative methods, including autoethnography and cultural studies methods, such as analyzing films and books, scientists in different fields have dismissed feminist work on sexuality as not objective enough and inappropriately political in its values and objectives.[3] The lack of engagement with feminism does us a significant disservice, hampering our complete understanding of sexuality as a political force.

This scientific approach showcases how sex and sexuality are socially constructed and imbued with power and how they serve as sites for resistance. As we will observe, sexual science has played a significant role in establishing the norms that the rule breakers in this book resist.

"I regard sex as the central problem of life. And now that the problem of religion has practically been settled, and that the problem of labor has at least been placed on a practical foundation, the question of sex—with the racial questions that rest on it—stands before the coming generations as the chief problem for solution," writes the English physician and eugenicist Havelock Ellis.[4]

Ellis is often cited as one of the so-called fathers of modern sexology, and his now-famous quote, which opened *Studies in the Psychology of Sex* in 1897, is one of those rare moments where people are actually using their full chest and not their dog whistles. At that time, especially during the Victorian era, religion and capitalist labor already had people on lock, Ellis gestured. Still, when it comes to sex, even religion and work can't always keep people ashamed and exhausted long enough to stop them from having all types of sex, from the vanilla to the freakiest, with all the wrong people. Gay panics and racial-sexual anxieties permeated the air that was breathing life into the science of sex.[5]

Sexology, the scientific study of human sexuality, was born out of a need to control people's bodies and, around the world, it became yet another site for the political weaponization of scientific knowledge to uphold heteropatriarchy, white supremacy, and capitalist wealth accumulation. Dominance requires controlling how people use their bodies, especially in sex. You can't build wealth and maintain patriarchal monogamous marriage between cisgender white women and white men if people do not stop getting it on across racial, gender, and class lines. Sexology, like all sciences, was shaped by the political and cultural context in which those ideas emerged.

The landmark publication that put all of the findings and flaws of these early scientists of sexuality on display was Richard von Krafft-Ebing's *Psychopathia Sexualis,* published in German in 1886 and translated into English in 1892. Setting the stage for the focus on deviance that would define the research that followed, this text essentially amounted to a laundry list of sexual behaviors that Krafft-Ebing deemed to be disorders.

This perspective didn't come out of the clear blue, and the social context for the work of Krafft-Ebing and his peers gives us crucial insight into *why* deviance was such a magnet for research. When Krafft-Ebing and his peers were developing this new field of scientific inquiry, social and legal prohibitions on sex were primarily focused on preserving the institution of heterosexual marriage under a system of patriarchy—*heteropatriarchy* for short. Perhaps, unsurprisingly, most of these scientists worked to establish scientific legitimacy for heteronormativity, building their work on the assumptions that sex between cisgender women and cisgender men is normal and that sex between people of the same gender is abnormal.[6]

Like many people in the nineteenth century, Krafft-Ebing understood sex in relation to procreation only. Any aspect of sex that diverged from this procreative function was, by definition, abnormal. This is another way of saying that some cultures of the time were most concerned about how any given sex act mapped onto a procreative/nonprocreative binary. It's also why one of the first scientific definitions of heterosexuality, written in a medical journal in 1892 by a US doctor named James Kiernan, referred to heterosexuality much differently than we do today. He defined it as a sexual disorder, in that it described people with "inclinations to both sexes," engaging in "abnormal methods of gratification," or nonprocreative sex acts.

In the United States, Kiernan's writing about disordered sex was occurring during the lead-up to and introduction of Jim Crow segregation codified into law under *Plessy v. Ferguson* in 1896. White people were obsessed with so-called miscegenation, and the idea of white and Black people fucking drove them up a wall. Stopping interracial sex and procreation was a key, yet underdiscussed, objective of Jim Crow, with long-lasting effects on the domains of sexuality.[7]

In the United States in the nineteenth and twentieth centuries, *scientific racism* was used to uphold the existing order. Scientists across disciplines created and used pseudoscience to lend support to white supremacist ideologies and political projects.[8] The United States has long been a nation obsessed with categorizing bodies and establishing systems to ensure the preservation of racial capitalism and heteropatriarchy—systems that have always been bedfellows. And at the time, economic shifts and migration into cities meant that sexuality was increasingly moving from behind closed bedroom doors into public view.[9] It is of little surprise that US doctors and scientists would have had an interest in ordering and disordering sexuality.

At the time of Krafft-Ebing's writing, Germany, too, was experiencing an economic boom and rapid industrialization, which meant that more and more people were moving into cities and into closer proximity to one another. Like many cities during modernity, urban life was entangled with what we might call the *sexual spirit of modernity*. Rapid economic and political shifts catalyzed new sexual cultures and sexual exploration with new people in new places. Urbanization and economic growth, alongside people's sexual curiosity and thirst for eroticism, led to increases in access to early film-based pornography, the number of brothels, interracial and interethnic sex, gay sex, public gender-bending, public drunkenness and partying, and so-called sin. And the early sexologists, near and far, were taking notes and names.

The lesson here is that we should never let the pretense of scientific objectivity fool us. Scientific knowledge is always shaped by the cultural and historical moment in which it is created, and it is always a site of power and resistance. Krafft-Ebing's work was no exception. This early sexology was part of a larger cultural project to define and condemn homosexual or any other nonprocreative relations as deviant.[10] Such efforts aimed to keep sexuality locked up and caged, behind closed doors—back in private—as if that were even possible.

Yet just as social forces worked to control and regulate piping-hot human desires, people stepped forward, privately and publicly, to resist. As normative and heteropatriarchal ideas took root, the German physician Magnus Hirschfeld was one of the key figures to defy them. In 1897, Hirschfeld founded the Scientific Humanitarian Committee, whose motto was "through science to justice"—a mantra I, like many Black feminists, live and write by. The Scientific Humanitarian Committee used science to counter the growing movement in psychology and politics that labeled LGBTQ people as abnormal and criminalized them.

Challenges to early pathologizing scientific work on sexuality came from many places within the academy, although with varying degrees of pushback and refocus away from heteronormativity. As the science of sexuality moved into the hands of psychologists, we can observe a slightly more progressive view, and I'm being generous here, in the work of Sigmund Freud, the founder of psychoanalysis, even as scientific investments in labeling so-called pathologies and a heteronormative order came with it.

Unlike his predecessors, Freud, living and writing in Austria, argued that humans can and do find gratification in many ways. In the *Three Essays on the Theory of Sexuality*, Freud theorized on human psychosexual development, arguing that at birth and early childhood, our sexual desires are "unfocused sexual libidinal drives" that have yet to be oriented in a normative direction. In other words, as humans, we are not sexually born one way or another. We are born with unfixed desires that must be tamed and socialized.

However—here come those heteronormative investments again—Freud argued that over time, and with healthy socialization, humans would sublimate non-normative desires and adopt heteropatriarchal standards, ensuring genetic fitness and maintaining social order. So, Freud still had much in common with his predecessors, letting his study of our sexual desires and psychosocial sexual development be defined by the relationship to socially constructed sexual abnormalities.

Another front opened up against the psychological focus on disorder when the biologists entered the fray, seeking to connect our erotic minds to our bodies. In the 1930s, biologist Alfred Kinsey led the US movement to establish a field of science that would conduct experiments and studies on human sexuality—sexology. In 1947, Kinsey founded the Institute for Sex Research, where he published *Sexual Behavior in the Human Male* (1948) and *Sexual Behavior in the Human Female* (1953). His was an attempt to embrace and understand the sexual spirit of modernity, not pathologize and condemn it out of fear or personal and religious sensibilities about sex. Each of Kinsey's books, with their never-before-seen statistics and data about sexuality in the United States, drove people to clutch their pearls, aghast at the goings-on happening behind their neighbors' curtains. Extramarital affairs, gay sex, sex with sex workers, and so much more! Kinsey reported that sexual desires and behaviors are fluid and often defy social norms governing sex.

None of these landmark moments in sexual science occurred in a vacuum. As products of German and US society, they were marked by the place and time of their creation—but they also circulated worldwide as scientists traveled and delivered lectures and as their published work was read across borders and translated into other languages. And though the conventional telling of the history of sexual sciences focuses on the work of Western white men, scholars in Asia were prolific—and the way that they absorbed the nascent ideas is instructive in its own right.[11]

Scholars in India and Japan were deeply influenced by the latest insights of Western sexology, and yet they updated and expanded such ideas to fit their cultural milieux, challenging white scientists' hegemony in the ongoing history of establishing normative and hierarchical systems of sexuality. In India, Alyappin Padmanabha "A. P." Pillay (1889–1956) was a prominent sexologist, physician, and editor of scientific journals such as *Marriage Hygiene* (1934–1937), renamed the *International Journal of Sexology* (1947–1952). Pillay wrote numerous books in the 1940s and '50s, and also had an interest in sexual socialization and disorder.

Around the same time, Japan's Takahashi Tetsu (1907–1971), influenced by Freud and Kinsey, conducted research and wrote on sexuality, and his work had a profound impact on cultural understandings of sexuality in mid-twentieth-century Japan. He was so famous for his empirically informed sex advice and his writing about sexual perversities that in the 1950s, police detained and fined him for ostensibly breaking obscenity laws.[12] Meanwhile, his *Seishin Report* was merely documenting and reporting case studies of people's sex lives. Tetsu was a forerunner for sexual rights, yet he is not remembered or celebrated like Hirschfeld or Kinsey. Let this brief snapshot of the transnational flow of sexology and the marginalization of sexologists of color also serve as a reminder of the scientific racism that plagued this burgeoning field.

By the 1960s, a new generation of sexologists, following in Kinsey's footsteps, capitalized on the continuing proliferation of discourse and public visibility of new sexual cultures, mounting ever more overt challenges to psychology's dominance and emphasis on disorder. Several of them, including William Masters and Virginia Johnson, began conducting controversial in-lab sex experiments designed to explore physiological responses to bodily stimuli.[13] Their work was so defiant of sexology's norms, medical journals and others in the field lambasted their work as pornographic. They studied up close how the body moves through the stages of arousal: excitement, plateau, orgasm, and resolution. Masters and Johnson asked what sex does to our bodies—from the minute we first make eye contact, signaling it is game on, to the minute we shiver and sigh.

As groundbreaking as Masters and Johnson's model was, their focus on physiological responses failed to capture or interrogate the role of desire in cycles of sexual arousal and response. To remedy this, in 1979, Helen Singer Kaplan offered a new and revised three-stage model of sexual response, including desire, excitement, and orgasm.[14] Kaplan underscored the importance of desire in understanding arousal and all the eroticism that follows, but did so in a way that, unsurprisingly, given the history of sexual science, made disorder the focus of the story.

Kaplan's work focused extensively on how a lack of sexual desire adversely affects relationships, and in doing so, she followed a long line of psychologists pathologizing low sexual desire. Unfortunately, it was her model and research that laid the groundwork for the addition of Hypoactive Sexual Desire Disorder and Female Sexual Arousal Disorder to the psychologist's bible, the *Diagnostic and Statistical Manual of*

Mental Disorders, or the *DSM*, for short. Stay tuned for more on this, but for now, I'd like to note that desire exists on a continuum, and I believe that nobody should be labeled abnormal or shamed for where they fall on that spectrum.

Not coincidentally, sexology's moment in the Western academy dovetailed with the global health community's new commitment to sexual health, which, as the World Health Organization wrote in 1974, included "having pleasurable and safe sexual experiences, free of coercion, discrimination and violence."[15] The sexual revolution and antisexist and antiracist movements swelling in the streets had a profound impact on sexual science and health.

In the United States in the 1960s and 1970s, people began talking more publicly about sex than ever before. Journalists and writers cited the new scientific research on sex in their stories. Sexologists' studies helped upend public perceptions of sex and drove unapologetic calls for sexual liberation. Sex is political, and the science of sex is political, and the erotic realm of life shapes our institutions and is central to change.

As sexology developed in the 1970s, the political landscape outside of academia in the United States was filled with debates around reproductive justice. Feminists won hard-fought battles that legalized birth control and abortion, and, in the process, legalized sexual pleasure. Feminist ideas and texts circulated through the mainstream into the mouths of liberal supporters and conservatives alike. The ideas of the 1970s that got the tradwives, masses of men, and some sexologists the most riled up were the ones about women's sexuality, freedom, and pleasure.

Kate Millett's *Sexual Politics* fiercely called out how heteropatriarchal structures and cultural norms controlled and constrained women's sexuality.[16] Surely making Freud turn in his grave, Anne Koedt published the essay "The Myth of the Vaginal Orgasm," challenging the prevailing Freudian notion that clitoral orgasms were immature and advocating for women's sexual literacy about their bodies and women's sexual pleasure.[17] And, forget it, heteropatriarchal defenders shook when The Boston Women's Health Book Collective, part of Bread and Roses, a socialist women's liberation group, published *Our Bodies, Ourselves*.[18] It was one of the first comprehensive sex-positive texts to reach the mainstream about women's sexual health, sexuality, pleasure, and reproductive and sexual justice.

While all this is only a snapshot, feminist sexual politics in the 1970s challenged heteropatriarchy. It makes sense, then, that studying human reproduction and the preservation of heteronormativity became a significant focus of sexology, given its history. Amid increasing cultural backlash to the feminist, LGBT, antiwar, and antiracist movements of the 1960s and '70s, evolutionary biologists assert themselves the dominant authority on sex and bring the focus of the science of sex back to its roots.[19] And, from my perspective, to put us feminists back in our so-called place.

Calling back to ideas from the late nineteenth century, in the 1970s and 1980s evolutionary biologists ramped up their writing, refocusing sex on reproduction and evolutionary processes. Because sex ensures the continuation of the human species, these researchers often reduced sexuality to a handmaiden of evolutionary biological destiny. Take, for example, bestselling author Matt Ridley's position in his gender essentialist and heteronormative book, *The Red Queen*: "Reproduction is the sole goal for which human beings are designed; everything else is a means to that end."[20]

Even now, two decades into the twenty-first century, contemporary sexology focuses on risk, disease, and dysfunction, continues to reinforce heteronormativity, and ignores feminist ideas. This limited and negative vantage point cannot provide us with a holistic portrait of human sexuality. In my 2019 study, "Sex Is Not a Problem: The Erasure of Pleasure in Sexual Science Research," a small team of brilliant undergraduate student research assistants and I analyzed three hundred studies published from 2010 to 2015 in the leading international sexual science journal *The Journal of Sex Research*. We showed that the vast majority of studies ignored sexual pleasure and reproduced heteronormativity and that people of color, transgender and nonbinary people, and disabled people were underrepresented, generally, unless the research focused on discrimination and risk.

Lost in the push and pull of psychological, biological, and physiological accounts grappling with the sexual spirit of modernity was a sensitivity to culture, politics, and broader social arrangements. Fortunately, beginning in the 1970s, a stream of sociological thought offered up much-needed insight into the social life of sexuality, alongside the growing body of feminist thought. These insights remain underexamined in mainstream perceptions of sexuality—understanding them opens up a new view of human sexuality's dynamics and eroticism's true power.

Revolutionizing how we talk about sex means thinking not just about what a single, solitary person should or shouldn't do in bed, but why we as humans do all the things we do, what it means that we do them, and how these choices reflect and influence the society we live in together. It's about recognizing sexuality as social, rather than solitary.

Transforming how we understand sexuality is also about seeing beyond our genitals. Sexologists always focused on genitals: where they went, how they functioned or were dysfunctional, and how they became vectors of disease. Evolutionary biologists got even more granular—genitals be damned, it was all about the sperm and eggs!

Sociologists, in contrast, focused on people and social institutions. Specifically, when it came to sex, sociologists called out sexologists for ignoring how people are socialized into sexuality and how culturally specific norms shape people's relationships to their bodies and sexual behaviors—*sexual socialization*.

The 1970s kicked off a series of insights into sexuality that upended the status quo. In their 1973 book *Sexual Conduct*, sociologists John H. Gagnon and William Simon directly challenged the authority of psychologists, evolutionary biologists, and sexologists. They proposed a new set of sociological concepts and theories to describe how socially and culturally constructed *sexual scripts* govern sexual behavior.

But sociologists weren't without shortcomings of their own. Like the sexologists before them, they ignored the flourishing body of feminist writing that was happening right under their noses. They were missing out—as second-wave feminism focused more on issues of bodily autonomy and reproductive freedom in the 1960s and '70s, sexuality began to play a prominent role in feminist scholars' work.

Sociologists also had a tendency to ignore crucial social dynamics in their studies of sexuality—especially race,[21] and what Ariane Cruz terms *racial-sexual alterity*, or the insidious ways that sexuality and race are intertwined.[22] Initially, they missed the value of concepts powered by Black feminist analyses of the 1970s and afterward, like *intersectionality*—which encompasses the intertwining of systems of power, such as capitalism, white supremacy, and heteropatriarchy, and the social categories they produce—and *marginality*, or the disadvantages resulting from one's position within systems of power.[23]

It is only by bringing together the insights of feminism with those of contemporary sociologists that we can grasp the true nature of human sexuality—the social life of sexuality that sexologists, liberals, and reactionary politicians can never quite come to grips with. When Gagnon and Simon conceptualized the notion of sexual scripts, or the social rules that shape how we desire, fuck, love, and live, they didn't go far enough.

To fully connect the concept of sexual scripts to the workings of power and domination in our society, they could have looked to the words of contemporaries in The Combahee River Collective (1974–1980), an important Black lesbian organization operating around the same time:

> We believe that sexual politics under patriarchy is as pervasive in Black women's lives as are the politics of class and race. We also often find it difficult to separate race from class from sex oppression because, in our lives, they are most often experienced simultaneously. We know that there is such a thing as racial-sexual oppression, which is neither solely racial nor solely sexual, e.g., the history of rape of Black women by white men as a weapon of political repression.[24]

Since the 1970s, and especially in the 1980s, feminist scholars have disrupted sexology's focus on the biology of sex, which emphasized disease, dysfunction, and disorder. Feminists demonstrated the importance of studying sexual freedom and pleasure, especially for women, whose sexual oppression was a significant yet under-discussed part of heteropatriarchy.[25] Second- and third-wave feminists emphasized sex positivity as a political tool for challenging the ongoing capitalist, white supremacist, ableist, cissexist, and heteropatriarchal assaults against women's bodies and lives.[26]

For decades, feminists have been calling out what Jenny Higgins and Jennifer Hirsch call "the pleasure deficit" in the science of sex. The *feminist framework of pleasure and danger* teaches us that, first and foremost, sexuality is socially constructed. As such, it is the site for both exploitation and inequity and empowerment and pleasure. This theory was born out of feminist debates about sex work, which were dubbed the feminist sex wars.[27]

On one side of the sex wars debate were culturally conservative radical feminists who focused on only the exploitative characteristics of sex work, particularly misogyny in pornography.[28] Pro-sex feminists clapped back, focusing primarily on the agency of sex workers and experiences of empowerment found in erotic labor.[29] However, challenging this binary, sex radical feminists gave us the pleasure and danger framework, positing that the theoretical and political debates among feminists over whether sex work is inherently exploitative or empowering were reductive and unhelpful. Sex work, like all matters related to sexuality, is contingent on both danger and pleasure.[30] Since the sex wars, there has been a proliferation of Black feminist theorizing and writing on sexuality, power, and pleasure that recognizes the symbiotic relationship between pleasure and danger, which is indispensable for understanding contemporary sexuality—these ideas make up what I call the Black feminist erotic imagination.

There is a way to resolve sexology's deficits and to help everyone understand contemporary sexuality a bit better. The Black feminist erotic imagination sits in sharp contrast to much of both academic and popular sexology. Using this mindset and maintaining a commitment to the Black feminist traditions and values it represents allows us to chart a better, non-normative, nonheteropatriarchal path to understanding sex and sexuality. This book uses this approach to turn the sexual sciences' focus on sexual abnormality, despondency, and disempowerment on its head.

First and foremost, Black feminist approaches are rooted in a profound commitment to liberation, what scholars call *praxis*, a stand-in for social change. Black feminists' unapologetic commitment to praxis and freedom is not antithetical to empirical research—it deepens researchers' commitments to applying outcomes and fostering justice through science. So, even as this book offers insights that are helpful to individuals, it also illuminates the structures of power that need to change for people to access empowerment and have more pleasurable, shame-free erotic lives.

Following the core tenets of the Black feminist erotic imagination, this book focuses on how eroticism, not just sex, provides a far more inclusive and helpful way to comprehend sexuality. *Eroticism*, the human desire for intimate connection, transcends a mere sexual, libidinous desire. The profound desire for social connection and intimacy is eroticism's drumbeat and its baseline, and is key to the social understanding of sexuality. And, in these pages, I'll hopefully convince you of the benefits of opening ourselves up to a broader concept of what counts as sex and to the expansive forms of eroticism and intimacies that bring us tons of pleasure and help people form supportive communities of care.

Sexual scientists across disciplines too often refuse to talk with and learn from one another. Fortunately, interdisciplinarity is a hallmark of Black feminism. Applying interdisciplinary thinking means my analyses lie at the crossroads of physiology, psychology, and sociology. Rather than trying to disentangle this heap of knots, I acknowledge that these dimensions of our embodied sexuality are inseparable. My scientifically slutty approach rejects intellectual silos and embraces concepts from across branches of science. I sprinkle ideas from anthropology, biology, history, neuroscience, philosophy, political science, psychology, and sociology into my cauldron and mix them all with feminist magic. In doing so, I offer us new, holistic ways of understanding sexuality.

Black feminism also teaches us that our sexuality is a site of power and pleasure, not of abnormalities and inadequacies.[31] In Jennifer C. Nash's *The Black Body in Ecstasy* and Mireille Miller-Young's *A Taste for Brown Sugar*, both agenda-setting books, the authors delve into the concept of *illicit eroticism*, demonstrating how Black women in porn have reclaimed agency over their bodies, manipulated racist and sexist ideas to make money, empowered themselves and other Black women, and carved out spaces for pleasure.

But don't get it twisted. Centering pleasure doesn't mean we need to let systems of power off the hook. Black feminists assert that we can simultaneously analyze how systems of power control and restrain us and how such regulation sets the stage for people to resist, demand pleasure, and make social changes that everyone can benefit from.

Focusing on power alongside pleasure can help people better connect their individual sexualities to the world around them, identifying how social institutions and norms shape our sexualities in ways that have nothing to do with biology or so-called hardwiring. Understanding the embodied nature of our sexuality and how society's norms and values shape our bodies is critical to developing a complete awareness of our sexuality and creating a more caring, affirming, and shame-free relationship with both our bodies and sexualities. As Audre Lorde tells us, "the erotic is the nurturer or nursemaid of all our deepest knowledge."[32]

Drawing on studies of marginalized communities and people across the spectrum of gender and sexuality, across age groups, and from various racial and ethnic categories around the globe, this book looks at the world through the prism of the erotic power model of sexuality—focusing on desire, behavior, identities, relationships, and communities. All these are modes for acquiring human connection, sociality, pleasure, joy, and power. In particular, this analysis centers on what social justice facilitator, doula, and writer adrienne maree brown calls *pleasure activism*, celebrating the colorful ways humans prioritize pleasure that can lend themselves to transformative social justice.[33]

I should warn you, though, that centering sexually rebellious people doesn't mean this book is filled with nonstop hedonistic sexual delight. I take feminist insights seriously and believe we must understand that our erotic lives are simultaneously bound up in pleasure and danger. Just as our sexualities are sites for joy, pleasure, and freedom, they are also spaces where we encounter socially and politically produced shame, stigma, harm, and trauma. So, friends, even as I highlight resistance, pleasure, and freedom, such experiences can never be divorced from the structures of power that work to control and deny those very experiences.

People have often gone to hell and back to free themselves from intense sexual repression. I believe everyone can learn something from people's stories of pleasure *and* pain. Such stories give us a direct view into the *social life of sexuality*, *sexual socialization*, *disciplinary power*, and the *social functions of sex*—all key concepts to help people know their sexuality fully and understand the political nature of sexuality.

Sex is not a social phenomenon because we do it with other people. When we masturbate, we engage in solitary sex. Yet, even masturbation is a social action because its meanings and prohibitions are not part of a natural order.[34] Sex, in all its definitions and forms, is a social and political phenomenon because cultural scripts and mores, politics, and economics shape how people think about sex and enact it.

Many people around the world grow up in heteronormative cultures. *Heteronormativity*, a concept coined by queer theorist Michael Warner, refers to the culturally constructed and deeply institutionalized idea that straight sex and relationships are normal and natural and all others aberrant. It creates a heterosexual/homosexual binary that ignores sexual fluidity. Heteronormativity also rests on an essentialist binary-gendered logic—that sex and relationships should be formed between cisgender women and men—and that these are unwavering standards for all human relationships.

So, heteronormativity establishes a hierarchical system of social control, privileging straight cisgender people and excluding anyone whose gender and sexuality fall outside of this limited framework. Queer people actively challenge this system, as Warner recognized, arguing that "heteronormativity can be overcome only by actively imagining a necessarily and desirably queer world."[35] bell hooks, too, explained that being queer is not simply about the gender of your sexual partners. Queerness, she writes, is "about the self that is at odds with everything around it, and it has to invent and create and find a place to speak and to thrive and to live."[36] And this is precisely why this book focuses on various queer or non-normative sexualities. Centering people who actively resist political systems like heteronormativity can help everyone better understand the political nature of sexuality.

Feminists have also called out the compulsory nature of heteronormativity and its imbrication with patriarchy—hence their use of the term *heteropatriarchy.* In her classic 1980 essay, "Compulsory Heterosexuality and Lesbian Existence," the feminist and poet Adrienne Rich made plain that heterosexuality is not natural, but is rather a coercive and violent political institution with patriarchy as its beating heart. *Compulsory heterosexuality* socializes people into heteropatriarchy in ways that take away their ability to recognize alternatives and make them feel shame and fear if they realize they have desires that differ—thus regulating and denying sexual freedom.

Further, as feminist Jane Ward explained in her book *The Tragedy of Heterosexuality*, heteropatriarchy produces straight cultures predicated on gendered scripts that not only produce inequality but often make straight people unhappy.[37] Heteropatriarchal relationships are built around artificial notions of difference—men are from Mars, women from Venus. The *misogyny paradox* suggests that men are socialized to both desire women and dominate, degrade, and devalue them. The point is that heteropatriarchy often suffocates genuine intimacy and thwarts equality in straight people's sexual lives. Heteronormativity and heteropatriarchy are harmful to everyone, not just queer people.

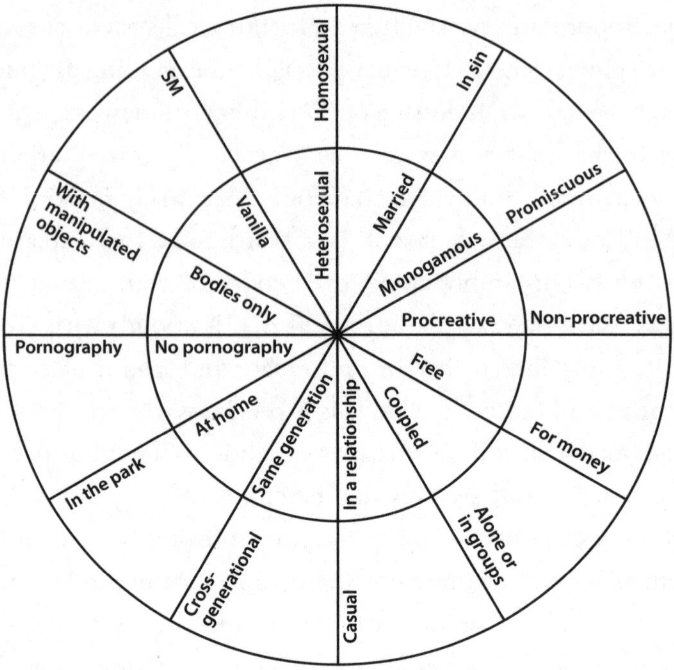

The charmed circle, from Gayle Rubin, "Thinking Sex: Notes for a Radical Theory of the Politics of Sexuality."

Under heteropatriarchy, cultures divide the universe of erotic possibility into "a charmed circle" of socially accepted practices and a danger zone of the abnormal and unnatural. This is what feminist anthropologist Gayle Rubin famously aimed to show—societies and cultures create all sorts of rules for sexual practices in ways that deny people human freedom and pleasure.[38]

Through the examination of the specific sexual hierarchies produced under heteropatriarchy in the United States circa 1984, Rubin explored the implications of a system whose governing standards demand that sex should only occur between similarly aged cis women and cis men who are married and monogamous, presumably with the goal of procreation.[39] If sex is primarily about procreation, then nonprocreative sexual behaviors (see the outer limits of the circle), or even sexual acts that take place outside of the home, become taboo. Forms of sex that take place outside of the socially constructed charmed circle are regulated through stigma and social sanctions. When individuals internalize such norms, sex outside the charmed circle creates undue silence and shame.

Conformity is insidious and often operates at an unconscious level. When you're deeply assimilated into a culture, the ideas about how you are supposed to think and act are so normalized and internalized that your choices are not always conscious. You can't make a choice if you have no other available options. If all your life, your parents and culture only described love as something that happens between a man and a woman, or marriage as this, or sex as that, this becomes your worldview.[40]

To sharpen our understanding of how heteropatriarchy and cultural context shape the realm of sexual possibility, let's consider anal sex for a moment. Stick with me because we can learn a great deal by exploring how it is perceived in, for instance, the rural South African community of KwaZulu-Natal.[41] In the mid-2000s, researchers set out to explore the knowledge and perceptions of anal sex across gender and regional differences. A set of eleven focus groups revealed that many participants, especially rural women, did not know what anal sex was; their language did not even have a word for it. So, researchers described it as "sex in the place of feces" (*ucansi embotsheni yendle*) to minimize confusion.

Men were more likely to recognize the sexual practice. Across gender and region, those who had heard of anal sex associated it with white and Indian people, men who have sex with men, prisoners, or as something a man might do with a sex worker, but certainly not with his wife. Context, in other words, shaped how people thought about sex and how they can and do have sex. In the rural KwaZulu-Natal context, anal sex was in the outer limits, not the charmed circle. These research findings underscored how social and political factors such as gender, race, and nationality shaped ideas about what types of sex were "normal" and for whom.

Let's consider additional contexts and how political context shapes the world of erotic possibility. In 2018, the Supreme Court of India ruled that the prosecution of same-gender sex was unconstitutional. The law in question, Penal Code 377, deemed any sex considered "against the order of nature" an "unnatural offense" and illegal. The law was first introduced in 1861, under British colonial rule.[42] India was not the only country to inherit this kind of anti-sodomy law from its British colonizers. Section 377 of the Indian Penal Code has parallels with Section 53 of the Belize Criminal Code and Sections 76 and 77 of the Offences Against the Person Act in Jamaica, for example.

Nigeria has an anti-sodomy penal code, too, and in 2013, the National Assembly of Nigeria intensified it by passing the Same-Sex Marriage Prohibition Act. The law made it illegal for gay people to participate in any form of gay cultural life, such as holding political meetings or attending social clubs, and violations of the law can carry up to fourteen years in jail. Even politicians seem to recognize that sexuality is not simply about sex, but that it has a distinct cultural life, which they seek to regulate. While many gay people fled Nigeria in 2013, other gay and trans people stayed. They had been resisting anti-LGBTQ laws and social norms well before the law, and they would continue to do so after the passage of the Act.

Reading the laws of nations in the Global South as repressive and backward ignores the importance of understanding what feminist sociologists call *postcolonial sexualities* and reifies what Edward Said famously termed *Orientalism*—the view of nations and people from Africa, Asia, and the Middle East as exotic, "Other," and backward, to uphold the supposed superiority of the Western world. In *Imperial Leather*, Anne McClintock uses the concept of *porno-tropics* "to highlight how the European male imagination of Africa and the Americas was profoundly gendered, sexualized, and racialized, thereby mediating colonial conquest and control."[43] Thus, these policies were not rooted in indigenous cultures; in most cases, these policies came from their colonizers.[44]

Nations globally have used sexuality and the regulation of sexuality and gender to establish themselves as a legitimate state.[45] The regulation of sexuality is fundamentally tied to the creation and enduring existence of the state.[46] Still, people in many of these nations have spent decades organizing and resisting these policies, and fighting to change them. People to this day are actively fighting penal codes that, in some cases, are hundreds of years old, resulting from the imposition of colonial ideas about appropriate sexuality.

In countries such as Nigeria, these are the people who find ways to live authentically, tear at the seams of power's suffocating blanket, build community, and find joy. In northern Nigeria, anthropologist Rudolf Pell Gaudio studied people known as *yan daudu*, who break the rules for gender roles and sexual behavior. Gaudio explains, "As men who are said to talk and 'act like women,' they are widely perceived to be witty and clever, but they are also persecuted for their presumed involvement in heterosexual and homosexual prostitution."[47] Yan daudu use language, aesthetics, their bodies, and aspects of culture such as media to, in their words, "play" with social boundaries regulating gender and sexuality, which are inextricably linked.

Throughout the African diaspora, there are similar groups of people who practice erotic resistance and find pleasure despite strict forms of sexual governance. In the book *The Sex Lives of African Women*, Pan-African feminist and writer Nana Darkoa Sekyiamah interviewed women from across the continent of Africa and the diaspora, including those who'd migrated to nations such as Barbados, Costa Rica, and Haiti.[48] Each chapter centers on a different interviewee's experiences, allows for the nuances of each woman's stories, and forefronts the utility of the feminist pleasure and danger framework for understanding sexuality. Yes, women talked about confronting abuse and exploitation, but this was the context for their stories of fighting for and discovering erotic empowerment and joy.

Without a doubt, some people derive pleasure from crafting repressive laws and controlling others' desires. Yet others find deep pleasure in resisting these laws. While scientists, cultural institutions, and governments regulate sexuality in coercive ways, this book showcases the people all around the world who resist prohibitions and regulations every day.

So, before we push forward, I want to ensure my first point is crystal clear. Sexuality has a distinct social life. Understanding how cultures and systems of power shape our erotic lives gives us the perspective we need to glimpse the pleasures that come from intentionally straying from the path and pushing back on systems that control and regulate our sexualities.

Throughout my life, I have been a bad girl. I did drugs, was friends with miscreants, had tons of sex (lots of it queer and kinky), faced time in jail (forever grateful I got out of this one), dropped out of college, had an abortion, did sex work. Although not necessarily in that order. Too often, loved ones, friends, political pundits, talk show hosts, and other cultural kibitzers make us feel like failures for violating these and other kinds of social norms. Social pressures to conform to culturally determined normative standards of behavior are pervasive, and social sanctions for transgression are ubiquitous.

In some parts of the world, being yourself and standing out loud and proud can cost you your life. As Palestinian and Jordanian writer and LGBTQIA+ activist Madian Al Jazerah explains, "for many in the Arab world, being yourself requires living a lie. For those brave enough to try living an honest existence, the implications are prison, exile, or death."[49] This is true for all components of our sexuality—our sexual desires, behaviors, identities, relationships, and communities.

One of my goals in this book is to help people counter sexual shame and understand its social and political origins and manifestations. But changing society starts at home—to fully understand and map out the workings of *sexual socialization*, the complex social processes that form how we develop and comprehend our so-called sexual preferences, the best first step is often to turn the camera on oneself. I encourage everyone to delve deep and reflect on the social, economic, and political forces and life experiences that have shaped how they understand their sexuality.

I interviewed Lorena, who was recently outed as a sex worker and kinky, and she talked about her own experience of sexual socialization in the United States of America. She was currently estranged from her immediate family members, who had reacted terribly to learning about her job. Lorena spoke about her cultural upbringing and being mixed—having Black and Mexican parents who both worked in law enforcement—and their effects on her sexual socialization. She shared, "Well, let's just say I didn't get the sex talk. I learned from friends; at home, that wasn't really discussed. Both my parents are from the hood. So, there's that cultural aspect that certain things aren't really talked about. You find out through other means."

This messaging created a heteropatriarchal environment laced with shame. "I didn't realize there are so many sexualities because, you know, you're brought up in a cultural environment. I grew up with more conservative parents . . . and there are certain rules of a culture for different ethnic groups. So, [culture] plays into that. . . . I grew up in a Christian environment where the idea was that you wait until marriage or the right man to have sex, and there was shame . . . it affected my thinking. . . . You know, growing up in that environment, it's not really healthy. But when I got into BDSM, it was freeing because it broke those shackles."

To understand a person's sexuality fully, we first need to pay attention to how they learned about sex in the first place. Individuals often grow up in households like Lorena's, where everyone silently agrees not to talk about sex. Or, when a discussion does occur, it is filled with sex-negative and repressive ideas that bring home the heteropatriarchal, ableist, racist, cissexist, and allocentric (not recognizing people on the asexual spectrum) ideas that surround us in the media and other cultural messaging.

Lorena's reflection underscored the payoff of deep introspection, at least where our sexual socialization is concerned. It's taken years, but she finally feels free of what she calls the shackles of her own heteropatriarchal sexual socialization. In this work, she asked herself searching questions: "When did you first learn about sex? How have you learned about sex, and from whom? How has your upbringing shaped your sexuality? Was the sex education you received sex-positive and inclusive?

As you map your socialization, think critically about the world around you. How have its systems shaped your desires, behaviors, identities, and relationship preferences? And, have the communities around you made you feel supported in your sexuality?"

Understanding sexuality demands we take a hard look at these biographical truths, which is not always easy. Tricia Rose writes in *Longing to Tell*, "We are all deeply shaped by our histories in this world; histories that have seeped into places many of us find it difficult and painful to go."[50] I know this not just because of my scholarship, but also because I have applied this lens to my own life and asked myself all of these questions. It has taken me years of personal introspection to understand how my sexual socialization has affected my sexuality today. So, don't be hard on yourself if it takes you some time to figure yours out fully.

I have spent much time thinking about all the aspects of sex education that I did and did not receive and how they affected me. In my house, sex was framed as something pleasurable that straight adults do. So, while my mother was intentional about sexual literacy, I was socialized in heteronormative contexts that, at a young age, did not help me understand my gender and sexual fluidity—but they did teach me shame.

As a young person, the limited access I had to information about sexuality left me without the tools to manage sexual propositions or interactions, also without a language to talk about consent. So, when kids around the way suggested we spend time in Jamir's dad's van to "hump," coercing me and others to engage in sex acts, I went along with things that I didn't want to do. When I got a little older and, for the first time, had a guy say, "Just the tip," I didn't understand that this wasn't playful banter. It was fucking coercion.

Our sexual socialization is not simply what our parents and caregivers did or did not explicitly teach us, but what we learned about sexuality through social interaction in the world. My heteropatriarchal socialization into girlhood was marred by sexual objectification and gendered and racialized social messaging from media, educational institutions, peers, and other social institutions that all programmed me to believe my body and beauty were my most important assets—that I was an object of others' sexual desire, *not* that I had sexual agency.

When I was five, I was tested for what, at the time, was called Alpha, a so-called gifted program in New York City public schools. As part of the testing for placement into the first-grade program, I received an IQ test and met and interacted with a psychologist. In the full report, the first line read: "Angela is a very pretty five-year-old girl." The *very* first line of a report ostensibly about my aptitude for study, academic excellence, and social skills doesn't begin with my Mensa qualifying score or notes about my advanced vocabulary, but rather that I was a very pretty little girl.

When I was growing up as this "very pretty" biracial girl, strangers and family friends never hesitated to tell me that I was uniquely beautiful—emphasis on the "unique" part. My light caramel skin tone and loose, kinky hair texture have always produced a racially ambiguous blend of erotic mystery. I recall that people, typically white folks, would say I looked so much like model and actress Shari Belafonte, who is twenty-four years older than I am—the politics of comparing a seven-year-old child to a thirty-one-year-old adult were apparently lost on them.

Nobody ever prepared me for or gave me tools to grapple with the sexualized realities of heteropatriarchal socialization into how to be a girl. Take the boy in the fourth grade, who showed me his penis and made me touch it. Or when I was twelve, a man working in the fried chicken joint around the corner from my house, where my friends and I would sometimes hang out, pushed me up against a wall, held me in place, and with a nasty, menacing grin gyrated his pelvis against me. And even as I was working to scrub his stench from my soul, kids in the neighborhood said I made a big deal out of nothing. "He was just playin' around," they said.

As a teenager, I was unprepared for the number of eighteen- to twenty-something-year-old men who'd try to fuck me and the never-ending experiences of men of all ages whistling and hollering at me and commenting on my body as I merely walked down the street. And y'all, nobody prepared me for all the penises I'd see or have accidentally on purpose rubbed against me while riding the F train from Queens to the city.

I was a girl socialized into a world that normalized women's sexual objectification. My direct experiences with boys and men led me to understand my body as an object of sexual desire. Yet I also received contradictory messages about needing to respect my body as a young woman. For all the people who told me that as a girl or woman, I needed to respect my body, none questioned or cared about men's disrespect of women's bodily autonomy and humanity, seemingly viewing such behavior as routine, normal features of everyday life.

And sexual socialization is not just a product of our childhoods or adolescent years—it is an ongoing, lifelong process. My evolving physiology and health over the years—my disabilities and abilities, a history marked by childhood abandonment, years of childhood bullying with racialized and classed dimensions, and experiences of sexual assault—intertwined with my neurodivergence (ADD linked to complex trauma, if diagnostics are your thing), privileged educational background, media consumption, weight fluctuations, and years spent exploring spirituality in various settings, including Black Pentecostal churches, Jewish temples, and Tibetan Buddhist temples, converging to make me who I am.

My circuitous journey also includes navigating drug abuse and recovery in self-help spaces like Narcotics Anonymous, experiences with both excellent and ineffective therapy, my political beliefs and extensive activism, a history of engagement in sex work, the transformative experience of parenthood, and the unique backdrop of growing up and spending most of my adult life in New York City, a progressive global hub. These, among many other hidden curricula within my social communities, represent just a few of the multifaceted factors that have shaped my ongoing socialization into sexuality.

Our sexual socialization directly affects our self-concept, relationship to our bodies, and sexual behaviors. We can make choices in our erotic lives that are more autonomous and pleasurable when we have a fuller understanding of our sexual socialization and take intentional steps to fill in knowledge gaps and undo what has been done to us. Now, that is sexual agency!

In my own study of the adult pornographic camming industry, I interviewed Luiza, who shows us how people defy systems of power and how contemporary sexuality is governed through what scholars call disciplinary power. Luiza is a Brazilian cisgender woman who was thirty-two years old at the time; she had been camming off and on for fourteen years. She started at age eighteen for the same reasons anyone looks for work—she needed income. After working briefly at an exploitative studio that took the lion's share of what she made on the cam sites, she moved to independent cam work from home.

Luiza did well for herself. She spoke English fluently and was conventionally attractive, so she was well positioned to flourish in an industry that catered to affluent white men from the United States and United Kingdom. However, after a year and a half of this work, she married her boyfriend, and he grew incredibly jealous. Even though the conversations, performances, and sex she was having with clients were digitally mediated in private pay-per-minute sessions, he felt it violated the holy bonds of marriage. So, she stopped.

After several years of marriage, Luiza grew bored, both sexually and professionally. She was now working as an accountant, and she described her husband to me as a "very serious vanilla person." Luiza expressed her frustrations to her husband about the monotony of both her work and their sex, and she even got him to agree to go to a swingers club. But once they got there, he was unwilling to have any sexual encounters. After a series of discussions, he suggested that perhaps they could have sex on camera, since the cam sites now offered spaces for couples (they did not in the early days). He ultimately decided that he couldn't bring himself to do that, but he agreed not to stand in her way if returning to camming would help her feel sexually adventurous and more satisfied.

Luiza continued to work in her job as an accountant even after she returned to her work in adult pornography. When we talked about her accounting job, she told me earnestly, "It's boring. . . . I'm not a super good accountant; I know that. I don't get home, and I'm like, 'Oh my God, I'm gonna read those accountant books because I'm gonna be a great accountant.' I don't . . . but when I'm on webcam or shooting porn videos all by myself, and it's just solo, I love it. And I put my videos online, and guys buy my videos, and they just make comments. I love to read my reviews. I feel so proud, and I wanna do more. I love the attention. I love the feedback I get. I get to know people. I like to talk to people. So, it's fulfilling. . . . My dream is that maybe in the future, I can stop my other job, my accountancy job, and do only webcam. I think I'd be strapped for money, but I'm saving—I'm saving it all, and when I have a good amount, because I'm always investing, I hope to stop my accountancy job and do only webcam and videos for fun."

As Luiza described the pleasures she got from her porn work, her face lit up on the other side of the screen. Her giddiness was palpable as she bounced slightly on the foot of her bed. So, of course, I inquired if there were other reasons, outside of the financial constraints, for why she didn't pursue what she characterized as her dream. She turned immediately somber: "At work, it would be horrible if anyone found out. I am afraid of people from my husband's work knowing, too, because in Brazil, people are very conservative about sex things, so it would be really hard. And my father is a really religious man, my mother is the same way, and my friends are religious."

In camming, and in enjoying the work, Luiza was breaking many of the cardinal rules of her husband and family's charmed circle. She was performing sex acts for money, often involving lots of sex toys, and doing so for a cadre of consumers outside of her marriage. Further, Luiza recognized the culturally specific sanctions she would face from the devout Catholic, sexually conservative people in her life if they found out about her sex work. She nevertheless refused to sacrifice her desires. Still, she does her adult work in secret, knowing that both she and her husband could lose their jobs and face social ostracization and excommunication if word got out. Sex work indeed remains in the outer limits in most parts of the world.

Luiza's story demonstrates what French philosopher Michel Foucault called *disciplinary power.* Luiza sacrificed her dream and her sexual and professional desires, knowing the social sanctions that would otherwise await her. Social systems of rewards and punishment govern all social behavior, especially sex, and disciplinary power keeps most people in line with the sexual norms of the milieu. Designated experts and laypersons alike gaze at one another and hold each other accountable to societal norms. In many cases, simply the fear that others are watching us guides conformity.

Before Foucault's work in the 1970s, most theorists understood power as the product of domination. In the West, power has usually been held by a person (e.g., Queen Mary I of England in the sixteenth century, who murdered hundreds of religious dissenters) or a group (e.g., the bourgeoisie in Marxism) that maintains authority and keeps people in line through brute and merciless force and exploitation.

Foucault challenged this understanding of power by highlighting a change that accompanied the onset of modernity. In the modern era, throughout the world, power and the social control of bodies are no longer enacted solely through governmental authoritarian violence and brutality, whether in the form of a guillotine, lynching, or mass incarceration. Rather, power now exerts its control through self-policing. Beginning in the seventeenth century, what Foucault called disciplinary power emerged as a new mode of governing and controlling behavior that operated through social systems of surveillance and a looming fear of social consequences and punishments.

Foucault drew heavily on Jeremy Bentham's notion of the *panopticon* to explain how this disciplinary power works in the modern world. The following picture is Bentham's original depiction of how the panopticon works in a prison setting. Suppose a prison were built circularly and a guard stood in a central position. In that case, they would have a line of vision that ostensibly allowed them to monitor all the

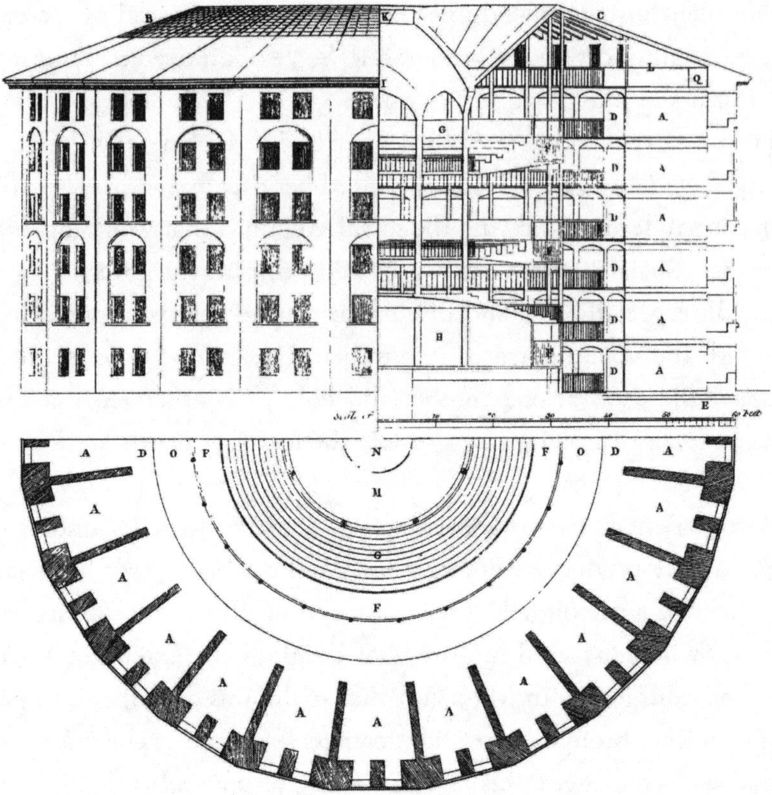

Plan of Jeremy Bentham's Panopticon
penitentiary by Willey Reveley, 1791.

imprisoned people from their post—an all-seeing eye, that is, a panopticon. The imprisoned knew they were being watched, so, for the most part, they abided by the rules out of fear of being caught and punished.

Bentham's illustration described a place designed explicitly for control and punishment: the prison. However, Foucault suggested that this form of internalized disciplinary power governs much of social life in the modern world. Systems of surveillance, coupled with the fear of punishment, ensure conformity to these social rules.

Disciplinary power particularly applies to sex: The fear of sanction drives conformity to the sexual rules of any given culture. But in naming how self-policing relates to structures of power, the idea of disciplinary power also suggests paths for resistance. When we push past our fears of social sanction, actively choosing to go against the grain and draw outside the lines, it's a political act—defiance can also feel *really* pleasurable.

People navigate modern sexuality in ways that often simultaneously adhere to some aspects of what we might think of as sexual laws for safety, while they also find ways to push back and reclaim bodily autonomy and pleasure. Luiza found much pleasure in her porn work, even as she navigated cultural and political regimes of social control around her. She knew that she would face hostility, maybe even financial consequences, if her community found out about her work, but continuing her sex work gave her a way to tap into the joys of the erotic and make connections with her own body, with her sensuality, and with her clients.

One person's actions, like Luiza's, yours, or mine, can't topple an entire system of sexual regulation or norms. This is why erotic communities are essential, both to individuals as a space for affirmation and to social change—the collective pushing back against sexual taboos and prohibitions creates change and sometimes allows for experiences of erotic empowerment. The more people push boundaries and sexual mores, the more changes occur. Foucault famously argued, "where there is power, there is resistance."[51]

We cannot live outside of systems of power. A person can't just wake up and decide, "Well, racism is bad, so I choose not to acknowledge race or label myself." Of course, they can say that, but it does not make it anything but a fantasy. We cannot live outside of power, but people can and damn sure do push power's boundaries. As new sexual practices, identities, and subcultures emerge, new regulations and forms of social control follow, and new forms of control create more public discussion and resistance. The progressive cycle of erotic power continues.

So, let's move beyond our own sexual socialization stories, and take these tools onto new terrain: How do people come to decide how to spend their erotic capital? We can answer this question by exploring the *social functions of sex*. The reasons people have sex would appear to be obvious: to procreate or fulfill sexual scripts in relationships or, alternatively, for pleasure and fun. But I want us to trouble this *procreation/pleasure* binary. If we accept that sex is social, then our reasons for doing it get more complicated. The motivation for sex may have nothing to do with an orgasm, and personal corporeal pleasure is not always an endgame.

Acknowledging the social functions of sex isn't just a theoretical exercise. Recognizing that sex has social functions and that people seek it out for multiple and changing reasons complicates how we think about consent. Popular debate tells us that sex must include enthusiastic consent. What contemporary sex-positive consent culture misses is that sometimes, people *are* unenthusiastic about sex; sometimes, people do it because sex is a tool for some other goal. People have myriad physiological, psychological, and social motivations for having sex. The emotional states that accompany those motivations don't have to be ones of enthusiasm and joy in order for sex to be consensual.[52]

So, why *do* people have sex? If you can think of a reason people might have sex, researchers have probably studied it.[53] In the widely cited study "Why Humans Have Sex," psychologists Cindy Meston and David Buss reported that participants in their sample offered 237 individual reasons, outside of procreation, for having sex. They grouped these motivations into four categories: physical (e.g., reducing stress, obtaining pleasure, gaining new experiences), goal attainment (e.g., obtaining resources, social status, or revenge), emotional (e.g., expressing love, intimacy, and commitment), and insecurity (e.g., boosting self-esteem, fulfilling a duty, and guarding a mate).

While Meston and Buss documented gender-based differences in motivations, they rooted them in evolutionary–psychological perspectives, suggesting they were part of a natural order of things—there goes the science of sex again. But even a cursory knowledge of the social life of sexuality troubles this interpretation: If cisgender men were more likely to be motivated by physical factors and cisgender women by emotional ones, the reasons were rooted in heteropatriarchy, not biology.

The reasons people have sex are often multiple, overlapping, and complicated, and systems of power shape them. My personal experience and interviews with sex workers globally underscore this point. Many sex workers consent to sex for work. Some do not desire or enjoy the sex acts themselves, but they seek the sex out and are enriched by it because of the monetary incentive. Still, in some cases, sex work also simultaneously provides an opportunity for pleasure and other emotional and psychological benefits, such as boosting self-esteem.[54]

Sex work is an umbrella term for a wide range of commercial sexual industries. It was initially coined in 1978 by sex worker and activist Carol Leigh, a.k.a. The Scarlot Harlot (1951–2022), to underscore that prostitution (what I hereafter refer to as full-service sex work) is a form of service work and that people should treat it as just that—work.

Today, the category of sex work has expanded, no doubt in part due to the Internet. Now, *sex worker* is a catch-all term, including not just people who provide full-service sex, but also those who perform porn work on- and offline, stripping, and telephone sex, as well as professional dominatrices.

I use sex work to make my case about the varieties of motivations for participating in sex because it so clearly demonstrates the practical benefits of sex. At the same time, make no mistake that, as feminist sociologist Viviana Zelizer argues in the book *The Purchase of Intimacy*, we mix business with pleasure all the time. Like Zelizer, I believe there is much value in troubling the "twinned beliefs that intimacy corrupts the economy, and the economy corrupts intimacy."[55]

Sexual grit is a term I use to acknowledge that sometimes we use sex to get what we need and want. As part of their sexual socialization, many people have been taught that sex is sacred. So, to use sex instrumentally is a no-no; yet, people use the erotic this way all the time—even if they don't formally sell sex as their occupation. Have you ever been sexually gritty—have you ever used eroticism and sex to achieve some other goal, to get something you needed or wanted? Be honest! Fine, I'll go first.

When I was younger and had a drug problem, there were occasions when I engaged in sex acts with drug dealers I knew for access to more cocaine, ecstasy pills, or ketamine (depending on what year it was). My attitude was that my New York City rent was high, and why keep paying for drugs when I had erotic capital to barter? This experience of what I call sexual grit did not generally feel pleasurable. Still, later, when I more formally did sex work, I came to sometimes experience both pleasure and empowerment in that labor and community.

Sometimes, when we have sex, we satisfy physiological, psychological, and social needs. I worked as a stripper for about five years in the late 1990s and early 2000s and saw a few of my regulars outside the club. While sex industries are plagued by the same kinds of workplace exploitation, racism, sexism, and ableism we find across capitalist markets, there were things I loved about sex work. I loved being naked (and still do). I loved dancing sensually for audiences. I loved having people appreciate and compliment my body. I loved that entranced look in a man's eye that told me he was so captivated with me that he'd empty his wallet when I commanded him to.

Like Luiza, I recognized that I had control over these men and agency over my own body, sexuality, and destiny despite the stigma I feared from friends and family. This was especially critical for me as someone who, like many other people who have lived as a woman, had experienced sexual assault and trauma from an early age. I discovered the power of the erotic as I took back control of my body and sexuality. I found pleasure and joy in the sex worker community and in my friendships with other dancers and bartenders, who showed me love and provided me with myriad forms of support. And to dispel popular myths, it was this sex worker community that educated me and protected me from getting involved with a neighborhood pimp, not law enforcement.

In my interviews, trans and nonbinary sex workers, in particular, talked about income and access to resources as primary motivations for having sex with clients. Consider Francisco, a Mexican trans man living in the United States, who was eighteen years old when we spoke. He explained, "I started because I know I am not very good at speaking English sometimes. I started to be an escort because first, I still have my legal name and my gender marker on my documents. And here in [Southwestern Conservative State], I cannot get a job easily because they see my documents as female, and I can get in trouble. I decided to be an escort because I heard that you can get easy money, and I'm also saving money for top surgery."

Roger, too, talked about trans medical care. When we spoke, Roger, thirty-one, British in origin, had lived in Thailand for some time. He said earnestly, "My health insurance doesn't cover trans medical anything, so I'm racking up huge bills."

Noah, twenty-five, from the United States, similarly said, "I got chest surgery in 2015. At the time, insurance didn't cover it, so I had to scrape up like eight thousand dollars on my own."

Coen, twenty-two, from Australia, talked to me about how long it took to save for top surgery. "I've been trying to save, but it takes time. It's a lot of money. People think that if you come out as trans, you just get surgery because we have universal health care in Australia. So, they're like, 'Oh, don't they just pay for it?' They don't cover any of the costs at all. So there's no funding or support for any sort of gender-related surgeries in Australia."

It was common for trans escorts in countries without access to universal health care and free or affordable gender-affirming care to talk about doing sex work to access these specific resources. This is but one example of how the systems and institutions around us shape sexual behaviors and underscore the social functions of sex.

People can have sex to access a resource, human connection, and pleasure, all at the same time. Many sex workers I spoke to explained how, over time, they developed complex motivations for the sex they had professionally. Some sex workers come to enjoy the connections and intimacy they share with regular clients. In escort markets, consumers of sex are often looking for what's called a girlfriend experience, not just a quick half-and-half (blow job and intercourse).

Henrik, twenty-seven, from Norway, had worked as a nurse, but with his physical disabilities and chronic illness, he could not keep up with the demands of the job. He told me that initially, he did sex work for income only, out of what he described as desperation. Still, his motivations and experiences changed over time. After he had acquired regular clients, he said, "I still definitely would not do it if not for the money. But it's shifted. . . . I have regular customers I enjoy being with and genuinely enjoy seeing."

Like Henrik, Jalen talked about viewing sex with clients as motivated by money, erotic connections, and personal fulfillment and empowerment. Jalen, twenty-nine, from the United States, said, "Of course, it started with I needed coin. I needed to make large amounts of money in short periods of time for survival reasons. . . . Then, especially post-transitioning, I found it to be really empowering sexually. Not only am I owning my sexuality and my being as a sexual person, but . . . people are paying me because I'm that good." When sex challenges sexual hierarchies and norms, it can feel empowering.

In many cases, the sex and the relationships that trans sex workers built with regular clients helped them minimize gender dysphoria, love their bodies, and find gender affirmation and euphoria and, ultimately, trans joy. Transgender people do not inherently need or desire affirmation or validation from cisgender people, and they often intentionally seek out t4t, trans-for-trans, sex and relationships to avoid harmful encounters with cisgender people altogether. However, in sex industries designed for and dominated by cisgender men, the choice to not service cisgender men would leave them broke. So, transgender sex workers found ways to set boundaries and terms that created conditions for affirmation, gender euphoria, and pleasure, while keeping themselves housed and fed.

Adeline, a twenty-five-year-old trans woman from the United States, and I spoke online about her work in the camming industry. We spent much of our time talking about her BDSM services and relationships with regular clients, for whom she served as a submissive in private one-on-one sessions online. She began to explore BDSM more deeply while working as a cam model. In porn industries, a pervasive sexual script rooted in transmisogyny dictates that trans women should have penises and use those penises to top/penetrate men. Adeline started exploring her submissive side, in part to resist this trope. She found that the BDSM role-playing she engaged in for work was pushing boundaries related to her gender identity in ways that gave her multiple and overlapping pleasures—*gender euphoria*.[56]

Adeline described the embodied pleasures of allowing a cisgender man to dominate her and call her words like "sissy"—something she'd typically never allow in her nonprofessional life. Adeline elaborated on her experiences of pleasure in these play scenes. "I felt endorphins in my chest. . . . Being a sub on cam was a score for me because sometimes I would have to be a Dom or vanilla-y, and those cases were sometimes more like acting to me. When I got to be a sub, I would feel lots of pleasure from the experience."

When sex workers cultivate long-term relationships with regular clients, they can, in the process, develop the trust necessary to have intimate and pleasurable experiences with them. For some, it will always just be a job and a means for paying the bills. And sex work does not have to be pleasurable or empowering to be recognized as a legitimate form of work.[57] In Adeline's case, she engaged in these erotic sex acts for money, intimacy, gender affirmation, trans joy, and bodily pleasure.

These are not just academic insights. We all stand to benefit from taking stock and asking ourselves: "If you desire sex, what does it do for you? What are your motivations for the sex you are having or have had? Is it for you; is it for someone else?" When we stop to reflect on these motivations, that introspection can help us take ownership of our choices, deepen and complicate our understanding of consent, and develop more agency around our sexuality.

Revolutionizing sexuality means going beyond the worldview that cheapens sex by boiling it down to a set of individual ethical decisions—but it also means seeing the social life of sexuality at work in our individual erotic life. Breaking the cycle of sexual repression and upending the assumptions that rob sexuality of its social power isn't just a matter of political maneuvering and intellectual debate. It means bringing these ideas into our own lives, too.

While what follows is not a how-to manual, I hope that this book will help each reader know, interpret, and act on their own sexuality. Understanding the pivotal role of sexuality in society makes us more deeply informed and better political actors and community members—it also helps individuals cultivate more empowered, joyful, and pleasurable erotic lives and combat shame.

So, with all the heady introductions out of the way, join me as we move on and demystify the first part of our sexuality—desire.

Chapter 2

DESIRE

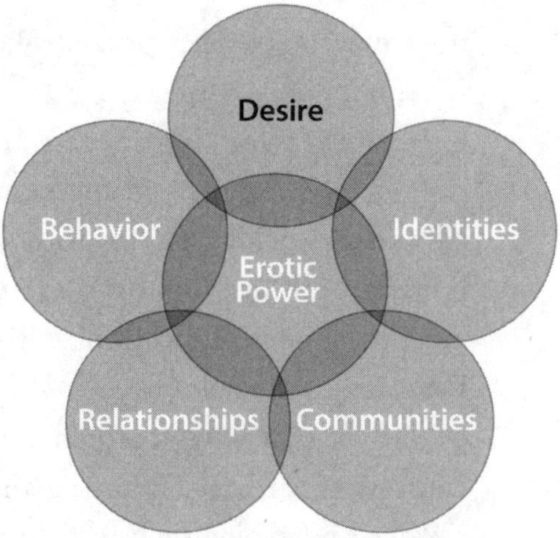

Desire is elusive. Scientists can't seem to agree on its origin story. Then again, few people can put their finger on where their desires come from. Instead, many people experience erotic desire as a kind of mystical force of nature, pulsating through bodies and living rent-free in minds. At times, it is a hedonistic force that people can't live without; otherwise, it's a biohazard that most societal structures insist be contained.

Of course, there are exceptions. Not *all* desire is forbidden. Movies, social media, and advertisements bombard us with messages that shape and appeal to our desires. They attempt to impose on us a socially acceptable vision of what we should or should not want, one that matches the kinds of products on offer, if only we are daring enough to act on our desires.

So much in our society depends on the management of desire, one might expect that the established sexological and psychological experts would make a priority of getting a handle on the subject. We know enough to shape desire through advertising—surely, we have enough data to explain the basics of what desire is and how it works. The ramifications would be massive—after all, if our erotic cravings are biologically determined in each individual at birth, then shaming someone for their hunger would be pointless. On the other end of the spectrum, if we had total conscious control over our appetites, we could save ourselves a lot of heartbreak.

In truth, there's a lot we *could* know about desire, but the reigning experts have been stuck in the nineteenth century. Groundbreaking advances in fields from feminist sociology to neuroscience have offered tantalizing hints about desire's true inner workings, but commonly accepted understandings of desire and eroticism remain locked in a Freudian choke hold.

The most widely accepted way to understand desire comes to us courtesy of the father of psychoanalysis, Sigmund Freud, and the generations of psychologists he influenced. Freud saw desire as purely intrinsic, stemming from an innate sexual drive that he called the libido. Individuals with sexual desires seek sexual activity to feel good or to avoid feeling bad. They want specific sexual acts for their own sake, and the locus of that desire is within them. Freud believed that anxiety about society's judgments of our desires plays a critical role in people's minds—that it creates shame, neuroses, aberrant behavior, and psychological disorders. And most importantly, our libido keeps powering our desires, deep down in the most primitive, childlike parts of our mind.

While this model of desire as a self-authored, self-serving impulse can be helpful to psychoanalysts helping their patients cope with socially unacceptable desires, outside of a one-on-one talk session, this model falls apart almost immediately. Over the course of daily life, our desire is constantly influenced by external stimuli, whether we are taken in by advertisements or aroused by interactions with other people. Furthermore, just about everyone reading this book surely has *some* experience articulating their erotic desires in socially acceptable ways. If desire leads us to derive pleasure from belonging, intimacy, and connection with others, then we can hardly call it self-serving.

Society may do its best to police our desires, but shame is not a given; as we will see in the pages ahead, there are deep pleasures to be found in rebuking its sexual scripts. Far from being a simple psychological drive or motivating force, pleasure has a social, economic, and political life that extends beyond our minds.

But we honestly don't even need to dive into the scholarship and interviews to prove Freud wrong about desire being an innate individual drive. How could it be, when everything we know about sexuality we learn from the world around us! All of our desires are social products, even as they are experienced in our bodies. Nor are those desires and attractions fixed or immutable facets of our being. They ebb and flow throughout our lives.[1] Our erotic desires are deeply embodied consequences of the interplay between our physiology, social experiences, and the *erotic fields* or social contexts we inhabit and move in and out of.[2]

Get ready, because I'm about to shake up your understanding of desire and address many lingering questions on the subject: What are erotic desires? Where do they originate? Are they biologically determined? Politically constructed? Do we consciously control them? Why must we control them? Are we ashamed of our desires? What is the source of this shame? And what if we have none of these desires?

The answers to these questions and many more await, and people who break societal rules are among the best suited to help us understand desire and attraction. To make sense of desire, there could hardly be a better authority to consult than those who have explored its absence. Asexual, or ace, individuals are erotic rule breakers who challenge our core assumptions about sexuality by demanding that we reimagine attraction as existing across a continuum of desire.

In cultures across the world, asexual activists are pushing back against the constraints and harms imposed by *compulsory sexuality*—the norm that everyone should want and need sex as a fundamental part of the human condition. Sex is not the only path to empowerment and pleasure. My interviews with asexual sex workers, alongside the writings of asexual writers and activists, will lead us to new ways of thinking about desire and eroticism. This chapter outlines five valuable lessons readers can take away and apply in their lives. These lessons underscore the political nature of sexuality, contest social norms like compulsory sexuality that affect everyone, offer us more fluid and dynamic ways of understanding desire and attraction, and highlight the importance of supportive communities for nurturing affirming, shame-free, and joyful relationships with our bodies, desires, and sexualities.

My interview with Bree offers a taste of these lessons.

Bree and I talked for over two hours on Zoom. The entire time, I sat captivated and enthralled by her unpunctuated, ebullient storytelling, transported into but a few chapters of her extraordinary life. She talked me through her incredible life journey: its joys and adventures, and some of its pains. Bree had worked in the sex industry for over four decades by the time we connected. She moved between industry segments as she moved through life, following men and work opportunities across the United States and back again. That meant working as an escort, a stripper, a sensual masseur, a pro-domme, a phone sex operator, and, most recently, as a cam model.

After years of working as an escort, Bree grew tired, physically and mentally, of full-service sex work. Her relationship with her labor, clients, her body, and her own sexual desires was changing. And so, the first time a colleague told her about a different kind of work—sensual massage—she was eager to learn more. Moving into sensual massage meant Bree could earn the same $250 per hour, but with less of the exhausting physical and emotional labor that full-service sex work demanded. In her words, "I didn't even have to get naked. . . . I was blown away. . . . There was a happy ending, but I did not have to suck a dick." But after some time, sensual massage, too, came to take a financial and physical toll. "I would see sometimes five, six to seven people a day, because I'm a workaholic." Market saturation exacerbated the situation, driving prices down and her hours up.

Bree talked about how corporeal changes, from perimenopause to menopause, the long-term physical tolls of her labor, and a sexual assault in a romantic (not professional) relationship affected her sex drive in and outside of work. In her fifties, she came to see herself as asexual. Now that she's in her sixties, she said, "I'm totally asexual now. I mean, sex doesn't turn me on at all."

She paused before providing an important caveat. She had loved and found so much enjoyment in all the sex that she'd had throughout her life. Her asexuality, in other words, wasn't retrospective. Still, for over a decade now, she had become sex-averse. When she thinks about sex in and outside of work, with all its "smells and textures," she told me she feels no desire for that physical experience.

Like Bree, many people's sexual desires wax and wane throughout their lives. Desire does not only disappear, contrary to the ageist, ableist tendency many societies have of assuming that an interest in sex simply falls away as one ages. Rather, our brains adapt to changes around us and within our bodies, something that feminist sociologist Laura Carpenter has explored through the *gendered sexuality over the life course (GSLC) model*.[3]

As Bree herself noted, lots of people her age and far older have active, pleasurable sex lives. Her own declining sexual desire and increasing aversion to sex developed over time and reflected her shifting desires and the circumstances of her economic, political, and social life.

Bree's story illuminates critical aspects of desire, as well as its physiological, psychological, social, and political underpinnings, but to make sense of them, first, we need to update our understanding of the language and science of desire.

How should we define desire? Desire is both a noun and a verb, and deeply embodied either way. It exists on a spectrum from asexual to allosexual. I am an *allosexual* person, meaning that I experience sexual desires and attraction.

To take the word in its noun form, I have many sexual desires. One of these is strap-on play. For many, there is a naturalizing tendency and embodied resonance in having such desires. If I have a desire, it resides within me. I own it. Strap-on play is *my* desire. That desire becomes part of us.

We also *feel* our desires—we experience desire in its verb form. But the tense of that verb isn't always straightforward. If I say, "I desire strap-on play," it could mean that I want to embark on a specific act using a particular object or with a specific person, but it could also mean I am accessing an embodied feeling and experience that isn't in the here and now. My experience of desiring strap-on play might look like me lying nestled in the soft linen exterior of my white goose-down comforter and fantasizing—sparklers dancing in my mind and fingertips jostling in the nether, wanting and harkening back with bated breath to a particularly magical night in bed with a former lover while traveling internationally. The disapproving stares from the airport security agents were well worth it.

Scholars have studied the complex nature of human sexual desire, fleshing out its dynamic physiological, psychological, and sociocultural underpinnings. As a result, we know a lot more than Freud did—enough to be cautious about identifying any of these particular aspects of desire as the being in the driver's seat.[4] Yet much of the latest work still fails to integrate the insights of sociologists and, feminists, because of scientific sexism, there's only so much that it can teach us.

Some biologists have started to recognize that this is a problem. As Frederick Toates explains in his book *How Sexual Desire Works*, understanding sexual desire requires a new theory or framework, "one that does justice to the influences of both biology and culture and which can mesh with evolutionary psychology."[5] This is where I come in.

Learning how erotic desire works demands that we come to grips with what is happening within our bodies, reckon with the dynamic relationship that this embodied experience shares with the sociocultural ideas about appropriate desires, and grasp how all of these factors are, in turn, bound up with pleasure. The biological, the sociological, and the feminist, all working together as one.

Our first lesson about desire requires us to peek inside our brains. This doesn't mean strapping on electrodes and looking at what neurons fire when we see something we want—we need to see the things happening inside our bodies as being in a dynamic relationship with external stimuli. Rather than taking for granted that our gray matter is in the driver's seat, or that its inner workings are the key to understanding why we want what we want, we need to adopt a completely different perspective.

Instead, let's visualize the body as a computer, coded to all of the things it does by a set of programmers—the external world and its social institutions. When it comes to erotic desire and sex, these programmers are *agents of normative sexuality*. They shape our emotions, behaviors, and beliefs related to sexual desires in ways that are deemed socially, economically, and politically appropriate in any specific context. Our brains are important, but they are just one part of our bodies, connected to a network of other parts, and influenced by external programmers.

The first major insight that recent scientific investigations can confirm for us is that desire isn't an inborn drive that spontaneously arises within us—everything we know about desire, sex, and relationships comes from the world around us. *The Biology of Desire*, a compelling and fascinating refutation of the disease model of addiction by neuroscientist Marc Lewis, reminds us that, while some portions of the brain respond directly to stimuli, most of the brain depends on learned responses. "Humans learn almost everything they ever come to know or do. That's why babies are completely helpless. They can't do a thing, because they haven't learned how," he writes.[6] Just like the baby who learns that crying may make someone appear and satiate a troubling feeling within them (what we non-babies all know as thirst), we have to learn specific erotic desires. We are not born with them.

Seconding Lewis's insights was another of my interviewees, Charlie, a twenty-three-year-old demisexual, bisexual, and polyamorous British cam model and pornographic content creator. In our delightful conversation, Charlie talked about her background, being on the autism spectrum, what she referred to as the "cis male gaze," and how other sociocultural factors combined with physiological factors have shaped her desires, attractions, and sexual behaviors throughout her life.

She underscored the importance of sexual socialization in our conversations about her sexual fluidity. She remarked, "I don't necessarily think you're born with your sexual preferences. I think they develop. . . . I think, obviously, some of it is just innate, like the way your brain is working when dopamine rushes when you look at certain things. But I do think that a lot of it is because of development. . . . I don't think I was born straight by any means. I think I was probably just born a baby, not attracted to anything—because I was a baby."

A second critical key to understanding sexual desire: neuroplasticity. Put simply: Our brains change as we learn. As we navigate through cultural spaces with varying semiotic messaging and find new lovers and new friends, we learn new ideas about desire and sex, which in turn keep reshaping how we understand sexuality. We learn the sexual scripts as we settle into a specific social network and its norms—and then life changes, we find ourselves in a new community, and we trade out the old scripts for new ones. Learning brings new desires, neural pathways, synapses, rewards, pleasures, and experiences—rinse and repeat. This is why social experiences in new cultures, spaces, geographies, media, languages, and terms are critical for achieving erotic empowerment and understanding our sexuality fully.

The stimuli our brains must respond to and learn from include socioeconomic–political cultures, especially oppressive systems. In *The Brain's Body*, feminist sociologist Victoria Pitts-Taylor maps out how neuroscientists have often overlooked brain diversity and its relationship to social inequities. In fact, the brain is so adaptable, and power takes so many forms, we must remain open to what Pitts-Taylor calls *epistemic multiplicity*, the many ways of thinking and knowing shaped by racial capitalism, heteropatriarchy, and domination of all shapes and flavors. This brain diversity and these systems influence the workings of sexual socialization and desires just as surely as diverse cultures overwrite sexual scripts and spark new connections.

The third revelation about desire is that our brain *does* have a pleasure circuit. The mesolimbic dopamine system, with its ventral tegmental area and nucleus accumbens, works in tandem with our various senses to help humans navigate the treacherous waters of social life and find pleasure amid the constant threat of undertow and sharp rocks.

But this is no nerve center dictating our desires. Instead, the system performs its work much like an anthropologist taking meticulous field notes, reporting back on an experience that was particularly joyful and pleasurable. Based on this data, our brain signals: "Let's seek that reward again; that was delightful."

Now that we have a sense of how desire works within the brain—that it is learned, that it is endlessly shifting, and that it is responsive to new opportunities for pleasure and eager to seek out new things to desire—we can move from gray matter to psychology. This doesn't mean leaving the brain behind, of course—remember, all these systems are networked, not separate—but it does mean we can see desire more completely than before.

Desire is experienced as a dynamic mental state that invokes corporeal responses. A psychological perspective allows us to see the ways that a variety of emotional, physical, and cognitive states and processes interact. As I fantasize about my desires, I recall past rewards and pleasures. Dopamine kicks in; I feel excited. I may lick my lip or caress my skin.

We can break this experience down further into three different levels—the ABCs of psychological desire.

A. At the **affective** level, erotic desire affects our feelings and emotions. If a person's erotic desires include not what most people typically define as sex but instead, say, hand-holding or cuddling, the soft touch of another's hand may generate joy and a smile. What we desire sexually, *if* we desire sex, reflects the emotional states we associate with sexual activity. For example, I desire oral sex because it makes me joyful when performed well, and my entire body feels blissful when I cum.

B. Sexual desire has **behavioral** connotations. When we ruminate about our desires, we often simultaneously fantasize about them in action. When I date, I will communicate my love of cunnilingus to my partners or harken back to a particularly pleasurable past sexual experience of a partner going down on me. In fantasy, my accumbens fires, and dopamine ignites a blaze, sparking embers that radiate through my skin.

C. The **cognitive** aspect of desire involves our beliefs about our attachments to erotic activity; for instance, I believe cunnilingus is super pleasurable. There are no universal beliefs about what is pleasurable. Pleasure has a social life and functions, and norms are culturally specific. Some people believe performing oral sex is sinful. One's relationship to erotic desires is entirely subjective and based on *our* bodies, identities, culturally specific sexual norms, and gendered, racialized, and classed sexual scripts that shape our sexual socialization, or upbringing.

Though our grasp of desire's story seems to be coming into focus, brain science and psychology can only tell us so much. Without considering the social life of desire, our understanding remains incomplete.

Social forces shape desire. All of our internalized desires—the neurological and psychological aspects of desire—are formed by externally imposed *social hierarchies of desire*.[7] Here, then, is a sociology of desire.

Let's start simple, by looking at "normal," socially accepted sexual desire in a predominantly white Western capitalist society. In such places, it is commonplace to think and talk about erotic desire, the so-called sex drive, in stereotypically masculine terms. The desire for sex is healthy when it is robust, powerful, and dominant. This is a heteropatriarchal society we're talking about, so it almost goes without saying that cisgender men are the ones encouraged to act on the desire for sex—this allows them to embody and perform what scholars call *hegemonic masculinity*, the idea that being a so-called real man is predicated on dominance, especially over women and other marginalized people.[8]

Desire works in mysterious ways, even in a suffocating heteropatriarchy. Not only is the pursuit of sexual desire an opportunity for cisgender men to celebrate masculine dominance, it also provides a handy way of excusing and normalizing the same men's unacceptable behaviors. Such societies tend to treat men's sex drives as so intense, so all-consuming, that sexual desire is seen as an instinctive, almost irrepressible response to stimulus. According to this logic, if men are often pushy when it comes to sex, it's simply in their nature. In a heteropatriarchal milieu, as writer and academic Katherine Angel explores in *Tomorrow Sex Will Be Good Again*, men's desires and sexual needs take center stage.[9]

Desire's cultural masculinization normalizes visceral, uncontrollable sexual impulses, and often legitimizes men's sexually coercive behavior. This is how we get to, for instance, questions about whether a woman might have done something to attract a sexual assault—as in, "Well, was she wearing provocative clothing, or did she lead him on?" In the book *Sexed Up*, Julia Serano aptly called this pervasive gendered trope *the predator and prey sexual script*.[10] The idea that men's sexual desires are hardwired and uncontrollably ravenous is a social norm, not a scientific fact—and frankly, either way, neither is an excuse for sexual assault!

These dynamics help explain how white men's insatiable and predatory desires and sexuality are celebrated as healthy and normal. It is why the 2016 release of a video of Donald Trump bragging about "grabbing women by the pussy" prompted his supporters to rally to his defense. Yet these dynamics don't apply monolithically to all men—men of color, especially Black ones, are rarely given the same grace.

Donald Trump may have built a public image out of posing with models and bragging about his fondness for *much* younger women in the '80s and '90s, but when Black music mogul Luther "Uncle Luke" Campbell and 2 Live Crew made music videos around that same time with young, scantily clad Black women, public outrage spawned congressional hearings and, ultimately, a Supreme Court case on the nature of obscenity.[11] When Black erotic desire takes center stage in a white supremacist culture, the focus shifts from celebrating masculine power to protecting the purity of delicate white children.

Uncle Luke does not get a pass for his misogynoir. He wasn't the first man of any hue to build an empire off the backs of women—serving up Black women's bodies on the altar of heteropatriarchy in exchange for his political and economic advancement. Yet there's a reason I'm citing his example. Uncle Luke's objectification of women notwithstanding, the unmistakable racism in the political establishment's response to 2 Live Crew's music and performance offered Black feminists of the early 1990s a political opportunity. Black feminists writing inside and outside of academia seized it, offering new critical frameworks for analyzing racialized and gendered media as well as a call for action to fight against the long-standing issues of racialized sexual violence and its cultural depictions under racial capitalism.[12]

Clearly, race and gender are inseparable from the sociological story of desire. Black sexualities and desires are routinely cast as aberrant, and in many regions and countries throughout the world, including the Caribbean, Germany, the United Kingdom, and the United States of America, racist discourse has associated Blackness with hypersexuality.[13] The Mandingo trope—the image of physically powerful Black men with huge cocks who prey on white women—has been central to global definitions of Black masculine desire and used to justify their imprisonment, lynching, and rape.[14] Also, in the US context, white Christian colonists used hypersexual *controlling images*, such as the "sexual savages" trope, to describe Indigenous people, ostensibly to protect white women, but really to bolster their power and continued occupation.[15]

Over and over again, Indigenous, Black, and Brown straight men, gay men, and trans people's desires have been culturally, politically, and economically constructed as too carnal, rapacious, aggressive, and abnormal—as a social threat.[16] Historically, due to their so-called high sex drive, gay men have become the focus of moral panics and witch hunts, branded the arbiters of public health crises and vectors of disease, and falsely accused of pedophilia.[17] Trans people, especially trans women, have often been stereotyped in similar ways. Bigoted and bad-faith "concerns" about trans people's desire to corrupt and harm children loom large in global culture today. These aptly called sex and moral panics that surround queer and trans desires in global culture wars are also highly racialized.

Alongside the convictions that white male desire is powerful, masculine, and uncontainable, Black male desire is dangerous and aberrant, and the desire of non-straight, non-cis people is a social threat, heteropatriarchy tends to maintain that cis women, particularly white cis women, have low sex drives. Being coded as feminine means being seen as passive, simply responding to, rather than instigating, sexual desire.

Black, Latina, and Indigenous women are forced to abide by a different set of rules. In the United States, from chattel slavery onward, Black women's desires have been cast in similar hypersexual terms that demonized Black men and were used to legitimize the rape and forced sterilization of Black women at numerous junctures in history, constituting a unique form of domination that Shatema Threadcraft calls *intimate injustice*.[18] In Canada and the United States, use of the word *squaw*, a term white colonizers co-opted to sexualize Indigenous women, is pervasive and also used to routinize and normalize men's ongoing sexual violence and exploitation of Native women as well as the governmental inaction surrounding such harm and injustice.[19]

Saartjie Baartman, a.k.a. the Hottentot Venus, is often cited as the classic example of how racist sexualized norms about desire and sexuality have propagated racialized stereotypes of Black women. In 1810, British doctor William Dunlop brought Baartman from Africa to Europe under false pretenses and promises of economic enrichment. For years, the living Baartman was put on display in European cities, with the doctor pointing to her large buttocks and genitals as pseudo-scientific evidence for Black women's dangerous hypersexuality.

Even after she died in 1815, Baartman's body was kept and used as a scientific artifact. The Musée de l'Homme in Paris displayed a cast of her body and jars containing her brain and genitals well into the late twentieth century. Her remains were not given a proper Khoikhoi burial until 2002.

What do all of these ubiquitous gendered, racialized, classist, and ableist messages about desire add up to? On the simplest level, they dictate what kind of behaviors are allowed, reward some categories of people, punish others—but the actual effects of the dominant society's messages are not as straightforward as we might think.

We can compare the content of one of these society's messages with survey data gauging sexual desire. The United States is a heteropatriarchal society that condemns and punishes a broad spectrum of sexual behaviors—but desire tends to respond to social condemnation in unpredictable ways. In his 2019 book, *Tell Me What You Want*, psychologist Justin Lehmiller reported that the vast majority of Americans in his sample—84 percent of straight cisgender women and 81 percent of straight cisgender men—fantasize about having sex in public. Now, in most jurisdictions, outside of a few public parks like Copenhagen's Ørstedsparken, sex in public spaces is illegal. And yet, clearly, public sex is deeply desirable to a lot of people, regardless of gender.

That isn't to say that there aren't marked gender differentials in Lehmiller's findings. Take the fantasy of watching other people having sex. Lehmiller documented that 72 percent of cisgender straight men, but only 48 percent of cisgender straight women, fantasized about voyeurism and watching others in flagrante delicto. Clearly no particular configuration of chromosomes, level of estrogen or androgens, or possession of a vulva or testes can explain why one might be aroused at the thought of watching others shag. Rather, the sexual norms of heteropatriarchy socialize people into different sexual scripts based on their gender and, in so doing, shape their desires.

If neurological and psychological models of desire have allowed us to understand it from a physiological perspective, the sociological and feminist analyses complete the equation, laying bare why and how people desire and fantasize about this and not that, how nations and cultures regulate and attempt to control people in unjust ways, and how desire and sexual expression bump up against those restrictions and find ways to defy them altogether.

One of the most defiant responses a person could have to a society that mandates the performance of desire is simply not to participate. Scientific and mainstream discussions of desire are allocentric, which is to say they are overwhelmingly focused on people who experience sexual desire and attraction. Mainstream cultures are smattered with endless depictions of people with insatiable sexual appetites, from hot and horny singles on reality shows, to mainstream films that walk right up to the pornographic line, to thirst traps on socials. People with minimal to no sexual desire, people who don't or rarely experience sexual attraction, are seldom depicted. Their absence from public and scientific view can make asexuality seem aberrant or rare. It is not.

We've used numerous perspectives to make sense of desire—now it is time to deploy the image of a spectrum of desire and attraction. Contrary to the Freudian impulse to say all humans are driven by libidinous desire, there are those who rarely ever or do not experience sexual desire and attraction at all.[20] Some people are *asexual* or are on the *ace spectrum*. The Asexual Visibility and Education Network (AVEN) defines an asexual identity as "someone who does not experience sexual attraction or an intrinsic desire to have sexual relationships."[21] Similarly, but focusing their definition on attraction, the 2023 *Ace in the UK Report* defined ace as "an umbrella term used to describe a wider group of people who experience little, fluctuating, or no sexual attraction."[22]

Asexual people underscore the social functions of sex because even though they do not or rarely experience sexual attraction, they may choose to have partnered or other forms of sex. The definition from ace activist and writer Sherronda J. Brown makes space for this—not all aces are sex-averse. In *Refusing Compulsory Sexuality*, Brown writes, "People on the asexuality spectrum, also called ace, experience little to no sexual attraction and/or little to no sexual desire, and these things are not evidenced by either the presence or absence of sexual arousal or activity."[23]

Importantly, asexuality and celibacy are very different things. Someone who chooses to abstain from sexual activity for political, religious, or other social and personal reasons has adopted the practice of celibacy. Asexual people are not inherently celibate. As Black feminist sociologist Brittney Miles explains, choosing to abstain from sex is a choice; asexuality is an orientation.[24]

And, even as asexuality is an orientation, I urge us all to resist born-this-way narratives that suggest that any sexual orientation or identity is biological or innate. As Brown argues, it is critical that we not define allosexual desire as the default and asexuality as abnormal. Such binaries only serve to reify the pervasive medically, socially, and culturally constructed idea that there is something wrong with not having sexual desires *or* experiencing sexual attraction.

Some ace activists, writers, and sex educators make a point of drawing sharp distinctions between desire, libido, and sexual or sensual attraction. Some define asexuality as a lack of sexual attraction and distinguish it from the experience of a lack of or little desire for sexual activity. The latter is sometimes labeled as simply having a low libido—and not asexuality. At the same time, there are ace people who understand asexuality in terms of desire and libido, and others who recognize just how tough the terms *desire*, *libido*, and *attraction* can be to disentangle.[25]

So, you will hear from people across the ace spectrum who define and understand asexuality in different ways. I told you, friends, sexuality is messy. While much debate exists about the definitions of these terms, here, I use *desire* to refer to our personal levels of interest in erotic activities, and *attraction* to mean the embodied desire or impulse to engage erotically with specific people. As some ace folks say, consider hunger and craving. A person may experience hunger (desire) but not crave anything in particular (attraction), and sometimes, people crave something but aren't hungry.

Like all sexual terms and identities, asexuality is shifting and changing. As ace people have made their lives more visible to the public and challenged compulsory sexuality, or the globally pervasive idea that everyone should want and need sex as a fundamental part of the human condition, more people are finding a home in the ace community—although not always with an enthusiastic reception. *Boundary policing*, debates over who belongs and who doesn't, and actions to control those places of belonging are commonplace across communities—especially marginalized ones. Ace people have experienced this themselves, as some queer folks have not been welcoming of the "A" as an addition to the LGBTQ umbrella.

There is a history of boundary policing within asexual communities around who is ace and who is not, especially regarding aces who do not experience sexual attraction but who desire sex or have sex.[26] So, the separation of attraction and desire is, in part, a reaction to this boundary policing, and many ace community members use the term *attraction*, and not *desire*, as a way to be more inclusive of sex-favorable aces. Despite efforts toward inclusion, aces who are not sex-averse have reported feeling unwelcome in some ace spaces.

Ideas and debates about who is ace, who is not, and who can be are evolving. As is always the case when it comes to sexuality, things are constantly changing. Increasingly, people who experience sexual attraction but who have never desired sex or have over time found themselves no longer wanting it have begun seeking refuge in asexual identity and communities as a way to ward off the medicalized and shame-inducing stigma of a diagnosis of hypoactive sexual desire disorder.

Whether people define and understand *their* experience and identity as asexual in terms of attraction, libido, or both, all are taken as valid and serve a social function. As David Jay, founder of AVEN, has remarked, "a definition is a tool." As an allosexual person, researcher, and writer, it is not my place to tell people how they can or cannot identify themselves. Still, even as an outsider, I'd say that if the language of asexuality provides people with a frame for understanding themselves better, helps them be more authentic in their erotic lives and relationships, and connects them to supportive communities, then isn't that a good thing?

The ace community has not only challenged the fundamental meaning and place of desire, but it is by all appearances growing, particularly among Gen Z. On the 2021 England and Wales Census, twenty-eight thousand people identified as asexual. Further research suggests that the asexual population encompasses between 1 and 2 percent of adults, skewed toward younger generations.[27] According to a 2020 Trevor Project survey in the United States that sampled over forty thousand LGBTQIA+ youth, 10 percent of respondents identified as on the ace spectrum.

Nor is the phenomenon specific to Gen Z. As young ace people create a new language for describing their experiences, a wider range of sexual labels are becoming available for everyone. Bree, the asexual sex worker in her sixties, is just one example. As ace scholar and activist Megan Carroll gave a name to in a conversation with me, Bree exemplifies what scholars have only just started documenting: how, with newly available identities, people are *aging into asexuality*.

Black ace people have called out the whiteness of ace spaces. Studies suggest the vast majority of asexual people are white, and not long ago, British model, award-winning asexual activist, and writer Yasmin Benoit sternly wrote, "the ace community has a racism problem."[28]

Consider what we learned about the sociology of desire. An underrepresentation of people of color in asexual communities on- and offline does not automatically mean that there are simply fewer Black folks and other people of color who experience low or no sexual attraction. Instead, how people experience and understand their desires, or their lack of desires and attractions, is shaped by social expectations and the availability of community.

We can partly understand the whiteness of the ace community as a consequence of the uphill battle that asexual Black people are forced to fight. In a white supremacist society in which Black and Latinx people have been typecast as having hypersexual desires and appetites, compulsory sexuality can be particularly difficult to navigate for Black asexual people. As Sherronda Brown has observed, the very existence of Black asexual people threatens and upends this racist worldview. Critically, these stereotypes not only shape cultural depictions of people's sexualities, but also people's internal understandings of their own desires. In this, there is a lesson for everyone—it can be really tough to see one's own true desires clearly in the face of suffocating sexual scripts and systems of power.

But there's another reality, one that will become a recurring theme as we center erotic dialectics and spend time with a variety of communities of sexual rebels over the course of this book. Just because a community came together out of a collective need to combat discrimination and find affirmation, it does not mean they are free from other forms of bigotry. As Brown poignantly writes, "what is true of whiteness in every space, even in 'progressive' and 'inclusive' spaces, is that it will always work to create some form of exclusivity as a means to reassert white superiority."[29] People often create community spaces that include some and exclude others, whether intentionally or due to cognitive biases that reflect broader historical patterns of social and economic exclusion. As I will continue to point out, racism is all up in our sexuality!

Regarding gender and the ace community, only 13.9 percent, or just over one in eight, of the 2019 Asexual Community Survey respondents were men. Cody Daigle-Orians, who is a gay asexual man, acknowledged the potential sociological underpinning of this statistic in his introduction to the anthology *Being Ace*.[30] Socially produced ideas about what it means to be a so-called real man may shape whether people come out as asexual in a world where both heteropatriarchy and compulsory sexuality dominate.

Nevertheless, there is something incredibly subversive about asexuality. Women socialized under heteropatriarchy are subjected to cultural messaging that depicts feminine desire as passive and, in many global contexts, they are rewarded for chastity. Yet, women are often told their greatest source of joy and fulfillment should come from being mothers and wives, and that having sex regularly is vital to sustaining a happy marriage. So, embracing and owning an identity that entails having *no* or little sexual desire is a rebellious act of defiance.

Meanwhile, men socialized into systems that equate manhood with a high sex drive and that measure their worth by how many people they've slept with and the size of their dick have a lot to lose. By openly admitting that he does not desire sex or experience sexual attraction at all, he risks punishment and shame. In the face of such risks, it's not hard to see why even people who recognize that they are asexual might not admit it publicly. The ace community may be growing, but the power of heteropatriarchy and white supremacy's sexual scripts remains hard to overcome.

We can learn five critical lessons about desire and attraction from ace people's experiences, if we're willing to listen.

The first is that compulsory sexuality, the norm that everyone should want and need sex as a fundamental part of the human condition, shapes everyone's sexuality. Compulsory sexuality makes people feel shame if they have no desire for sex, for any length of time. People across sexual identities and communities often feel pressured to desire sex, and experience discrimination and shame when they do not. In resisting that pressure, ace folks are lightening that load for everyone.

So, I want us to broaden our thinking about desire. The impulse to center sex itself in understanding desire, or the idea that people's libidos or sex drives lie at the heart of our behavior, is a limited frame. One likely reason my intellectual mentor and muse Audre Lorde was so critical of sex work and hard-on porn was precisely because erotic expressions that center sex obscure the broader sociological and feminist underpinnings of desire, which is rooted in a thirst for human connection.

People on the ace spectrum have erotic experiences and desire intimate human connection—just not necessarily in the form of sex. Ace people may experience *sensual attraction*, not sexual attraction. Ace writer and activist Coyote notes that sensual attraction is an "involuntary, internal impulse to initiate physical contact," such as hugging, hand-holding, and cuddling. Ela Przybylo, author of the book *Asexual Erotics*, offers, "erotics thus provide a promising language for discussing forms of intimacy that are not simply reducible to sex . . . and that further challenge the Freudian doxa that the sexual is at the base of all things."[31] This is all to say that part of the problem is a misguided cultural and medical overemphasis on sex drives.

What's more, a wide range of social conditions might leave people uninterested in sex. Bree's story underscored this point well. People are often overworked and tired from capitalist labor, whether they work in or out of the sex industry. People are exhausted from chasing around children. Let me tell you, I love my kid, but especially when he was young, single-parenting and working a lot often burned me all the way out—making me sometimes crave sleep more than sex. As ace people frequently joke, sometimes people would simply rather bake and eat cake than have sex. My sweet-toothed mother, who was incredibly sex-positive, used to quip that sometimes, if given the option, she'd, too, choose a piece of cheesecake or key lime pie or a box of hazelnut truffles over sex. And she loved sex.

Evolutionary biological, psychological, and medical perspectives on desire either erase or pathologize people on the asexual spectrum who experience little to no sexual desire. As writer and journalist Michele Kirichanskaya underscores in the book *Ace Notes*, clinical professionals are still trying to "cure" asexuality, apparently having missed the point of a prior generation's activism rejecting diagnoses of lesbian, bisexual, and gay people as sick.[32] With pens for pistols, psychologists and medical practitioners produce studies and ideas and engage in practices that incessantly tell people that their normal and healthy desires are *paraphilic* or abnormal.

When it comes to low sex drive, we see scientific sexism yet again, as these experts have especially targeted women, whom they have specifically diagnosed with female hypoactive sexual desire disorder

(FHSDD).[33] Historically, many cultures have often emphasized, quite coercively, that women must restrain their sexual desires and refrain from recreational sex outside of marriage and procreation. Given this, one way to interpret this hysteria around some women's low or absent interest in sex is that the FHSDD diagnosis is retribution for failure to uphold heteropatriarchal familial obligations.

Scientists and clinicians have enormous power to pathologize sexual desire, including a lack of sexual desire—libido. But despite their efforts to police and regulate desire, and much to the chagrin of Freudians, it is valid to have no sex drive or one that is low, high, or anywhere in between. This spectrum of desire reflects the rich and beautiful diversity of human bodies and experiences.

I also believe, in some cases, medicine and psychology's pathologization of low libido is precisely why, politically, some people on the ace spectrum prefer to define asexuality in relation to attraction and not desire or libido—a linguistic coat of armor to shield themselves from the ongoing harms and marginalization caused by medicalization and pathologization of healthy and normal sexualities.

Compulsory sexuality and its corollary, *allosexism*, or the privileging of allosexuals, also help explain why so many people on the ace spectrum do not come out or otherwise identify as ace. In a 2022 study, "I Didn't Know Ace Was a Thing," sociologists reported that 65 percent of ace folks had previously identified as straight, and 47 percent had identified as bisexual or pansexual at some point in their lives. As these sociologists explain, "this phenomenon appears to stem from a lack of knowledge about asexuality as an identity option."[34]

These findings were in line with many of the conversations I had with ace sex workers. Lorena, a twenty-seven-year-old asexual sex worker from the United States, shared: "I didn't come into asexuality until recently. I didn't even know it was a thing until a year and a half ago, actually. In high school, I leaned more toward bisexuality. And then, as I got into understanding about sensuality, and then I got into BDSM, I learned about asexuality through my [current] slave. They mentioned to me, 'Since the way you see relationships, you might wanna look into asexuality and see if that, you know, works for you.'"

After exploring online and learning more about asexuality, Lorena began to feel at home. So, I asked Lorena, "Do you still use the bisexual label?" She responded, "No, not anymore. Just because I wasn't aware of asexuality. So, I thought, there was, you know, gay, straight, bi, and I didn't really have other vocabulary. And then I hear asexual, and I'm like, 'Oh, damn . . . like, fuck.'" She reflected on the limited language available to articulate her desires when she was younger. "I just wasn't aware of the other sexualities because, in high school, I did hang out with more of a queer crowd. So, we were all still learning, and I was still kind of seeing where I define myself because growing up, it was basically like straight and gay."

Lorena explained to me how she experienced compulsory sexuality. People are socialized to believe that having sexual desires and experiencing sexual attraction is a fundamental part of the human condition and that everyone must fit neatly into available sexual categories. One's cultural milieu dictates just what those options are. Lorena came from a conservative home with parents who emphasized heteronormativity, but her friend groups were primarily queer in high school. Like all of us, she could use only the language available in her cultural worlds to understand her own desires and sexuality, and she did not, at that time, have access to the language of asexuality.

A sociological lens shows that individuals on the asexual or ace spectrum still have a social relationship to sexual desire, even if some do not experience embodied sexual desire or attraction. This is because compulsory heteropatriarchal sexuality is a system of power that none of us can magically step outside of. But people can and do resist and contest sexualized social control, creating new languages and communities around forms of eroticism. They embody non-normative forms of desire that lead to social change.

It is critical that everyone takes a moment and asks themselves how compulsory heteropatriarchal sexuality has affected their desires and sexuality. People feel social pressures around their sexuality all the time. To move toward erotic empowerment, we need to locate the external sources of these pressures and understand how the world and people around us have shaped our understanding of our desires.

From this first lesson, I hope it is clear that nobody should ever feel pressure to have any erotic encounters or sex they do not want. People do not have to desire sex ever, much less frequently, in order to have a healthy sex life—a healthy erotic life—and sex positivity involves honoring your desires, be they nonexistent, nonstop, or somewhere else on the continuum of desire.

Sexual liberation for all will only be possible when we recognize and honor the fact that desire exists on a spectrum, and it is sex-positive to stand up and fight against the system of compulsory sexuality and the societal shaming of anyone based on where they fall, at any given time, on the sexual desire continuum.[35]

The second lesson we learn from people on the ace spectrum is that desire exists across a continuum. It ebbs and flows throughout our lives, just like a breaking tide pounding the shoreline.

Linguistically, words make the world intelligible. Still, languages often rely on limited and binary forms that conveniently support the social order but defy empirical and human realities. As journalist, writer, and ace advocate Angela Chen puts it, "language is a form of power. It creates categories that help us interpret the world, and that which is not easily available in language is often ignored in thought itself."[36] What happens when people don't fit into categorical schemas?

One way we can answer this question is to reckon with what still happens to babies and children with intersex traits when doctors discover that their bodies defy the sex binary—female/male.[37] In the words of Anne Fausto-Sterling, people with intersex traits "have unruly bodies. They do not naturally fall into a binary classification [and] only a surgical shoehorn can put them there."[38] Around the world, cultures literally mutilate the bodies of babies and children born with intersex traits to make them conform to medically, politically, and socially constructed binary classification systems of human sexuality. We must accept that the living world exists on a continuum!

It has been more than half a century since Alfred Kinsey, a pioneering sexologist in the United States, attempted to shake up these binary ways of thinking about sex and desire. As he wrote in his groundbreaking 1948 study, "not all things are black nor all things white. . . . Only the human mind invents categories to force facts into separate pigeonholes. The living world is a continuum in each and every one of its aspects. The sooner we learn this concerning human sexual behavior the sooner we shall reach a sound understanding of the realities of sex."[39] To underscore this position, Kinsey introduced the Heterosexual–Homosexual Rating Scale, most often colloquially called the Kinsey scale, to capture his core thesis that whom we desire is fluid.

As part of the research for two works published separately, *Sexual Behavior in the Human Male* (1948) and *Sexual Behavior in the Human Female* (1953), Kinsey interviewed 5,300 white cisgender men and 5,940 white cisgender women about their sexual histories. Before I say anything more about what Kinsey found, I do have to share with you what one of my favorite humans and disciplinary colleagues, Brandon Robinson, is saying in my head as I type: "What people *say* they do is different from what they *actually* do." So, readers, please keep that caveat in mind when you read about research, including Kinsey's, that claims to have studied sexual behavior. Only when researchers conduct in-lab experiments, like Masters and Johnson, or watch people fornicate in the wild, as I have done in my fieldwork, are we documenting sexual behaviors.

Methodological and linguistic gripes aside, Kinsey reported levels of same-gender attraction (which he called *homosexual attraction*) in both men and women that audiences at the time found shocking. Nearly four in ten cisgender men and just over one in ten cisgender women reported at least some overt same-gender experience to orgasm over the course of their lifetimes. About 10 percent of men reported a nearly exclusive preference for same-gender sexual experiences, while lower

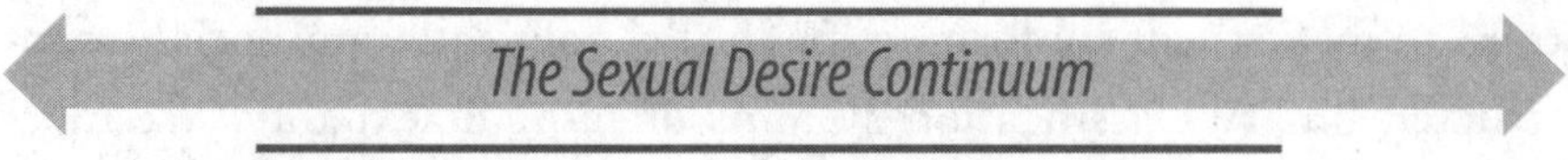

The sexual desire continuum.

percentages of both men and women reported exclusive same-gender preferences for shorter periods in their lives.

Kinsey's point was that sexuality is not binary, and it is not static. People often have desires and sexual behaviors throughout the course of their lives that are not in line with their sexual identities or with normative standards of the day. We can draw on the Kinseyan notion of sexual fluidity to rethink a more expansive understanding of desire that accounts for both asexual and allosexual people. I call this the *sexual desire continuum*.

Human desire exists across the sexual desire continuum. On one end of the spectrum lies asexuality, and on the other, allosexuality. However, as Angela Chen writes, "the world is not a binary of aces and allos."[40] So, I ask you to consider human sexual desire in terms of volume, not as an either–or proposition. Some people never experience sexual desires. Some people do experience sexual desire, but infrequently. For others, desire is context-specific, something that happens only after they form intimate and emotional bonds. Some people experience sexual desire frequently, and others can't stop desiring sex, fantasizing about sex all day long.

Critically, people do not stand on the sexual desire continuum with lead boots—many people's desires fluctuate throughout their lives, based on social, economic, and political conditions. The terms *aceflux* and *acefluid* capture this phenomenon.

RJ is a bisexual and ace trans and nonbinary online sex worker. Originally from the United States, RJ has been living in New Zealand for the past five years. In our conversation, RJ underscored the fluidity and contextual natures of desire. "I could go years without masturbating. I could go years and months without sex and without thinking about it . . . I could take it or leave it. Sometimes, I have sex; sometimes, I like sex. Sometimes I masturbate, but, like, that's why it's a spectrum."

In my conversations, I also spoke to people on the sexual desire spectrum who were currently sex-averse—emphasis on *currently*. Their nonlinear stories disrupt born-this-way narratives and complicate binary thinking—that people are born with specific desires and are either ace or allo. Joanna, for example, is a cisgender woman and an asexual full-service sex worker from the United States. She had not been in a relationship in ten years because she did not currently desire sex or a romantic relationship. Still, she had sex for a living and has not always been sex-averse.

Joanna explained her current relationship with sex in this way: "It's really not important to me. . . . I guess I'm just over sex from work. The idea of it just makes me feel tired, to be honest." Joanna's comments underscore how people can and do age into asexuality and how our lived experiences can reshape our relationship to desire and sex.

I also spoke to people who are demisexual. These folks sometimes experience sexual attraction, but generally only after they have formed an emotional connection and bond with someone. Eevi, for example, a demisexual nonbinary full-service sex worker from Finland, is not entirely sex-averse: "It can take me a year into a relationship to feel open to sex with a partner." Many of the ace people I talked to enjoy romantic relationships, but they desire partners who respect, understand, and validate their sexualities.

Research has shown that when asexual people are romantically involved with allosexual people, they often consent to sex because they want to please their partners, express affection, and connect. As several of my research participants noted, sex can be a vehicle for intimacy with their partners.[41] This is a finding that once again showcases the social functions of sex and the sociological nature of eroticism.

Samantha, a twenty-five-year-old demisexual Scottish sex worker, explained her relationship to sexual desire: "I can go a year or longer without sex. It's not something that I need. . . . And I have been in relationships. I'm currently in one, and the best way to make it work is to allow them to have sex with other people if that's what they choose to do."

Through polyamory, Samantha only has sex when she wants. Explicitly discussing her levels of sexual desire with her allosexual partner, who has high levels of sexual desire, allows the two of them to make choices that honor both their desires, make their relationship work, and allow for control and agency over their sex lives.

A public understanding of the sexual desire continuum, compulsory sexuality, and allocentrism can help everyone. Productive discussions of sexual desires with partners, especially in the context of romantic relationships, involve sharing where we currently are on the desire continuum. Partners need to find ways to connect so that each feels seen. Nobody should feel pressured to have sex they do not want. And, I believe, sex is better and most empowering when we communicate our desires clearly and in detailed ways to our partners.

Communicating our sexual needs and fully understanding our sexuality also requires that we "split" our understanding of desire and attraction. People in the asexual community have embraced a model of *split attraction*.[42] So, a person might be asexual in their sexual orientation but bisexual in their romantic attraction. Just because someone doesn't experience sexual attraction doesn't mean they don't experience romantic attraction. Ace people show us that just as desire exists on a spectrum, so, too, does attraction. People on the ace spectrum offer everyone a much more nuanced way to understand human attraction.

The third critical lesson is that attraction, like desire, is complicated, takes many forms, and is not just limited to sexual or physical attraction.

For allosexuals, attraction is physical attraction. Most of the time, this takes the form of *aesthetic attraction*, which is primarily based on specific aspects of another person's physical appearance. Most people are reluctant to talk openly about how race, nationality, ability, body size, and class shape their romantic desires, fearing being labeled a bigot. Still, we can clock allosexuals' aesthetic preferences in everyday life. People talk about having a type, maybe "tall, dark, and handsome." Open gay dating apps, and you'll see profiles defiantly announcing, "No Fats, No Femmes, and No Blacks or Asians."[43] These folks may use the language of personal preference to legitimize their fatphobic, femme-phobic, and racist cleansing of eligible matches or what scholars call *sexual racism*, but such choices reflect the political nature of attraction and sexuality.[44]

I spoke with asexual sex workers who talked to me about their personal romantic lives outside of work, their experiences of attraction, and how being raised in an allocentric context shapes their lives. Samantha told me, "I can identify someone who's attractive and someone who's sexually appealing to the majority. But just because I know these things doesn't mean that I'm interested in them. I know they're attractive in society, but that's just all I can really say about them. . . . That doesn't mean I can feel anything."

As she told me about her attraction to her current partner, she explained, "I wasn't in the beginning. I thought, Oh, they're a good-looking person, but I'm not interested, and it wasn't until four months of knowing each other, I became more attracted to him. And that's when we started dating. . . . But it wasn't like an instant attraction. That's something that can vary. I probably only felt that once in my life. I don't really have the instant attraction or feeling that some people might have."

The cultural dominance of sexual and physical attraction in an allocentric world can make dating challenging. Samantha told me that, particularly on the apps, potential partners place aesthetic attraction on a pedestal, like high-value art. "Look at the way relationships are portrayed in films. You see the way they fall in love straight away. And then you've also got things like dating apps, which, you know, you're uploading five photos, and that's what people are judging you on. And you write a tiny little paragraph about yourself."

What people on the asexual spectrum teach us is that aesthetic or physical attraction's cultural dominance under compulsory sexuality obscures other forms of attraction. First, consider *romantic attraction*, which refers to the desire to form a relationship that extends beyond friendship, including culturally defined practices related to dating, courtship, and expressions of love. Some people assume that everyone inherently desires to find a special someone and experiences romantic attraction, which is just not true.

Experiences of romantic attraction are also not a monolith, and people have created new, valuable terms to help us understand romantic attraction more deeply. So, first, some people are *aromantic*, or aro, for short, experiencing little or no romantic attraction. People can now use the terms *gray-romantic* if they do not often experience romantic attraction or *demiromantic* if they do not experience romantic attraction until after a close emotional bond has been formed. We can learn a lot from aromantic people, too, about challenging romantic norms and designing and reimaging relationships that work for us.[45]

New terms are also available that highlight how orientation shapes romantic attraction. For example, someone who experiences romantic attraction and is bisexual might identify as *biromantic*; a pansexual person, *panromantic*; a person who is gay might use the moniker *homoromantic*; and a straight person, *heteroromantic*. Using such terms allows people to present their sexualities with far more nuance than terms such as ace, gay, straight, or queer. It is a recognition that not everyone experiences romantic attraction or desires a relationship.

According to the *2020 Ace Community Survey Summary Report*, based on over fifteen thousand survey respondents from more than one hundred countries, "over half of aces claimed at least one aro [aromantic] orientation," whether aromantic, demiromantic, or gray-romantic. Another third also claimed polyromantic orientations. In terms of gender attraction, about a sixth identified as heteroromantic/straight, a quarter claimed a queer romantic label, and another quarter "were questioning or unsure about their label."[46]

Perhaps we are *emotionally attracted* to another human. This means we desire a deep form of intimacy with a person, sharing personal aspects of ourselves and our lives that generate feelings of closeness.

Ace and aro people often use the term *alterous attraction* instead of emotional attraction to reference attraction and desires for close relationships that are not romantic but are also not necessarily platonic, because people frequently tie emotional attraction directly to romantic attraction.

Whichever term most resonates with us, emotional and alterous attraction connote that, rather than being drawn to a person because of their physical appearance, we can be captivated and enticed by their personality, spirituality, character, and inner qualities. Perhaps they have the sexiest mind—for me, intelligent people are so hot! In this case, we experience *intellectual attraction*.

Lorena also spoke to this point: "I'm very attracted to how a person speaks. I was a creative writing major and love poetry. I pay attention to how people speak, and that's actually what's attractive about a person, how they speak and their tone. . . . What attracted me to my slave was how he talked."[47]

So many new terms—I get it—but this language is important. Cultures build dating and courtship solely around physical desire, dismissing other forms of attraction. I believe the expansive ways that ace people understand attraction can help everyone think more deeply about their desires. It is a worthwhile exercise to consider what makes us feel attracted to someone: sexual, physical/aesthetic, romantic, emotional, alterous, or intellectual attraction? If we experience physical or aesthetic attraction, it is beneficial to take a moment to consider how the cultures around us have influenced our perceptions of what we find physically appealing.

We can all benefit from a fine-tuned understanding of attraction. People can experience one, some, none, or a combination of these forms of attraction, and our relationship with them can shift throughout life. Erotic empowerment is a deeply embodied experience, and the more precisely we can articulate how we do or do not experience attraction to others, alongside understanding the social origins of attractions, the more profoundly consensual, pleasurable, and empowering our erotic relationships will be, regardless of our orientations.

A fourth lesson we can learn from asexual people is that community can serve as a lifeline for countering the shame associated with desiring in a different way from the cultural norm. Erotic communities, in other words, are essential to individual sexual well-being.

Visibility really matters: As more ace people come out and create new languages and communities, their eroticism creates cultural change. Today, television shows like Netflix's popular series *Sex Education* and *Heartstopper*, about British teenagers navigating sexual exploration, feature characters coming out as ace. Off the screen and on the stage, Branden Jacobs-Jenkins's stunning play *Purpose* won a Pulitzer Prize for Drama and a Tony Award for Best Play in 2025. The main protagonist and narrator, Nazareth "Naz" Jasper, is an asexual African American man, and his sexuality is central to the story.

Young adult books feature asexual protagonists. For example, Jen Ferguson's novel *The Summer of Bitter and Sweet* tells a powerful story of an eighteen-year-old Canadian Métis woman named Lou grappling with racism and economic precarity and coming to understand her lack of sexual attraction better, eventually coming out as demisexual. In other aspects of culture, too, ace people are starting to see themselves represented.

Still, even as new forms of asexual media and language proliferate and asexual people and activists educate others, erotic change can be slow. Ace activist Yasmin Benoit has written movingly about the struggles of coming out as asexual. Even after she came out as asexual and found language to describe her sexuality, that language was unintelligible to the people around her.

Like Yasmin, many ace people find that those around them do not believe asexuality is real. They might call it a phase, or insist, "You just have not met the one yet." Others confuse it with abstinence or celibacy, or believe that it's an illness (e.g., HSDD).[48] Inviting, inclusive communities counter these feelings of dismissal, alienation, and shame. When the world invalidates your sexuality, discriminates against you, and tries to make you ashamed, an erotic community can not only keep you safe, but can also become a space where you find empowerment and joy.

Ace people demonstrate pride and rebuke shame in small cultural ways. Some people wear a black ring on the middle finger of their right hand to signal to other aces that they are community members. People wear Ace Pride T-shirts or paint their nails black, white, gray, and purple in a nod to the colors of Ace Pride.

On the asexual Pride flag, black represents asexuality, but ace people often wear purple instead of black because purple is the color in the flag that represents community. In wearing purple, ace people are repping their community, not just themselves. We need affirming and supportive sexual cultures to nurture our desires. These cultures are critical to our sexual well-being.

Ace people on every continent (except Antarctica) have created face-to-face social groups and online groups. They have created dating applications, like AceSpace. Community organizations such as the Asexual Visibility and Education Network and the Asexual Association of Denmark have hosted international conferences dedicated to education and community building. Community spaces like these are helpful for everyone. We all need educational and supportive systems in our lives.

Communities are a significant component of the erotic power model of sexuality. We can do endless work on ourselves and completely understand our desires and attractions. Still, humans are social creatures, and communities where we are supported and validated, where we can enact our desires, are critical to a healthy erotic life. Even though they are always imperfect, in these spaces, people not only take refuge from societal oppression, but find profound joy.

Finding supportive communities is essential because they provide affirmational, emotional, and instrumental support. This is the fifth and final lesson we can take from the ace movement: Erotic communities are spaces where we can bathe in the tingling hot springs of empowerment and cultivate joy and deep pleasures.

One thing I have damn sure learned from my immersion in ace writers' cultural output is that being ace and owning your sexuality is, as Yasmin Benoit puts it most directly, a source of immense freedom and joy.[49] As my disciplinary colleague in sociology Canton Winer writes, we need to make space to discuss *asexual joy*.[50]

It feels empowering to live authentically in our sexuality because this is a moment when we exercise bodily autonomy—to be in total control of what we do or do not do with our bodies erotically, despite what the world around us tells us. As Rebecca Burgess shares in *How to Be Ace*, living authentically as an asexual person in an allocentric world made them stronger and more secure in their relationships.[51]

In the blog post "My Asexual Joy Story," Tyger Songbird explains how challenging and harmful it was—to mind, body, and spirit—to grow up and live in a culture marred with compulsory sexuality and amatonormativity (the social norm that all human beings must inherently want to pursue romantic relationships, especially monogamous ones).[52] Songbird was in the doldrums when they learned about asexuality. Coming out as ace was the greatest source of joy they had ever felt. Living out and proud as their authentic self has made them a joyful person.

RJ's ace joy was palpable despite the computer screen that mediated our conversation. RJ explained how much, in her words, she loves "facilitating someone else's orgasm," even though she rarely has any interest in sex. She told me, "I want to be in ownership of my sexual experiences," which has meant exploring what she called being a "stone top," or someone who does not want to receive sexual attention but loves giving it. RJ has found much joy and pleasure in exploring sex with her partner, who honors these desires.

RJ spoke tenderly about the eroticism she shares with her partner and the joys of them making their own rules. "I can relate to wanting to feel attracted and attractive to your spouse. We don't have to be squelchy wet for how we engage and how we are enjoying each other sexually, like the whole concept, the queering of it. . . . But my spouse gives me massages. My spouse tells me I'm attractive. I tell them they're attractive to me. We cook a nice meal together, and we sit down to eat. And we say, "This is sex.'"

When people recognize and understand their desires deeply, when they develop agency in rebuking social shame and connecting with sexual communities that affirm who they are, they find deep pleasures and joy. As Cody Daigle-Orians highlights in *I Am Ace*, authenticity brings joy. Living your truth and not forcing yourself to be someone you are not is both liberating and intensely pleasurable.[53]

When ace people live their authentic lives and form communities and relationships that honor their desires, they open up access to the joys of erotic empowerment. When they develop new languages and communities around their sexuality, they are producing a form of erotic power. In challenging existing systems of power governing sexuality, their eroticism generates social change that sets the stage for sexual liberation.

Chapter 3

BEHAVIOR

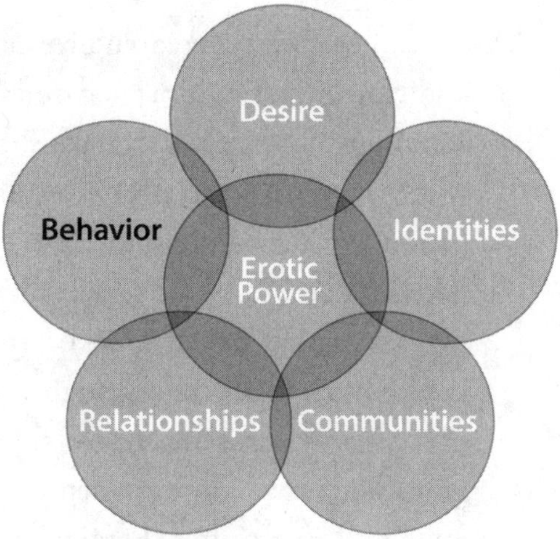

Segseu, seks, sēksa, seksi, seksiä, sess, sesso, sex, sexe, sexo, syeks, szex—there are countless ways to say *sex* around the world, and every language has a word for it. But what sex actually means to each culture is an entirely different story.

If we want to understand human sexual behavior—the second dimension of our sexualities—we must understand the contextual, cultural, and interactional variations in how people define sex. Tackling the question of sexual behavior requires us to examine all the forms of eroticism and sex acts that people think of as sex. When we talk about sexual behaviors, we are referring to eroticism in action. So, for those who find definitions helpful, I name *sex* as a wide range of consensual erotic practices that are qualified situationally and culturally, shaped by external systems of power. Remember, anything that is not consensual isn't sex—it's assault.

Still, rather than attempting to advance an all-encompassing, inclusive definitional slipper that magically fits every foot, I propose we accept the following simple fact about sex—sex means different things to different people. Not assuming that we know what "sex" means for anyone and leaving space to communicate exactly what it means to us is an excellent first step in establishing trust in intimate relationships, improving our sexual health, and accessing erotic empowerment.

Contemporary research gives us unique insights into how our social and cultural locations shape our sexual behavior and individual understandings of sex. Studies have shown that people residing in countries with progressive social policies and comprehensive, inclusive sex education are more likely to have expansive definitions of sex. Cisgender men, regardless of sexual identity, are most likely to define sex as penile–vaginal penetration or anal sex only. Queer and trans people are far more likely than straight cisgender people to adopt inclusive and expansive understandings of sex. People reporting high levels of religious faith have more set definitions, framed primarily around procreation and intercourse. Finally, as people age, physiological shifts often necessitate expanding one's definition of sex.[1]

If you ask straight folks to define sex, their answers sometimes still reflect what feminist sociologists call the *coital imperative*—the focus on penetrative sex between a cisgender woman and a cisgender man. Under what Rachel P. Maines, in *The Technology of Orgasm*, calls the *androcentric model of sexuality*, sex is not sex, especially medically, unless it involves penetration and the infamous money shot.[2] But, sit back, my friends, because the coital imperative dies hard in these pages.

The coital imperative perpetuates what researchers call the *orgasm gap*. The heteropatriarchal focus on intercourse and men's climax cums at a cost for women, with 95 percent of straight men reporting they usually or always orgasm during sex, compared to only 65 percent of straight women saying the same.[3] An overwhelming number of studies show that cisgender women are more likely to have orgasms through clitoral stimulation, especially oral sex, rather than through intercourse.[4] So, there is a lot of pleasure at stake when people hold tight to heteropatriarchal definitions of sex.

Today, is sex *really* just about the old in and out? In the now classic study "Would You Say You 'Had Sex' If . . . ?" published in the *Journal of the American Medical Association*, Stephanie Sanders and Jane Reinisch demonstrated that among their sample of college students in the United States, 99.5 percent defined sex as penile–vaginal intercourse, 81 percent included penile–anal penetration as sex, and 40 percent defined oral sex as sex. Sixteen years later, when researchers replicated the Sanders and Reinisch study, 98 percent of the sample defined sex as penile–vaginal intercourse, 78 percent also included penile–anal penetration as sex, and only one in five defined oral sex as sex.[5]

Even lesbian, bisexual, gay, and queer folks often define sex in ways that prioritize direct genital contact—cunnilingus, blow jobs, anal penetration, scissoring, penetration with fingers, dildos, butt plugs, and, of course, my favorite, strap-ons. In one study, researchers found that 90 percent of men described insertive or receptive anal–penile penetration as sex.[6] There was, however, far more variation for women, and no one definition came out on top: For example, women spoke of many different erotic acts: sixty-nining (80 percent), oral sex (77 percent), use of dildos (74 percent), scissoring (69 percent), and rimming (52 percent).

The coital imperative and the focus on genitals misses a lot—sensual kissing, heavy breathing, dragging nails down a back, joyful frottage, and a range of other erotic acts not involving direct genital contact. Sometimes people get so hung up on the final destination that they forget to enjoy the trip. Just think of the sexual bases in straight cultures. You don't score until you hit home. But, in fact, all the way along the diamond and much beyond, we find erotically gratifying behavior. Sex is not one heteropatriarchal moment when you round home plate.

People's definitions of sex are shaped by their interactions with one another, their social and cultural context, and the specific situations in which they find themselves.[7] If a straight monogamous couple is fighting over cheating, not defining a blow job as "real sex" is a semantic dodge. In the United States, in 1998, former President Bill Clinton famously tried to pull this fast one—emphasis on *tried*—iconically insisting, "I did not have sexual relations with that woman," because he had *only* received oral sex from Monica Lewinsky.

Here's another example: To avoid teasing, Jonah tells his boys he had sex with his girlfriend when she only gave him a hand job. Given the androcentric model of sexuality that guides his thinking, Jonah knows his friends define sex as intercourse, but the stain on *his* girlfriend's blue dress also reminds him that he did cum. So, he skillfully glides across the gray area, knowing he's socially on thin ice.

The point is that how societies and individuals define and regulate sex is a social, political, and economic phenomenon shaped by cultural and historical contexts. Consequently, definitions are fluid, not static. Sure, many hold tight to a definition of sex as the heteropatriarchal coital imperative, but the way people think of sex is changing worldwide. And once again, we can turn to marginalized people to learn about the benefits of more fluid, open definitions of sex.

Let's take a lesson from LGBTQ folks in India. In a 2020 study, researchers asked people across the gender spectrum, including trans and nonbinary people and cisgender people, in Chennai, Bangalore, and Kolkata, to define and discuss the meaning of sex with their own terms and in their own language. Respondents discussed a wide variety of sex acts, from forms of genital contact that did not necessarily prioritize penetration to phone sex. Many included various forms of touching and masturbation as sex.[8] Participants described sex acts along a spectrum, including any that made them feel close to a partner—Doly, a thirty-five-year-old lesbian, called sex "silently holding someone in a peaceful place."

One twenty-two-year-old from the case study, Pooja, pointed out that the fluidity of sex becomes more apparent when you actively reject heteropatriarchy. Pooja, who identifies as gender-fluid and homosexual, remarked, "Why would you realise that [it is fluid] if you're inside the binary because it's [the definition of sex] already given to you? 'This is sex,' and you perform it, and you know it's sex, but once you're out of the binary, you start questioning [the definition]."

Good news—more and more people *are* questioning heteropatriarchal compulsory sexuality and its sexual norms. And such sexual transgressions help everyone—regardless of sexuality.

If I were to get to the heart of what it means to *really* be open-minded about rethinking sex, I would start by interrogating what counts as sex and focus on the kinds of erotic connections that make us most hot, and the conditions we need to achieve this connection. Open-mindedness comes with a big payoff. When we widen and deepen our understanding of what counts as sex, we extend to ourselves a trove of possibilities for enacting our desires—no matter where we are on the sexual desire continuum. This way of thinking prompts us to consider more broadly what each of us wants on a truly inexhaustible menu—one that includes new sexual technologies, a ton of new spaces to explore, and alternative modes of reality.

To push our collective thinking about what counts as sex and probe contemporary sexual behavior, a critical domain of our sexuality, let's turn to sexual technologies—which today produce not just orgasms but also billions of dollars. In this case, human eroticism and sexual behavior drive markets, and capitalism in turn influences our sexual behavior. Sex tech teaches us so much about the power of sex.

I am going to showcase, in different ways, how our sexual behavior shapes the world *and* how systems of power shape our sexual behavior. I invite you, my reader, to think deeply about how systems of power, such as capitalism, heteropatriarchy, white supremacy, and ableism, inform your sexual behavior and how your sexual behavior and choices might play a role in reinforcing these systems—or possibly resist and challenge them.

The enhancement of erotic pleasure through sexual technology is not a new phenomenon in human history.[9] In 2023, archaeologists at Newcastle University and University College Dublin reassessed a two-thousand-year-old artifact found in 1992 at the Roman fort of Vindolanda in Northumberland, which scientists had previously labeled as a darning tool.[10] They now believe it is—drumroll, please—the world's largest dildo. This is not to be mistaken with the world's oldest dildo. That is a title held by the Hohle Fels dildo, found in Germany in 2005 and dating back some twenty-eight thousand years.

Those intrigued by these antique sex toys can satisfy their curiosity by taking a trip to see some of them—for an entrance fee, of course. Pay a visit to the Sex Machines Museum in Prague—three floors filled

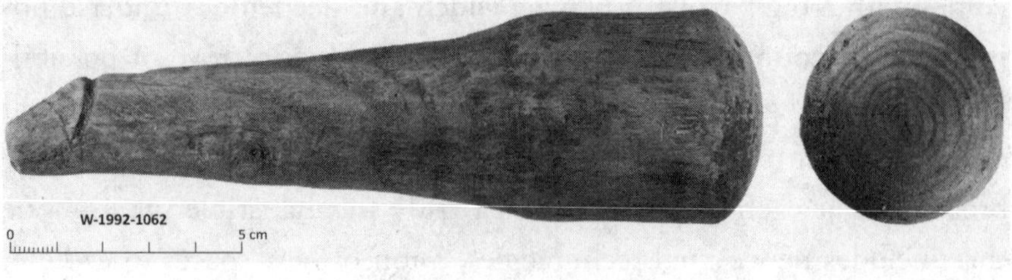

Vindolanda wooden phallus, from Rob Sands/Vindolanda Trust.

with over 350 erotic relics. In the United States, the Antique Vibrator Museum, located at Good Vibrations in San Francisco, California, features a unique collection of vibrators dating back to the late 1800s.

Sexual technologies such as vibrators were not initially *technically* designed to bring personal pleasure—they were medical devices. In 1869, a US doctor named George Taylor patented the first vibrator. The so-called Manipulator was a massive coal-fired and steam-powered device that doctors used to treat what was then called hysteria in women.[11] Using a medical device helped doctors legitimize the practice of getting women off as a medical treatment. Who knew that a mind-blowing orgasm would momentarily ease the pains of existing in an unsatisfying and soul-crushing heteropatriarchal jail?

Fast-forward a century, when feminists advocating for sexual liberation and bodily autonomy would come to frame vibrators, in the words of feminist porn studies scholar Lynn Comella, "as tools of liberation" for women "willing to pay for the promise of better living through orgasms."[12]

In the United States, feminist sex shops such as Eve's Garden (founded in 1974), Good Vibrations (founded in 1977), and Toys in Babeland (founded in 1993) became symbols of women's erotic empowerment. They rejected the heteropatriarchal systems that denied women sexual agency and pleasure. These sex-positive sex shops offered not just toys, but also sexual education and spaces for raising consciousness and affirming women's sexual desires, which compulsory heteropatriarchy had foreclosed for so long.[13]

Today, more than ever, sexual technologies—devices designed for sexual uses—are reshaping sex.[14] They are shifting people's definitions and resonances of sex, as well as how folks actually experience it. As more and more people engage in forms of tech-mediated sex, it changes how we talk about sex with partners, including how we think about consent.

I've seen this play out over the course of my research on the adult webcamming industry. Suppose a cam model in Bucharest, Romania, is in an online private chat room with a client in London, England. After exchanging pleasantries and discussing his desires for the session, she discreetly starts the playlist on her phone.

She performs a slow striptease, caressing her own body. Using the soft tip of her pointer finger, she seductively outlines the contours of her breasts, circling her areolas and gently touching her shiny stainless-steel nipple piercing.

After freeing both straps of her chiffon champagne-pink negligee from the grip of her toned shoulders, she lets the garment fall to the floor slowly, like an autumn leaf from a tree. She pauses, stares into her client's beaming face on the screen, into his baby blue eyes, and instructs her suitor to undress. He does so eagerly, rapidly unbuckling his Cartier belt from his Savile Row–tailored Kilgour pants. After about thirty minutes of online play and directed masturbation, they both cum. She goes on to another client, and he goes back to work.

So, what exactly happened here? Was this even sex?

Technology mediates sex all the time. During the lockdown phases of the COVID-19 pandemic, many people around the globe explored sex virtually for the first time. People partook in digitally mediated encounters as a survival mechanism. Sex parties moved from secret physical locations to Zoom. Swingers moved their monthly events online. Dominatrices moved webcams into the BDSM dungeon. People with more so-called vanilla appetites experimented with all types of sex acts virtually, too.

So—what even *is* sex if it's mediated by technology? Does sexting count? What about masturbating to Internet porn? What about sex acts with inanimate objects, such as dildos and vibrators? If one person takes remote control of a Bluetooth-enabled vibrator located in a partner's anus, is this sex? If someone has sex with a sex doll, is this sex? If someone visits a cyber brothel and has sex with a sex robot, is that sex?[15]

Hot take: It's all sex!

Widening our understanding of sex opens up space for everyone to experience pleasure. For Fatima, a seventy-eight-year-old woman, vaginal dryness can make intercourse with her well-endowed eighty-year-old partner, Ram, uncomfortable. And, for Ram, magic blue pills have caused severe dyspepsia (a.k.a. severe indigestion), plus, they are cost-prohibitive for the couple, given the USA's avarice-driven health care system. But when they began to rethink how to pursue mutual pleasure, they discovered gains in their sex life, even after taking intercourse off the menu.

I want everyone to consider: What's on the Michelin-starred fifteen-course tasting menu that fits your desires? An entire market of sexual technologies exists to satiate your sexual hunger—where there's a desire, there's a market to satisfy that desire—for a price. At the same time, it's important to remember that sexual technologies and sex toy markets are a microcosm of even bigger phenomena.

Sex toys teach us so much about contemporary sexual behavior. Sexual technologies, including toys, offer a unique vantage point for us to explore the power of sex. We can't tap into erotic empowerment unless we fully appreciate how our sexual behavior shapes the world *and* how systems of power shape our sexual behavior.

Fucking drives markets. People *are* widening and deepening their understanding of what counts as sex. Humans are constantly looking for new pleasurable ways to experience their bodies, sex acts, and erotic connections with others, and capitalist markets and enterprises are happy to meet that demand. In the sex toy market, we get a prime example of how human eroticism and our sexual desires and behaviors influence the institutions and the world around us. In this section, we will also observe how the world around us and its systems of power shape our behavior.

Sex toys are big business! And as people get more erotically charged up and more willing to communicate their desires to their partners, the market and profits get bigger—and bigger—and bigger. The global sex toy market was valued at $21.69 billion in 2017. Just five years later, sex toys were a $37.72 billion worldwide industry, with China serving as a manufacturing hub, producing 70 percent of products.[16] During this period, the global COVID-19 pandemic significantly increased online consumption, particularly during the lockdown phase. During lockdown, sales of sex toys increased 110 percent in Denmark. The German seller Dildoking reported an 87 percent increase in sales.[17] People used sexual pleasure as a coping strategy, and sex toys aided in our self-care.

At the current 8.4 percent compound annual growth rate, analysts predict the sex toy industry alone (not including porn or other sex tech) will be worth $62 billion in 2030. Some consumers might be surprised to learn that, in the United States, one of the biggest players in the sex toy market is Church and Dwight Co., better known for distributing fabric softener, kitty litter, and children's vitamins. They also own Trojan, the famous condom brand that also sells sex toys and other pleasure products—bringing in $5.31 billion in revenue.

E-commerce produces the lion's share of sex toy profits. However, unlike many industries that have suffered from the growth of e-commerce, brick-and-mortar sex businesses still thrive. For example, in the United States, over 8,700 sex shops employ over forty thousand people and generate approximately $11 billion in annual sales.[18] The US sex toy retail giant Adam and Eve has physical stores in twenty-two states, Canada, and Peru.

Drawing from the feminist sex shop model, contemporary sex stores often offer much more than opportunities for consumers to buy sexual gizmos and gadgets. Sex shops are sites for inclusive sex education, which is deficient in so many parts of the world. At the popular Come As You Are store, a feminist co-operative sex shop in Toronto, Ontario, people across the gender and sexual spectrum can access sexual health information.[19]

In much of the Global North, sex toys such as vibrators have become normalized and recognized, as they should, as vital tools for sexual wellness. This is precisely why vibrators, often labeled personal massagers, are now sold globally in drugstores and other convenience-style locations. In Canada, you can proudly march yourself into a Pharmaprix or Shoppers Drug Mart and get yours. In the United States, all you have to do is walk into a Walmart, Target, or Walgreens (except in Alabama, where sex toys are illegal to sell). In the UK, no problem—Tesco carries several Lovehoney options. In Sapporo, a large northern Japanese city, you can buy a Tenga-brand sex toy from a vending machine.[20] If you've traveled to Berlin and forgotten your toys at home, well, Berlin Brandenburg Airport (BER) also has vending options to solve all your traveling erotic needs.[21]

People are indeed using their purchases, especially the ones that go buzz. A 2009 US-based study reported that almost half of women used vibrators, and not just for personal use. Of the women using them, four out of five had used them with their partners.[22] Indeed, the popular British sex toy seller Lovehoney Group reported that nearly 70 percent of its buyers are in committed relationships. This data shows that sexual technologies are not simply gadgets that help individuals achieve individual pleasure, but tools for assisting people in romantic relationships to connect.

Fast-forward to 2023: In a robust US-based survey of over forty-four thousand people that additionally incorporated findings from over one hundred existing studies, researchers at Let's Talk Sex found that 82 percent of women in the United States owned sex toys (generally vibrators). More broadly, 76.6 million Americans owned a vibrator. Every month, Americans buy approximately one million vibrators.

Consumer enthusiasm for sex toys is not limited to the United States. In fact, on average, Europeans buy more sex toys than Americans. In Italy, for example, studies show that 70 percent of people have owned a sex toy. And even when accurate data on consumption rates does not exist, we know people are researching and ogling them online.[23] People in the Global North just can't get enough sex toys.

Okay, enough with the nerdy data. I suggest we think about the growth of the sex tech industry as an example of how the power of sex and eroticism shapes social institutions and the entire social and political world. As sexual commerce expands, it causes moral panics and often hasty attempts by governmental leaders to regulate sex, even as they amass huge profits.

Still, please make no mistake; my position that eroticism drives economics is not intended as a love letter to global capitalism. Quite the opposite: The world of sex toys illuminates erotic dialectics and how erotic power does not always foster politically progressive changes or shifts that further economic or social justice.

Even as sex toys enable pleasure for individuals, they are still commodities within an exploitative global market economy. The growth of sexual commerce lines the pockets of owners by exploiting workers. It's a buzzkill to consider that our tools of pleasure were likely made by a poorly paid factory worker on the "996" in China—this is where people labor for seventy-two hours a week, twelve hours per day, from 9 a.m. to 9 p.m., six days per week.

The way that eroticism drives markets ossifies existing forms of economic injustice, even as erotic power shifts ideas about what constitutes sex and sexual norms, and creates spaces for individuals to experience erotic empowerment. This tension reveals a reality that the quest for individual erotic empowerment sometimes comes at the expense of economic and other forms of justice. Sexual liberation entails eradicating and dismantling the structures of power that produce myriad forms of injustice. There's much to be repaired about these systems, and we have to dig deeper to see how people's sexual behaviors drive the change happening within them to understand how to go beyond.

People produce the energetic social force of erotic power. It is, therefore, our collective eroticism that generates change and influences the world around us—our economic, political, and social institutions. As David Allyn shows in *Make Love, Not War*, his book on the sexual revolution in the United States in the 1960s and 1970s, the era's shifting ideas about sex emerged from a potent stew of political movements for racial, gender, and sexual justice and the behaviors and communities of pornographers, sex party enthusiasts, kinksters, feminists, lesbians, and gay men. Collectively, their actions and behaviors not only shifted ideas about sex but also affected laws, markets, and systems of governance. These people, in Allyn's words, built "an era of erotic possibility."[24]

In the same way, we can trace the impact of real live erotically charged people behind the growth of the sex tech industry. Sex toys have developed to support the erotic needs of a vast array of people who, by making their sexual needs part of the public conversation, create demand and contribute to economic growth. Critically, in analyzing people's use of sex toys for personal pleasure or to serve the pleasures of others, an intriguing reality comes to light—erotic power drives change, just not always in the liberatory ways people might expect.

Members of queer communities, kinky people, sex workers, and other marginalized people have played a significant role in advancing an entire sexual pleasure economy. A vast array of sexual technologies has been made just for them, and often by them, all with the goal of fulfilling their desires. There are now sex toys, for example, that meet the sexual desires, needs, and bodies of trans and nonbinary people.[25] Sex toys have been made specifically for people with disabilities. BDSM practitioners need bed restraints, bondage tape, floggers, gags, nipple clamps, penis cages, whips, ticklers, and so much more, and those needs have also contributed to the growth of the market for sexual toys and equipment.

When I sat down with the prolific writer, podcast host, and sex worker Gabriela Herstik, she pointed out the critical role sex workers have played in the evolving sex toy industry and its success. She told me, "Sex workers are at the forefront of everything. . . . Sex workers are the ones that have been using these things forever, like floggers."

Gabriela Herstik pictured with one of her favorite floggers.

Gabriela explained that sex toys, while not necessary to all her erotic labor, are indeed important. Reflecting on working at a strip club, she provided an example: "You could totally strip without a pole. You don't need a pole, but that is also a part of the technology that has helped stripping evolve." In her BDSM work, she noted how certain sexual toys, equipment, and technologies are critical to orchestrating scenes and client fantasies for play sessions. Shifting to her work in camming, she said, "I have a vibrator that when you tip me on My Free Cams or Chaturbate, the vibrator vibrates. . . . I make more money with this vibrator because people want to feel like they can interact with me outside of the screen."

Gabriela pointed to a critical trend. In studio and amateur porn alike and in online cam shows, sex toys are a vital prop. In fact, I'd argue that camming performers are required to use sex toys if they are to remain competitive. In 2006, OhMiBod, a sex toy company based in the United States, created the first vibrator that could be operated remotely through an app. Today, OhMiBod is only one of many companies producing *teledildonics*.

Online sex workers were some of the first people to take advantage of this new technology. In my research on the camming industry, I observed models frequently using teledildonics, such as the one Gabriela described. Performers gave clients remote access to a vibrator they were using in real time. The new technology maximized income potential and created new consumer demands.

These toys complicate our understanding of what counts as sex. During my research, cam performers' use of teledildonics often went down like this: A woman used a teledildonic made by the popular company Lovense. Every time the customers in her virtual room tipped, the model's vibrator, which was inside her vagina, went off. A virtual battle of ego erupted, and one viewer after the other kept tipping. The toy kept right on buzzing until the performer ostensibly climaxed and removed it.

Performers' use of teledildonics also underscores how human's erotic ingenuity creates demand and thus drives industry growth. Aron, a thirty-one-year-old from Hungary, and I discussed his use of teledildonics in his shows and their use in the camming space more broadly. "Teledildonics skyrocketed a few years ago. You know, there are all kinds of dildos that you can connect to your smartphone. . . . When I'm using mine, I make the most money because people love it. Because you know, they can use a few tokens, and then they control something in you or on you or something, and they're just crazy about it. It makes a huge difference, actually. Or you can use it when you are not even online. For example, you can sell a package where you are saying, 'Okay, I am in this or this public place or whatever, I have my plug in, send me X dollars, and I'm gonna give control for ten minutes—and then you can control, and I will post videos on Snapchat that you can check out or something.'"

Sex is imbued with power, and teledildonics point to the sociality of sex. The client who wants to control Aron's vibrating butt plug feels empowered when they are in control. Clients may get off precisely because Aron was in a public place, defying conventional norms regarding the privacy of sex.

Performers like Gabriela and Aron find creative ways to use these toys in their online shows. Doing so makes them money in the short term, but the performers' ingenuity and artistry keep consumers coming back, creating demand for how the toys are used in online sex shows. It is precisely this combination of eroticism *and* pleasure that drives the contemporary sex toy market. At the same time, this industry growth generates large sums of wealth for owners through the exploitation of workers and the environment.

Now that we have observed how eroticism and our sexual behaviors affect one system of power—capitalism—let's talk about the inverse. To understand how systems of power shape sexual behavior, we can look to the uncanny world of sex dolls and the people who use them. This, too, is a window into how, in the personal pursuit of erotic empowerment and pleasure, individuals can perpetuate systems of inequality, which, I'd argue, is antithetical to sexual liberation.

We haven't yet quite figured out how to talk about sex dolls and robots. People are often rightfully mistrustful of new technologies, such as AI and robotics, and the exploitation and harm they can create. Even outside of sex, these days, I am reminded of this all the damn time, as my university colleagues and I lament about students' use of AI and commiserate about the good old days BAI—before AI.[26] When it comes to sex dolls and robots, fear combined with the exploitative ways that a relatively small group of people will likely use them pushes some people to embrace outright prohibition.[27] Much of the current writing on sex dolls and sex robots is primarily theoretical and, frankly, mostly conjecture. It also tends to fall into one of two camps: moral panics and diatribes about the harms of sex dolls and sex robots that don't even exist yet or, alternatively, love letters and hymns singing their praises.

On one side of this sex wars[28] reboot are SWERFs (sex worker exclusionary radical feminists) and academics such as Kathleen Richardson, who are associated with the Campaign Against Sex Robots and Women Against Sexbots in the United Kingdom. They argue that sex robots objectify women and have compared sex dolls and robots to slavery and sexualized labor trafficking—even distastefully co-opting the language of Black Lives Matter to protest that "Robot Lives Matter."[29] This crowd points to some truly egregious behavior in the sex doll industry—for instance, the existence of companies willing to produce dolls resembling children, knowing pedophiles will buy them—to demand the full prohibition of *all* dolls. They want no one who wants sex dolls to have them.

On the other side are proponents, such as David Levy, who romanticize this sex tech. He suggests that we should get ready because, by 2050, love and sex with robots will be a normalized and routine part of people's sex lives. In his book *Love and Sex with Robots*, he boldly claimed that people everywhere will not just be having sex with robots, but having long-term relationships with them.[30] This camp wants everyone who wants sex robots to have them.[31]

Once again, drawing from the feminist pleasure and danger framework, I find little utility in this doomsday/liberation binary. Like other aspects of our lives, sexuality has been and will continue to be shaped by technological developments. Some people resist the inroads that technology has made in sex because of its potential misuse. In contrast, others are hopeful that sex tech will challenge assumptions about our bodies, gender, sexuality, companionship, and pleasure.[32] We are not playing a zero-sum game and don't have to allow fear of a relatively small amount of inevitable misuse to shut down the pleasurable eroticism that sexual technologies provide to many. Still, this fear is pervasive, and aggressive knee-jerk regulations and prohibitions are born out of these fears.

Erotic change can be slow. AI and robotics are not being integrated into sex tech as quickly as the doomsday crowd makes it sound. On a practical level, the adult products industry faces a never-ending series of problems with payment processing, particularly online. Cultural taboos complicate advertising and marketing. And aside from selling torsos, which are undoubtedly off-putting to many, the industry has not found ways to produce lifelike adult dolls that the average person can wrangle, given their weight. Rapidly changing laws to protect children from exploitation are critical and present real challenges for the capitalist. Due to what sociologist Erving Goffman calls *sticky stigma*, many workers, especially those in robotics, may be reluctant to work in the sexual technology industry—there's disciplinary power at work again in the never-ending tug of war with eroticism.

The slow pace of this change is, in many ways, good news—it means nations and states still have time to use empirical data and ongoing input from industry stakeholders, especially workers, to develop sensible, scientifically informed policies that can address issues of abuse and harm while not putting people out of work, closing businesses, and shutting off the erotic power for everyone.

Sex dolls are global commodities. China has become the manufacturing hub for these life-size and lifelike dolls, which are generally made of silicone or thermoplastic elastomer. Companies such as WM Doll and Exdoll in China have dominated the space since 2012 and 2013, respectively. By 2022, there were over a dozen sex doll manufacturers.[33]

I spoke with Guillaume (founder) and Alice (chief customer support lead) from My Robot Doll, an internationally recognized sex doll dealer based in Brussels, Belgium. They provided me with an excellent overview of the current market, confirming much of what the data shows regarding client demographics. The vast majority of their customers are men, which they said echoes a larger industry trend.

Scholars Kenneth Hanson and Chloé Locatelli determined that, according to manufacturers, less than 10 percent of sex doll buyers are women; the industry primarily caters to straight cisgender men.[34] Hanson spoke to one representative from another leading manufacturer who said, "When it comes to dolls, the majority is probably people in their forties to seventies, cis white men . . . and there's probably more female customers buying female dolls than female customers buying male dolls."[35]

Hanson, a sociologist, has been at the forefront of empirical investigation into sex or love doll owners.[36] In a mixed-method study, Hanson conducted over a year of digital ethnographic fieldwork, in-depth interviews with forty-one doll owners, and social media content analysis in the online doll community. The interview study sample included thirty-one cisgender men, seven cisgender women, two nonbinary people, and one trans man.

These demographics are not surprising. They are examples of how heteropatriarchy shapes sexuality. In part because of the legacy of feminist sex shops and activism against sexual oppression, women are now more likely to own sex toys than men. Still, almost all other sexual commerce is generally built around men's desires, and capitalism exploits these patriarchal norms for monetary gain. Stick with me, though, because the story of gender in sex doll land gets more complicated.

I was surprised to learn that sex dolls are an interesting site for disrupting gender and sexual binaries. My Robot Doll has seen a growing interest from women, though they are still in the minority of customers. Guillaume and Alice showed me pictures of a male doll made for a client who is a woman, but they said that male dolls are primarily created for and sold to men who are presumably gay or bisexual. The sex entrepreneurs explained to me that customers who purchase dolls that are anatomically female often also buy gender-adaptive accessories, such as a detachable penis that can be inserted into the vagina of the doll. Guillaume said he believed these purchases suggested that these clients have a fluid understanding of sexuality.

Clothes are popular accessories among doll owners. As lead customer support person, Alice spends a lot of time corresponding with clients. Owners spend copious amounts of money purchasing clothing, wigs, makeup, and accessories for their dolls—items many men might feel uncomfortable walking into a store to buy. My Robot Doll cashes in on disciplinary power, selling accessories to consumers who prefer the anonymity of buying directly from the doll manufacturer. Plus, given that most dolls' bodies are thin and dramatically disproportionate (e.g., they have a tiny waist but very wide hips and ass), manufacturers know that customers might have a hard time finding clothes that will fit.

Alice described clients' pride and joy in dressing up their dolls. Dolls are generally feminine cultural artifacts—playing with dolls, combing their hair, dressing them up, and engaging in anthropomorphic play is traditionally relegated to the feminine domain. For many people socialized into masculinity, playing with their sex dolls allows them a sense of freedom from the gender regulations that choke them in other parts of their lives. There is a lot of pleasure in subversive gender play.

Research has documented these forms of gender play, too. Doll owners in online communities create personas and detailed biographies for their dolls, often staging elaborate photo shoots. They post on social media as their dolls. When men who own dolls interact with other men posting online as their dolls, they perform femininity by acting as their dolls; these men also interact as women with their dolls' followers.

As Hanson argues, sex doll companions provide cisgender men a portal to climb through, where they can float euphorically in feminine space—an opportunity to explore their own femininity without using or implicating their own bodies or manhood.[37] Their online gender play is a source of deep pleasure and eroticism. Even though this form of pleasurable gender play has nothing to do with what we generally see as sex, it is nevertheless erotic.

To prepare for my Zoom call with the sex doll retailers, I spent hours scrolling through page after page of doll sites. It was impossible for me not to notice a trend: Almost all the dolls were white, thin, and hyperfeminine.[38] So, I asked my sex doll tour guides to tell me about race and its intersections with gender in this world.

Alice and Guillaume told me that Caucasian and Asian female dolls dominate their bestseller list. The fetishization of Asian women and racist tropes of the China doll, lotus blossom, and geisha are quite common, both in and outside of sexual commerce and in media.[39] Under white supremacy and systems of colorism, whiteness and light skin are considered the pinnacle of beauty and sexiness. As sociologist Salvador

Vidal-Ortiz writes, whiteness is often the default regarding perceptions of gender and notions of beauty.[40]

When I asked the company reps specifically about Black dolls, they explained that Black dolls are undoubtedly underrepresented in their catalog and only sell sporadically. Guillaume said it was unclear if the lack of orders was due to customer preferences or a lack of choices. I'd say it is both, and that the structure of the market, the options within it, and consumer choices are inextricably linked and reflect pervasive anti-Blackness around the globe—especially when it comes to ideas about who and what bodies (yes, even silicone ones) are beautiful, desirable, and hot. In Tressie McMillan Cottom's words, "beauty is the preferences that reproduce the existing social order. . . . Beauty's ultimate function is to exclude blackness."[41] The lack of Black dolls puts the world's anti-Blackness and disdain for Black women's bodies on Front Street.

Keep in mind that there is nothing inherently racist about a sex doll, sexual technologies, or, for that matter, any technology. If these technologies reproduce sexist or racist tropes, it is precisely because humans designed them that way. As roboticist, engineer, and educator Ayanna Howard astutely argues in *Sex, Race, and Robots*, humans embed our systems of power, biases, and beliefs within technologies, algorithms, robots, and all AI technologies.

So, in the sex doll industry, we can observe erotic dialectics and how spaces for erotic joys, pleasure, and empowerment for individuals are simultaneously sites for the reproduction of sexism, racism, misogynoir, ableism, cissexism, and classism. When you select and customize a sex doll, you are asked to make choices about race, gender, ability, and age. Everything from the rooter to the tooter is customizable for a fee. It's not that different, really, from how people behave on subscription-based dating apps or the screening forms the affluent fill out for matchmaking services. People use modern technologies daily to filter their potential dating partners in socially and culturally appropriate ways, especially in ways that reinforce what sociologists have come to call *digital sexual racism*.[42] Consider how factors such as race, nationality, gender expression, ability, and body size influence whether people swipe right or left.

Regarding the size of dolls, most are thin. My Robot Doll was seeing an uptick in the demand for dolls with varied body types, but it's important to note that BBW (Big Beautiful Women) and male dolls often weigh above fifty kilos or one hundred pounds. This size, which presents a significant challenge for an average adult to move easily, undoubtedly affects customer choices, particularly for those with space or mobility constraints.

The existence and appeal of sex dolls underscore the importance of understanding the social functions of sex. It might surprise some readers to learn that most doll owners describe their dolls, whom they name and dress up, as companions. Studies show that doll owners do not spend thousands of dollars on a sex doll because they are horny and want to get off.[43] Or, at least, not solely. As Feona Attwood writes in *Sex Media*, "for some, a relationship with a doll of this kind is a form of 'synthetic love,' and one way of identifying as a 'technosexual.'"[44]

If this sounds strange, a thought experiment might be in order. When you were a child, did you ever have a blanket, a doll, or a toy that comforted you? I did. Mine was a blue, white, and beige blanket that my mother crocheted. I took it everywhere with me. Humans don't leave that behavior behind in childhood—think about your cell phone and the ways that it soothes you as you go about your day. Humans form attachments to inanimate objects all the time. So, I'll leave it to you to decide whether you believe genuine intimacy is possible with an inanimate object or not—but, I also do not think it is my job as a social scientist and sex writer to invalidate other people's experiences because I personally require reciprocity for intimate connection.

Owners often describe the vast benefits and therapeutic functions of their dolls. For people fatigued by the failures in their past relationships, a doll will not break their hearts, cheat on them, or leave them. Other doll owners report they have disabilities and illnesses that affect their ability to date and find sexual partners. Nancy Jecker argues that sex robots are a critical sexual health aid for people with disabilities.[45]

Some couples purchase dolls rather than explore swinging, sex parties, or other spaces for group sex. Couples have reported that dolls have made for more empowering, consensual, and pleasurable sex lives.

Sex dolls and their owners also highlight the role of shame in disciplinary power. Disciplinary power shapes the secrecy and behavior of doll owners who seek out online communities, fearing sanction and stigma from family, friends, coworkers, and various community members. In a study based in Germany, psychologists Lasse Peschka and Marius Raab found that 70 percent of doll owners kept their doll ownership a secret from people they knew in real life, but 92 percent participated in online communities where they could be open about their dolls. The only people in the sample who talked openly about their dolls were those who saw their dolls as companions, what the researchers called *synthetic partner users*, rather than as sex toys.[46]

Respondents' comments underscored the insidious nature of disciplinary power. Lucas said, "I don't think anyone is judging me for having dolls, but I know that doll owners are judged."[47] The distinction: People often engage in this type of furtive behavior not because someone is actively sanctioning them in words or deeds, but because they believe people will. Doll owners, therefore, look to sexual communities as a refuge from anticipated shame and stigma. Sex dolls and their owners underscore so well how systems of power influence sexual desires and behaviors.

After spending copious time on sex doll websites conducting research for this book, I asked myself just how far I intended to lean into the personal. After some thought, I concluded that having sex with one of these dolls could be a unique and valuable opportunity to examine the use of sex dolls from the perspective of a consumer.

Unlike some scientific experiments, I had no specific set of hypotheses going in. But I did suspect that it could be a unique vantage point from which to investigate how power shapes sex—how systems such as heteropatriarchy inform our sexual desires, behaviors, and choices.

If sex dolls are seen as just for men, why? What about them generally appeals to men and not to women, or anyone else on the gender spectrum? I knew I could bring a critical feminist lens to bear on this new sexual technology, all while not playing into reductive radical feminist critiques of sex dolls as representative of the fall of humanity. And, I'll confess, my perverted ass was curious.

Academic motivations and considerations aside, I initially felt ambivalent about purchasing a sex doll myself. On the one hand, I never felt particularly aroused while I was scrolling through pages of inanimate silicone dolls, almost exclusively thin, hyperfeminine white dolls that appeared to be twentysomething years old—and the price tags alone were a quick route to vaginal dryness. While you can get a low-end silicone doll with functional vaginal, anal, and mouth openings for $1,500, high-end models that integrate robotics and AI cost well over ten times that amount. Dolls are advertised with clothing and various accessories, but like so many products these days in e-commerce, you must purchase all these items as upgrades.

At the same time, my inner version of what Sara Ahmed calls a feminist killjoy was on the mat wrestling with my desires, until my sexual curiosity earned the point for the win. I acknowledge that I felt, like Roxane Gay, like a bad feminist.[48] I had been single for a while and was missing companionship. All the social scientific studies I read suggested that people, albeit primarily cisgender men, were finding intimate connections with these dolls, alongside orgasms—and I desired more of both in my life.

I finally found a doll with dark brown braids and caramel skin that looked cute. She was a bit more femme than I generally gravitate toward, but alas, I knew going in that these sites were designed for the cis male gaze. Still, she embodied enough of an aggressive femme aesthetic for me to hit the customize button.

After several customization selections, I put in my credit card information. With the detachable penis add-on, the cost was $1,339.00, far cheaper than for most sex dolls. I chuckled to myself; this expenditure was probably not what authors typically use publisher advance money for. When I tried to process the payment, it took two different cards before one worked: The banks kept blocking the cards on suspicion of fraud. Perhaps it was a warning from the feminist goddesses. Or maybe it was just a reminder that hackers are clever and understand how to exploit sexual shame for profit, as so-called adult sites are a feeding ground for ravenous online scammers.

When my doll was delivered, the good folks at DHL left the box, straight from the industry production hub in China, next to my garage, not on my doorstep. The garage and doorstep are roughly seven and a half meters, or twenty-five feet, apart. The dimensions of the doll's body, approximately thirty-three kilos (seventy-five pounds) and 166 centimeters (five feet, five inches), plus the packaging, tested my strength and reminded me of what I learned from my research interviews and the published empirical work of my colleagues.

The people who order only a torso don't necessarily do so because they are inherently sexist men who only see women as disembodied objects. This knee-jerk read is shaped by ableism. Many people cannot lift a full-sized doll for a matter of seconds, let alone carry one from the hidden chest in their basement or closet to a bed. That day, I was especially grateful for my regular power yoga routine.

Once unboxed, I decided, like most doll owners, to give my doll a name. I chose Cristal—like the champagne. She reminded me of an exotic dancer who used that name, whom I had a crush on back in the day. Her breast cup size, a B, was as ordered. I admit that while I am open to all body types, I especially love women's bodies with small breasts. But she was much thinner than I'd expected. I generally prefer thick bodies. She was also slightly lighter-skinned than I'd ordered, and came naked. Instead of the camouflage sports bra and shorts displayed on the website, Cristal shipped with packaged white hyperfeminine lingerie. Her vulva was the pinkest shade of pink, not at all resembling the shades of brown skin I'd come to expect to see in the beautiful genitals of other women of color.

My reactions as I unboxed Cristal reminded me of how social systems shape physical attraction and so-called preferences. My scrutiny of her body also made me think a lot about how a capitalist consumer mindset has come to shape sexual and intimate life. Increasingly, we are socialized to treat finding intimate partners like a shopping list. What a gut check this was. Here I was, a feminist, scrutinizing her! In heteropatriarchal societies, women's bodies are rarely good enough as they are. And remember, the patriarchal promotion of gilding lilies also waters capitalist gardens.

After fixating on her bodily configurations, I took her to my bed. I have decided to keep details to a minimum, and not simply for my own protection. I know a detailed retelling may be triggering to some. Some readers will want to know that depictions of sexual acts with Cristal and personal reflections of sexual assault follow, which end on page 119 if you'd prefer to skip over this content. Please take care as you read.

I use sex toys a lot in solo play and with partners, but sex with Cristal was unlike any prior experience. Cristal was not some disembodied plastic genital. I tried to relate to A. S., a woman who owned dolls in Hanson's study. She said, "I think it should be more acceptable to have something anatomically correct that resembles a legal adult human body than to have a body part."[49]

I tried to relate. A. S. suggested it is more objectifying to engage with replica human body parts than the replica of a whole human. This argument felt compelling when I read it, and Cristal was indeed a reproduction of an adult human body. Yet, her face and piercing eyes were disconcerting, not comforting, and they stared right through me.

Cristal, sex doll purchased and photographed by author.

Cristal was not incredibly flexible, and I had to work for a few minutes to position her on the bed. Beside her, I had set up a smorgasbord of sex toys, two small handheld vibrators, her detachable penis, and my favorite strap-on.

Once I had her positioned on the bed, legs open, I experimented with kissing her stiff lips, breasts, and nipples. It felt creepy and unsettling to have sex with a replica of an adult human who was unresponsive to touch and tongue. I certainly did not have the money to spring for one of the brand-new models that use AI and other robotic technologies to make her move, talk, and feel warm to the touch. Still, I'm honestly unsure how much this would have altered my experience.

I had initially wanted to experiment with the strap-on. However, when I looked down at the array of sex gadgets I'd assembled, I found that the desire to penetrate her had evaporated. After unsatisfyingly trying to duplicate sex acts with the doll that I usually enjoy with people with vulvas, I grabbed the detachable penis and inserted it into her vagina. This was neither smooth nor seductive—and, for me, it was triggering. Her vaginal cavity was tight, by design, of course, and unlubricated. Even with a bit of water-based lube, the detachable penis required hard shoving and twisting to get in properly. And then, I grabbed one of the vibrators and mounted her.

Cristal's body seemed simultaneously familiar and otherworldly. I kept my eyes closed almost the entire time. Her eyes were daggers, and looking down at her lifeless body triggered thoughts of shame and feelings of repulsion. Perhaps roboticist Masahiro Mori was right, and I was falling hard into the depths of what he called *the uncanny valley*—the idea that as a robot begins to achieve human likeness successfully, it triggers feelings of uncanniness and revulsion. But I knew it was more than this.

Our socialization into systems of power, such as heteropatriarchy, informs our reactions to sex dolls or robots. Understanding my sexual socialization and sexuality fully means that I know the origins of both the shame and repulsion bubbling beneath the surface, but not yet boiling over. The somatic experience of desiring sex in a body that is simultaneously triggered is complicated.

Looking at Cristal was triggering because I know what it is like to feel like a living, breathing sex doll. I know what it is like to have someone on top of you, riding away, moaning in ecstasy while you lie beneath them frozen.

This time with Cristal was not only a flashback to the sexual abuse I experienced as a kid at the hands of other kids, other forms of sexual assault in my adolescent years, or the rape in my early twenties, it reminded me a lot of the uninspired and one-sided sex I had with cisgender men from the time I was fourteen throughout the early part of my twenties—times when I felt just like Cristal looked. In this, I know I am not alone.

Systems of power shape our sexual behaviors. Compulsory sexuality tells people that an active sex life is part of a normal and healthy life, and heteropatriarchy can lead women to have sex with men they'd rather not. Research suggests that this may be particularly true for asexual people who are romantically involved with allosexual people.[50]

My conversation with Eevi, who is demisexual and from Finland, underscored how heteropatriarchal gendered sexual scripts shape our sexual behavior. During this conversation, I asked: "What was the motivation to engage in those sex acts or engage in sex that felt unwanted?" Eevi explained, "It's easier to have intimacy after it. I feel like things are expected of me, and then it's kind of difficult to have real intimacy, especially with cis men."

Joanna, a cisgender woman from the United States, also lamented about how porn and other social and cultural forces miseducate cisgender straight men about women's desires. Regarding her last boyfriend over ten years ago, she said, "He thought that women want to go on forever, and the longer, the better. And I mean, he was really sweet. He wasn't like being pushy or aggressive or trying to be macho. He just really was trying to be sweet. But I was just like, 'Oh, my gosh, I'm exhausted.' So it wasn't ever like I felt forced or anything. Sometimes, it was just like a way to end the night without hurting someone's feelings or just making him happy. I feel like all women kind of get into that situation at some point. I never felt like it was coercive or anything like that. . . . I guess they just need a release."

Heteropatriarchal socialization means that some men are not sentient of, or are downright dismissive of, women's lack of interest in sex with them. Given that heteropatriarchy prioritizes men's sexual pleasure, and that so many people see desire as rooted in biological drives, some men believe they have carte blanche over their partner's bodies, especially when they are in committed relationships. It is this very socialization that makes some men desire sex dolls; they are drawn to the dolls precisely because they are inert. Some men will remain oblivious to this without critical reflection on their sexual socialization.

When I laid myself on top of Cristal, given my socialization and identities, while I knew she was an intimate sex toy, her lack of response was an all too obvious reminder of everything that's wrong with heteropatriarchy. Yet another gut check.

Eevi and Joanna's comments also reveal a striking reality. Women are socialized into heteropatriarchy right alongside men, which disempowers many women to speak up. Sometimes, women end up having sex they do not want just because it feels expected. It is a worthwhile exercise for everyone to think long and hard about whether they've ever felt pressured to have sex, if they've ever had unwanted sex, and why. Often, the pressures people feel to have sex stem from social norms and not necessarily from anything a partner explicitly said. Hence, why Joanna emphasized that her ex hadn't forced her; as Eevi also noted, she still felt unspoken pressures to have sex.

I also encourage people to explore the other side of the pressure coin and introspectively think about any occasions in which they may have pressured someone into sex. Honestly, with introspection, I know I have done this to a couple of cisgender men in my past. My own heteropatriarchal socialization rears its ugly head—"Well, he's a dude, it's different!" It is not different—sexual coercion, unless consensual and part of carefully curated and negotiated erotic play, is never okay!

Even when people think they are being playful, a partner can feel pressured. Remember, motivation and impact are entirely different things. We can intend to be consensually sexually dominant and think of our advances as all in fun, but without necessary communication, someone else can experience that same behavior as coercive.

Systems of power can muzzle you when you are a woman, a person of color, an undocumented person, a trans person, a disabled person, or a poor person. That's why it is critical that people recognize their advantages within systems of power. For example, if aware of these dynamics, the person in a position of power would refrain from having sex with some people altogether in professional contexts (e.g., a boss in the workplace).

I want *all* of us to spend a lot more time thinking about how cultural expectations and systems of power shape our sexual behaviors and how we do or do not communicate before, during, and after sex. Lorelei Lee, writer, adult performer, and sex worker organizer, explains the idea of *constrained consent* so well. Systems of power always inform consent and the choices we make as individuals.[51] As Emily Owens explores in *Consent in the Presence of Force*, various historical, political, economic, and social forces and circumstances often force people to *perform consent* even when they don't want to consent, and especially if they fear reprisal for not consenting.[52]

Having a full understanding of our sexuality and how systems of power influence sex allows us to make choices where sex is concerned that are consensual and more autonomous, empowering, and pleasurable. Those of us who are sexually adventurous by societal standards often shy away from talking about experiences with sexual trauma and violence. We know all too well the ways that political pundits and others weaponize our experiences of sexual trauma to dismiss our desires as rooted in pathology, call us deviants, and drum up support for sexually repressive policies and actions.

Still, for so many of us, these experiences of systemic trauma have shaped our sexuality and our relationship with sex. Trauma, which has unfortunately become yet another overused and misused buzzword, is another term that people typically understand as an individual experience, divorced from its political origins. As Cara Page and Erica Woodland explain so well in *Healing Justice Lineages*, trauma is "an experience or threat that overwhelms our individual and collective nervous system. Trauma is not the experience per se but our physical, emotional, spiritual, and psychic responses to that experience, which are shaped by our lived experiences of intergenerational trauma and structural violence."[53]

If one in three women is sexually assaulted in her life, and she experiences trauma, that trauma was not only caused by the person who physically harmed her, but by the systems that cultivate and routinely encourage, ignore, or dismiss the behavior and that sustain a culture of transmisogynistic and patriarchal dominance and objectification. When feminists say that heteropatriarchy is a violent political institution, we are not exaggerating—heteropatriarchy is a well from which sexual coercion and violence spring.

This is systemic trauma. Heteropatriarchy, white supremacy, ableism, cisgenderism, and capitalism are dehumanizing systems, which science and infinite human testimonies unequivocally demonstrate cause trauma that, without intentional healing, can be passed down generationally and can live in our bodies forever. As Staci K. Haines, an innovator in the field of somatics and author of the groundbreaking book *The Politics of Trauma*, explains, "systemic trauma is the repeated, ongoing violation, exploitation, dismissal of, and/or deprivation of groups of people. . . . Systemic trauma overwhelms and breaks down safety, connection, and dignity in the minds, bodies, and spirits of individuals and communities. . . . When we live inside economies and social norms based on a model of power-over (domination), rather than power-with (interdependence and cooperation), many peoples and communities are traumatically impacted."[54]

Erotic empowerment comes from not shying away from histories of systemic trauma but from examining them—when it is safe for us to do so—so that we can understand why we like what we do and don't and what conditions we need to have pleasurable sex, taking complete control and ownership of our bodies back! We can only share these truths with others when we can define these terms for ourselves.

Sexual assault is not unique to my personal experiences. According to UN Women, who drew from a World Health Organization study from across 161 countries, almost one in three women, or 736 million women, have experienced sexual violence in their lives. These figures do not even include sexual harassment and forms of street harassment such as catcalling—what queer feminist Simone Kolysh has called everyday sexual violence.[55]

Sure, men experience sexual assault, but not on the same scale as women have historically. Around the world, rape and various forms of sexual violence have been legally and socially normalized, especially for poor women, women with disabilities, and women of color. Honestly, it really should not baffle anyone that some women and people with lived experiences of womanhood would rally against the objectification of women as personified sex dolls.

Many women who have not experienced sexual violence still fear it, and we live in global cultures that tell women this violence is inevitable. The objectification of women for profit drives global markets and is entrenched in cultures worldwide—what feminist sociologist Bernadette Barton and others call *raunch culture*.[56] And these conditions have consequences. Peggy Orenstein writes in *Girls & Sex*, "Hypersexualization is ubiquitous, so visible as to be nearly invisible: it is the water in which girls swim, the air they breathe. Whatever else they might be—athletes, artists, scientists, musicians, newscasters, politicians—they learn that they must, as a female, first and foremost project sex appeal."[57]

So many women are socialized into cultures that teach them, over and over again, that their bodies are their most important assets, and that men are entitled to them. In her book *Thick*, when reflecting on her childhood socialization into Black girlhood, Tressie McMillan Cottom shares that by the time she was only fourteen, it was clear to her that, according to the world, "being a woman is about what men are allowed to do to you."[58]

The cumulative effects of incessant objectification and misogyny affect women's socialization, relationships with their bodies, and especially their feelings toward and visceral reactions to men. As Jessica Valenti explores in her memoir, *Sex Object*, women's sexual objectification is pervasive, routine, and normalized—from the man who exposes himself to a woman on a train, to catcalling, to sexual assault, to the endless depictions of women as sex objects in media.[59] Thus, how we experience sex, the technologies we do or do not use in sex, and the ways we seek out sex all reflect our sexual socialization in a heteropatriarchal world.

For the record, neither my sexuality nor women's sexuality writ large should be defined by or reduced to sexual violence. But how we are socialized into and experience heteropatriarchy shapes our sexual behaviors and sexualities in tangible ways. As I take up in the next chapter, our identities are not just cultural markers. They reflect our positions within systems of power and sets of political realities that inform our erotic needs and lives—especially our sexual behaviors.

For me, sex with a doll was unpleasant and uncomfortable. It felt coercive—even though Cristal was an object, and obviously, we don't need consent from a sex toy. For me, reciprocity is key to intimacy and pleasure in sex. And, yes, acts with these sexual technologies are sex.

At the same time, some men say they find intimacy, deep arousal, and pleasure in the same encounter. Some women and queer folks find resistance and pleasure in using a product seen as taboo for them to own. I get that!

So, is my experience more valid? No! However—and this is the important part—I want us to think *really* deeply about how disparate socialization into heteropatriarchy and other systems of power has conditioned these different reactions and experiences. I want everyone out there in the world to think deeply about how various systems of power have formed their sexual desires and behaviors.

What I hope my trip to the Uncanny Valley illustrates is that power always shapes sex—our choices, behaviors, and erotic experiences. An understanding of our sexual socialization, alongside systems of power such as heteropatriarchy, white supremacy, capitalism, and ableism, can help us understand why people will have such different experiences with sexual technologies, whose sexual desires and appetites are satisfied by them, and, of course, whose pockets get lined through the sale of these technologies.

Political and cultural norms all around us influence how we think about sex, how we feel during sex, and how we communicate before, during, and after sex—if we choose to have sex at all. So, understanding how forces external to us may constrain and empower our ability to make autonomous sexual choices is critical for erotic empowerment. The most fundamental sexual freedom is the right to decide if, when, and how you have sex. Still, I also want us to move beyond our individual sexualities and think bigger.

Our tools of pleasure are often a site of exploitation. As sex positive as I am, and as much as I will advocate with my full chest, every day, all day, and twice on Sunday for people's sexual freedoms, I am also really skeptical about the centering of consumption as a path toward sexual liberation that I see playing out in popular discourse. Yes, sex toys and dolls are products designed to help individuals and their play partners achieve erotic delight and pleasure. Still, as we have seen already, they are also products enmeshed in oppressive systems that reify the social order.

Sexual liberation beyond the individual requires destroying the systems that influence why there are so few Black dolls and why sex dolls disproportionately appeal to cisgender men. Part of me wonders that if heteropatriarchy, capitalism, and white supremacy had never existed, would we even have sex dolls? Real talk: I highly doubt it.

Chapter 4

IDENTITIES

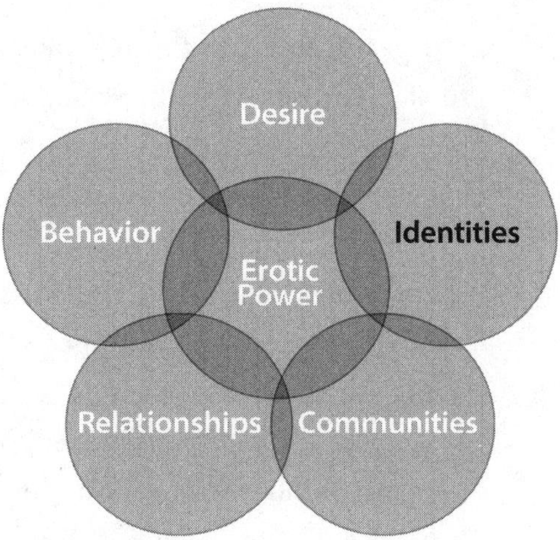

Have you ever looked through a kaleidoscope? As a kid, I had one that I loved so much. I'd place one of my little brown eyes on one side of the red scope and smile brightly as I watched the shimmering colors—reds, purples, and blues—shift and dance as I turned the toy's barrel.

Our sexual identities, the third component of our sexualities, intersect and overlap like the glass flakes in a kaleidoscope to create beautiful mosaics as we move through life and in and out of different social and geographic contexts.[1] Sexual identities make the parts of our sexualities, erotic desires and behaviors, relationship preferences, and community membership intelligible to others.

We've already seen the work of identity in action. The expansive new vocabulary and identity terms that asexual and aromantic people have created have allowed for more public recognition of their sexualities, challenging existing systems of power that exclude them, and demanding more fluid understandings of desire and attraction for everyone. New forms of language allow us to forge community, which is vital to our sexual well-being. Feeling seen in our identity by others produces affirmation and joy.[2] From ace folks to technosexuals to the ever-growing list of sexual identities—they all make up an even larger, more beautiful kaleidoscope of identities.

I get it, today it can feel like you must keep your head on a swivel to stay current with the sexual identity terms in play. Take, for example, the ever-expanding acronym LGBTQIA2SP (lesbian, gay, bisexual, transgender, queer, intersex, asexual, and two-spirit). Some queer folks in the UK and US jokingly call it alphabet soup. But there is a reason that the language and terms for sexual identity keep expanding. More identities mean that more people are getting to know themselves and living authentically.

As people tap into eroticism's power and explore their sexuality, they demand public recognition through new terms. That new language helps them to create supportive cultural spaces where they can express their sexualities fully, all while expanding public ideas and erotic possibilities. And in this expanded freedom, we witness erotic dialectics at work, since such erotic change is typically met with backlash from institutions and people resisting change—from those screaming online about the so-called tyranny of pronouns in bios and introductions to the pernicious attacks on trans people's humanity and rights all over the world right now. This is all yet another reminder that sexuality is always a site of political contestation and that our sexualities, especially our identities, are always a public matter.

Our identities are not just personal—they are political constructs. As French feminist philosopher Simone de Beauvoir famously stated, "One is not born, but rather becomes, woman."[3] The system of cisgenderism, for instance, prescribes that if doctors assign your sex female at birth, you should conform to femininity—be a woman. Similarly, if you were assigned male at birth, you should embody masculinity—be a man. These gendered identities and their expected performances are products of societal systems, not natural or universal truths. And they are intimately tied to our sexual identities.

Imagine a masculine-appearing woman or an effeminate man. Most people's knee-jerk reaction? Gay. Why? Because gender is the lens through which people understand sexual identity. But also, sexuality is the lens through which people see gender. People's so-called gaydar is a socially conditioned response to non-normative gender. When people see someone whose gender presentation conforms with normative standards, they likely assume they are straight. As feminist theorist Judith Butler argues, people police gender so hard because the system of heteropatriarchy collapses without it.[4]

Social systems create hierarchies that categorize and value bodies, determine who has access to rights and resources, and influence how individuals are perceived and treated—even determining whether people are recognized as human. Kimberlé Crenshaw, a legal and critical race scholar, coined the term *intersectionality* to underscore how systems of power, such as capitalism, white supremacy, ableism, heteropatriarchy, and cisgenderism, overlap.[5] As Black feminists have argued for centuries, our identities, born out of these systems of power, inform every facet of our lives.[6]

People often talk about identity in ways that are completely divorced from power—the systems that created them, and the complex webs of power and social relations that sustain those categories. In *Scenes of Subjection*, Saidiya Hartman explains that Blackness, for example, reflects a "social relational and structural position rather than identity; blackness incorporates subjects normatively, defined as black, the relations among blacks, whites, and the practices that produce racial difference. Blackness marks a social relationship of dominance and abjection, and potentially one of redress and emancipation."[7] All of our identities reflect our social positions in hierarchical systems of stratification and sets of cultural norms; they can also be a site of joy, pleasure, and resistance.

I want everyone to imagine that their identities are in the kaleidoscope and to spend some time considering the language they use to label their sexual identity, how that language has changed, if they've ever felt unsafe disclosing their sexual identity, and how their other identities, such as gender, disabilities and abilities, race, ethnicity, nationality, and class, have shaped their sexuality and sex life.

Here, put your hand on the shaft of my identity kaleidoscope and look inside. I am queer. I am nonbinary. I am Black. I am neurodivergent and have disabilities. I am from the United States of America. I am upper-middle class. Each one of these identities shapes every facet of my sexuality and erotic life. Yet, the complexities and nuances of my life experiences add color and texture to each identity category.

In my lifetime, I have identified as bisexual, lesbian, pansexual, and homoflexible. Currently, I use the term *queer* because of its fluidity. My sexual desires and attractions are messy, and no single term captures them perfectly. Like many people, my understanding of my desires and sexuality has shifted and changed over time—a reminder that coming-out processes are never one and done.[8]

I am nonbinary. I often use an expanded moniker, nonbinary aggressive femme, which, as a label, is also intertwined with sexuality and race. *Aggressive femme*, a term developed in Black lesbian subcultures, generally describes a lesbian who has culturally stereotypical masculine personality traits and likes to "top" sexually, but usually has a femme-leaning aesthetic.

I am Black, biracial, and light-skinned. Black feminist writer Alice Walker used the language of *colorism* to describe the privileging of light skin in a context of pervasive anti-Blackness. Black feminists have been integral in deepening my personal understanding of how proximity to whiteness produces privileges. My racial ambiguity has played an interesting role in my sex life, and coupled with aspects of my embodiment, such as my large tattoos or periodically shaved head, and now shaved sides and long dreadlocks, have contributed to what suitors have called my "exotic look." As a result, I have had both pleasurable and unwelcome experiences of *fetishization*, which is when attractions are driven by lust for a single attribute of a person.

I am neurodivergent and have disabilities. I have ADD, which is linked to my auditory processing disorder, which makes being in crowded and loud venues sometimes feel like a real drag. I only understand parts of conversations and often feel awkward. I have terrible chronic gastrointestinal issues. I have visual impairments. In the context of a sex club (this chapter's case study), I don't always like to wear my glasses for aesthetic and practical reasons.

I am also a citizen of the United States of America. My citizenship means that if I attend a sex club and it gets raided, I don't have to worry that I'll get detained and deported. I am also from New York, one of the most politically progressive states in the USA. The specific region where I live means I have access to sex galore: sex shops, sex parties, and sexual services. If I lived in Alabama, I could not even purchase a sex toy legally. Being born and raised in New York also means I've been able to live my erotic life authentically for most of my life—a privilege I have dared not squander and for which I am unbelievably grateful.

Living in the United States also means I live in one of the wealthiest countries in the world, with one of the highest rates of income and wealth inequality.[9] Our economic and social position shapes our relationship to survival—systems of inequality power our body's survival mode switch. Economic precarity and poverty cause trauma, which, as we know from science, affects our brains. I am now upper-middle class, but I've also been poor. That trauma still lives in my bones. When I hear the sound of a tow truck on the block or the swipe of a debit card, there's a split second when I must remind my brain, "We are not behind on the car payment," and "There is ample money in the checking."

But now, I enjoy the privileges of upper-middle-class life, especially where sex is concerned. I can afford sexual technologies. I can afford to travel to sex clubs. I can afford to pay for porn—seriously, people, if you have the means, pay for your porn! A theme you'll witness throughout this book is the importance of understanding how our class positions inform every facet of our sexualities, and how individual sexual exploration often reproduces class-based and other inequalities, stymying sexual liberation.[10]

Now, these are only snapshots of how my identities shape my sex life. The point is that the more we understand how *all* our identities inform our erotic desires, behaviors, relationships, and community membership, the better we can articulate our wants and boundaries to our partners and help our communities create safer and empowering spaces for sexual exploration. Advocating for our needs can feel deeply empowering and pleasurable.

Erotic empowerment is directly tied to our identity kaleidoscope. Systems of power and our intersectional identities mediate our sex lives and the spaces in which some people have sex—a point that comes to life in the sex clubs we are about to visit. As feminist anthropologist Katherine Frank explores in her 2013 groundbreaking book on group sex, *Plays Well in Groups*, our identities influence our access to and participation in sex-on-premises venues (SOPVs, for short) in complex ways.[11]

Sex clubs, quite literally, showcase sex in public. But figuratively, they underscore the point of this book—sexuality is public, not private, and political, not just personal. The political and social environments we exist in shape our sexualities, and our identities shape our access and experiences in cultural spaces, especially erotic ones. When we only understand our sexuality as personal, we miss how the people and spaces around us inform how we can and do embody and enact our sexualities.

Using what feminist sociologist Pamela Tsui calls *the erotic capabilities approach*, we can assess how well any context nurtures bodily autonomy and freedom, the foundations of empowerment.[12] We should ask: Does the space prioritize consent? Does the space provide access to information to enhance sexual education? Does the space have rules surrounding safer sex practices and contribute to supporting them (e.g., free condoms, dental dams, etc.)? Does the space encourage the participation of diverse bodies? Does the space support diverse forms of eroticism and fluid understandings of sex?

Sex parties that prioritize these goals, then, are a particularly productive place to explore notions of sexual identity and how they relate to systems of power. These spaces do not pretend that our identities do not matter—that as long as we are all sexual rule breakers, our race, nationality, ethnicity, abilities, disabilities, genders, and class backgrounds do not matter. Persistent racism, xenophobia, ableism, cissexism, sexism, and classism in the erotic realm undermine both personal empowerment and sexual liberation on a grander scale.

So, if gaining more erotic empowerment is a goal, then take note: Understanding the political origins of our identities can facilitate more empowering eroticism and more supportive community spaces for sexual exploration.

The first time I attended a swinger party, I went with Eric. He was a chain-smoking former rabbi I'd picked up on Christmas Eve in 2013 at a blackjack table in the famous gambling town of Atlantic City. It was a carnal type of night, and it was good fun. Time with Eric was erotically intoxicating and exhilarating—until it wasn't.

When we hung out that winter, Eric and I visited a swingers club in Queens, New York; various clubs in Manhattan, New York, including the legendary Le Trapeze, now closed; and one in Atlantic City, New Jersey. I'll never forget the first time we visited what became my favorite spot—a venue in Queens—on New Year's Eve.

That night, I was determined to serve femme realness. I was aware of the gendered and racialized beauty rules in these straight-swinger places. I rarely wear makeup or high heels, but I wore a short, tight black dress and high black heels that night. I had my makeup done at Mac—eyelash extensions and all.

My inner feminist killjoy was once again calling me a bad feminist. Still, mastering these beauty and sexual scripts made me feel safer entering these spaces. As Sesali Bowen underscores in *Bad Fat Black Girl*, "For those of us who are most marginalized, beauty actually becomes a tool that can be used to defend ourselves against racism, sexism, transphobia, classism, etc. We use it to lessen the impact of how we might otherwise be treated."[13] And, I won't lie, I find pleasure in this kind of drag.

Since it was our first time there and sex clubs are private, we had to pay a membership fee and agree to community rules and guidelines. We also paid the nightly entrance fee, which was higher than usual because it was New Year's Eve. The Queens venue, like many sex parties, was BYOB: Bring Your Own Bottle. So, all in, we are talking about a well-over-$500 night—a reminder that our class positions shape our sex lives.

We dropped our bottles of alcohol off with the bartenders, who served us our first round, and then we went off to explore. We sauntered around the area with the dance floor. After cruising the racially diverse crowd, populated by people who appeared to be in their late twenties through their forties, we headed to the outdoor area. There, we struck up some good banter with another couple and smoked cigarettes. At this time, I still enjoyed a Newport or two with my cocktails. Since my threshold for cold was crossed pretty quickly, we returned inside, grabbed another round, and ended up on the dance floor.

You'd never know it was –1 degree outside (that's 30 degrees Fahrenheit, Americans) because the crowd of scantily clad bodies on the dance floor made it feel like a sauna. I locked eyes with a strikingly stunning woman wearing tight white pants near the stage and the DJ. I remember approvingly smirking about her audacity to wear white after Labor Day. And she was thick in all the right places. She stared at me as she gyrated to the 1990s dancehall reggae beat—her lips didn't move, but I felt her invitation.

Destiny and I slowly made our way to the center of the dance floor. Eric stood off to the side, talking with her husband. We danced closely and intently. We slowly drew an audience as heat radiated off our knitted bodies. I got excited and aroused as people watched us. I felt the music around me—melodic hums vibrated across my skin and seeped into my body, controlling the rolling of my hips—my back—my ass.

We danced closely for many songs before my lips found her collarbone, and she opened her neck for me. A soft blow of air, a dance of my tongue on her neck. She temptingly pulled away and looked into me, and then—we magnetically kissed.

We had an erotic connection. For me, anticipation is erotic. I love to be teased, and I love to tease. Edging isn't just about orgasm play.[14] I want to want to fuck you so bad I might scream and implode if I don't. Destiny was giving me all these vibes.

After the music changed, we sighed and laughed, and both agreed we needed a drink as we fanned ourselves with our hands. When I was dancing, Eric had been taking notes and meeting other people. Destiny and her husband only *soft-swapped*, which in swinger terms meant that Destiny and I could make out all night long, but going upstairs, and Eric having penetrative sex with her, and her husband with me, was off the table for them.

I noticed that Eric and I had different desired outcomes in these spaces, which I attribute to our distinct identity kaleidoscopes. He would be annoyed, almost irate, if, by the end of a night, we hadn't ventured to a playroom with another couple for penetrative sex. Eric saw our adventures through the lens of the coital imperative and felt satisfied only when we fucked another couple.

That night in Queens, my favorite moments were the sensual dancing, the lingering trace of Destiny's fingers up the back of my skirt, my lips gently grazing her neck, and the hungry look on her husband's face as he watched. I find the eye contact between me and a cuckold profoundly arousing. In terms of swingers, a cuckold generally refers to a man who enjoys seeing his girlfriend or wife having sex with another man. So, FYI, I intentionally use this term to describe my experiences to challenge its androcentric connotations. Anyway, looking back, this erotic moment on the dance floor was the climax of the evening for me, even though we did ultimately have sex with another scorchingly hot couple later that evening, right before the club closed.

Don't get me wrong, I consented to the sex we had later. It almost felt like the moment in a pub when a bartender shouts, "Last call," and people run like Olympic sprinters to the bar. So, in this case, given that Destiny left me thirsty, I was happy for a final drink—even as I was disappointed it wasn't with her and her husband. However, given that the club was closing soon, the new couple, Eric, and I did not do much talking, and the four of us hastily took a room upstairs that had just become available after cleaning. It kind of went down like, "You're hot, we're all horny, you'll do, let's get it!"

Critically, we did not have as much of the advanced discussion with the couple as I now require. Our conversation was constrained by time and a language barrier with the Dominican couple, who did not speak English fluently. While I communicated a little with them in Spanish,

Eric spoke no Spanish, and the woman, in particular, was reserved and seemed self-conscious about her English. It wasn't until we were in the small room and starting to go at it that I learned the woman had hard limits around kissing, which was a bummer for me. I learned a lot from this, though.

This was a good lesson about consent for me. Consent is not simply about saying yes or no, or initially feeling enthused. Full consent is informed consent, which requires information and involves ongoing communication. In hindsight, if I had known that she was actually not all that interested in me, I am honestly unsure if I would have consented, especially after getting so worked up with Destiny. And if I am being *really* real with you, it just felt easier to finish the quickie than to withdraw consent. While I'd make different choices today, I've learned lessons through these experiences of sexual exploration—and so, for that, I wouldn't change them for one second. They forced me to think a lot about my identity kaleidoscope, consent, and how I communicate in sexual and romantic relationships.

These encounters were also a reminder of the benefits for all of us of centering eroticism and not just sex. The coital imperative and masculine gender norms that guided Eric's behavior are also part of what I call a *compulsory orgasmic culture*, which equates good sex with orgasms and disregards or undervalues all the erotic and sensual forms of play that come before.[15] My experiences that night were a reminder of the disparate ways Eric and I had been socialized into sexuality and how our different identities shaped our perspectives of the same events.

These critical differences, his chain-smoking, and other things led me to stop hanging out with Eric. I came to understand that he was what some swingers call a *Jimmy*, an overly aggressive single man. In Claire Kimberly's 2016 ethnographic study conducted at a swingers convention in the United States, a participant named Debra recounted her experiences with Jimmies at a swingers resort in Jamaica: "Some of them try too hard to hook up with a couple . . . and I mean, really try too hard to the point of being obnoxious."[16]

In the few months we hung out, it became clear that Eric was one version of what Myriam Gurba poignantly characterized as a creep.[17] As Gurba so poetically pointed out, sometimes creeps are charming. As a newbie in the scene, I can now see how I got lost in the fog of my exciting adventures and nights with him—an excitement that obscured his creepy behavior.

After I stopped chilling with Eric, I continued to meet couples online on SwingLifeStyle (SLS) and at the club I loved. I dated and had a couple of trysts with cisgender, mostly straight couples. In the lifestyle, I was what folks call a *unicorn*, a single, generally bisexual woman looking to hook up with a couple, who, like the mythical creature, can be hard to find and capture.

The heteropatriarchal swinging context meant that it sometimes felt like the women I was talking to in these dyads didn't particularly love being with women. They did it either to please their boyfriends and husbands, or simply because it was a norm in the subculture. More systematic research on the lifestyle globally confirms this observation.[18]

Part of what I enjoy so much about partnered sex is attending to someone else's pleasure. If the person I am kissing or touching has consented but isn't really into it, that's not pleasurable to me. So, it was a turnoff when I met women who seemed ambivalent and unenthusiastic about engaging in erotic acts with me.

A bisexual swinger named Nikki had similar experiences. She remarked, "The biggest issue as a bisexual woman is actually finding other bisexual women to have experiences with. I must wade through straight women pretending to be bi or suffering through it for their husbands just so I can find women who actually enjoy having real sex with other women."

These gendered scripts revealed an interesting theoretical point. Whereas many sexual cultures encourage or celebrate bisexuality among women, pervasive biphobic sexual double standards under heteropatriarchy too often make people demonize, mistrust, and avoid bisexuality in men. I saw this myself in the swinging lifestyle. Bi-curious women can get lost in the ecstasy of someone going down on them, regardless of the gender of the person doing the licking. But the men, not so much.

Though it felt like the women in the clubs were expected to have sex with other women, men went to great lengths to not even touch one another. As someone who loves bisexual men, this was super disappointing. I also experienced this as biphobic and sexist. Rick noted, "As a completely straight guy who's done it with one woman and two men before, the first time, it was pretty off-putting having a man touching, even if it was by accident, your naked body, especially in such a charged atmosphere." The social life of sexuality underscores how these sexual scripts and social rules reflect broader societal gendered sexual double standards. Our identity kaleidoscopes shape our erotic desires, behaviors, relationships, and communities in profound, yet often underappreciated ways.

Today, one of the most popular sites for sex parties is in the swinger subculture. Swinging, or what many simply call *the lifestyle*, is a sexual community where members consensually agree and negotiate sexual relations with other couples and people. Most of the swinger community is made up of straight cisgender couples, who sometimes also identify as bisexual (generally the woman in the dyad).

Cultural context shapes sexual scripts in the lifestyle globally. Still, across borders, heteropatriarchy tends to inform most swinger spaces. A study in Thailand, for example, documented how the lifestyle is incredibly centered around men's pleasure, with culturally specific sexual scripts requiring that the man initiate and arrange all sexual encounters.[19]

In China, too, research has shown that, due to the patriarchal cultural context, men are most often the initiators, frequently persuading women.[20] Still, as Dr. Fang Gang notes in *Swingers in Red China*, women are not forced to participate and always have the power to veto sex at any time. The women in Fang's study assumed a more passive role, but they reported enjoying caring for their partners' desires and said that these encounters strengthened their relationships. Inside and outside of these global swingers clubs, women often make what Deniz Kandiyoti calls *patriarchal bargains*, acquiescing to forms of gender inequality to achieve other benefits.

With the help of the Internet, swinging has grown into a global subculture, which underscores how eroticism shapes cultural, economic, and political changes.[21] Some meet on social platforms like Swingers Date Club (SDC) and SwingLifeStyle (SLS). Others use popular dating apps like Tinder or OkCupid, especially when couples seek a single woman. Once connected, people meet in hotels, private homes, and sex clubs.

Swingers use the Internet to increase public awareness, combat stigma, and share information. At the time of this writing, the r/Swingers subreddit had 467,000 members. In addition to the Swingers subreddit, people have created Discord spaces, other online forums, and YouTube channels. There are countless podcasts for swingers, many of which, like *Black n Kinky Lifestyle* and *Sapphic Swingers Podcast*, are built around explicit acknowledgment of how our identity kaleidoscopes inform people's lifestyle experiences.

The current number of swingers is impossible to track accurately, and available research provides wildly different numbers—ranging from 1 percent to 15 percent of the adult population. Most of this data is limited to married couples in the United States.[22] Even with these limitations, we know that we are talking about millions of people. Research on swingers has suggested that, compared to non-swingers, swingers are generally white, educated, relatively affluent, and likely to have mixed political views and affiliations.[23] Still, new research suggests that demographics are changing.[24]

Swingers often meet in private clubs with expensive entrance fees. Clubs like Paris's chic Le Mask are for couples only. Most clubs, like Fata Morgana near Amsterdam, only allow couples and single women to join. Others worldwide will sometimes allow single men, but only on restricted nights. Some clubs have takeover nights, or special nights built around identity, such as the Sapphic night I excitedly take you to later in this chapter. In places where sex clubs are illegal, swingers clubs are billed as private member-only social clubs. Depending on where you live, you might have to travel to access a club.

People with disposable income travel to resort hot spots, such as Scarlet Ranch and Secrets Hideaway in the United States; Desire Riviera Maya and Temptation in Cancún, Mexico; Hedonism in Negril, Jamaica; Village Naturiste in Cap d'Agde in the south of France; and La Mirage Swingers Complex in Gran Canaria, Maspalomas, in Spain's Canary Islands. People with dough can travel to Croatia to fuck on the sand at Punta Križ, a.k.a. swinger beach, near the city of Rovinj. You can set sail on a Bliss Lifestyle Cruise or board swinger cruises hosted by groups such as Naughty N'awlins from the United States. In Thailand, in 2023, Alternative Hospitality, a company registered in the United Kingdom, opened the first private members-only lifestyle club in the country, Sinful House. The club is in Bangkok, a hub for sexual tourism.

People in the lifestyle contribute to the global sexual tourism industry. A 2016 *Forbes* article reported that this global swinger travel industry was worth $20 billion annually.[25] Such travel raises interesting sociological questions about sexual access, privilege, and the politics of relatively affluent people from the Global North traveling around the globe to get their freak on. The commodification of eroticism, pleasure, and the bourgeois construction and commodification of sexual liberation are critical themes I want us all to talk about more.

Swingers often report that exploring their sexuality in the lifestyle helps add excitement to their relationship and strengthens their intimate bonds.[26] Participants in a study from Norway discussed how swinging allowed them to make their fantasies a reality—to explore desire, which produces feelings of freedom.[27] For individuals, swinging bolsters self-esteem and skills as a sexual partner. For women, in particular, swinging can provide sexual agency and a space to challenge sexual scripts that have fettered femininity to chastity and purity.

Swinging is also an erotic community. The lifestyle is a place where people can find friendship and various forms of support, a judgment-free space that helps counteract social stigma for practicing one of many forms of nonmonogamy. Swingers connected to the community sometimes attend conventions, like the ones hosted by the North American Swing Club Association.

The first time I attended that swingers party, I, too, saw the sex party as a space for challenging mechanisms of social control. Well, and of course, I was fired up and dripping with excitement, looking for a good time! Newly single after being in a sexless relationship for some time, I was so ready to play—it was game on!

In hindsight, part of the reason I went to my first swingers party in high-femme drags was precisely because I am visibly queer and not super feminine, and my hair had only just started growing back after I'd gone entirely bald. And I also admit that I was nervous yet excited, and I wanted to fit in.

The issue with my initial assimilationist approach was that our identities are not reducible to drag; they involve so much more than what we wear or how we present our bodies. Our identity kaleidoscopes reflect our life experiences, our cultural homes, and the shared values, knowledge, and histories of our communities.

So, the swinging scene exemplifies my proposition that sexuality has a distinct cultural life. I struggled to fit in despite my drag, because even as swinging is non-normative and challenges sexual mores in monogamous cultures, it is also *really* straight, and the kaleidoscopes of identities that often show up just aren't always ones that resemble my own. Straightness is not simply about people who desire PIV sex—if that's unfamiliar, it's shorthand for penis-in-vagina sex—being straight is also about sets of ideas and expectations, highly gendered and racialized cultural scripts and norms that govern behavior.

So, my feminist orientation, combined with my identities as a nonbinary queer Black person, made my first time in the swinger scene challenging. Why? Because I've always felt most at home in queer cultures. So, even if I could serve up femme realness and fit in the swinger scene, I did not initially feel at home there. It wasn't my culture. It wasn't characterized by norms that made me feel like I could show up as my authentic self. It felt profoundly heteropatriarchal, and those are cultural conditions that make me feel deeply guarded and sometimes unsafe, no matter how well I mask. In retrospect, these are the conditions that shaped my high levels of alcohol consumption while attending. And, to be really vulnerable, once, I even had to leave Le Trapeze because I got too drunk.

In these spaces, and being in my body, I often felt like I was navigating what Gloria Anzaldúa described as *borderlands*—spaces in which identities and cultures collide, and sometimes, a state of being as though one is suspended in liminal space, which can produce a unique opportunity for deep introspection and gaining of self-knowledge. It was through these experiences, which I remain grateful for, that I learned firsthand how critical it is to understand the connections between our identity kaleidoscopes and erotic empowerment, as well as how the spaces and people around us contribute to those encounters.

Locations are designed around people's identity kaleidoscopes. Humans design spaces in ways that make some people feel welcome and included, while excluding others. This is true of all cultural spaces, but we can observe it in full view in sexual ones. Like nonsexual bars and clubs, swingers clubs that cater to white patrons or want to draw in affluent crowds often use exclusionary practices to control who shows up. High cover charges or entrance fees often foreclose these venues to people with limited disposable income. Humans exclude other humans for all sorts of reasons, but in swingers clubs, the exclusion is most likely to be driven by classist stereotypes that suggest that working-class and poor people are less hygienic, less cultured, and less respectable—more ratchet.

In other words, the demographics of these spaces do not solely reflect the self-segregation of their members. Gender, class, and race shape the policies, practices, and symbols that structure organizations and the social interactions that people have within them. Club owners' hiring and staffing choices are sometimes strategic, and the identities of bartenders and other staff often reflect management ideals for patrons. Not hiring a Black or Brown bartender or entertainer may have been a conscious choice.[28] The more hip-hop, reggae, or Latin music you play, the more people of color will attend. So, when a sex club or bar refuses to play any of this music, it generally has an exclusionary intent.

This is why I loved the spot in Queens. It catered to an incredibly diverse crowd, with Black and Latinx people typically making up the majority. There was a working-class, nonpretentious vibe, and they played different types of music, including many of my '90s hip-hop and dancehall reggae favorites. This was unlike my experiences in other clubs.

In Manhattan, the clubs I attended were costly, generally not that packed, played almost exclusively club music, and were predominantly white. Echoing my experience in the city clubs, Cori, a Black swinging woman, noted: "I'm in an interracial marriage, and we live in a place with not a lot of Black people. So, immediately, when I enter a party, I feel on display." At the spot in Queens, I only felt like I was on display if, as I did with Destiny, I wanted to be.

But when I was in these sumptuous, white-dominated spaces, my identity as a light-skinned Black person seemed to simultaneously raise my sexual capital and exoticize me.[29] At first, I enjoyed being a hot commodity, a so-called exotic unicorn. Feeling wanted, pursued, or even being "hunted," as the controversial community expression goes, initially was profoundly validating. Being attractive to others in cultures that place a high status on physical appearance and hotness can feel *really* good. As I've argued in my previous work, experiences of fetishization are complicated, and context and identity shape when and if we find objectification offensive or pleasurable.[30]

Black men are often also in demand in these sexual environments due to pervasive stereotypes and desire for *BBC*—Big Black Cock. Some white couples are looking to fulfill a *Black Bull* and *Queen of Spades* fantasy, or interracial sex involving a muscular, well-endowed single Black man fucking a white woman while her white husband, a cuckold, watches.

Now, for some Black men, being desired and wanted in this way is hot, not a fetishizing turnoff. When we think about racialized sexual fetishization, it is critical to, as Mireille Miller-Young writes, leave space to "reread" these moments for "subjectivity, consensual expression, and sometimes, resistance."[31] As Xander, a Black swinging man, put it, "We came to fuck. I'm not here to educate anyone culturally. If this tall, athletic Black man is on your fuck-it lists and you have a squeaky-clean driver's license—I am your Lamborghini." As Jennifer C. Nash explores in *The Black Body in Ecstasy*, there is sometimes an "uncomfortable enjoyment in embodied racialization . . . pleasures in looking, pleasures in being looked at, pleasures in performing racial fictions, pleasures in upending racial fictions."[32]

But somewhat quickly, I personally stopped experiencing this type of fetishization as fun. Except for one couple, almost all the couples I connected with on SLS were not looking to date me. They were only interested in meeting up for sex—no public dinners or hanging out in addition to sex. This felt objectifying, like I was Cristal, a sex doll they could play with and then put back in the closet. In this, I know I am not alone. Studies have shown that some single women in the swinging scene feel similarly objectified.[33]

In messages off and on the site, the constant refrain about me being "exotic" added a layer of fetishization that made me uncomfortable, irritated, and annoyed. Kaya, a Black and Brazilian swinger, noted, "The stuff folks have said to me has been insane . . . we get enough bullshit in the real world. No one wants to deal with that in an environment meant to be fun."

People across sex club types have used the term *exotic* as a compliment. I even heard it at a lifestyle sex party, years later, with an ex-girlfriend in Brooklyn, New York, where those present were overwhelmingly young nonmarried people. Years later, too, at a sex club in Berlin, a white expat woman asked me if I was Brazilian because, in her words, I looked like "an exotic, powerful Amazonian woman."

Don't get me wrong, as a really short person who often feels socially awkward, hearing that I exude power is affirming, but I so wish folks would ditch the racialized parts.

Even though people across racial groups have fetishized me in this way, it hits differently when it rolls off the tongues of white folks. There were occasions when I felt like the white couple was interested in me because they'd never been with a Black woman before, but I was light-skinned enough, passed enough, and was racially ambiguous enough for them to want to try it out. Being a vessel for racialized sexual experimentation was just not a voyage I was down for, then or now.

At this point in my life, I am generally uninterested in experiences of fetishization in my erotic life—especially for free! I am deeply mistrustful of white people who only date people of color *and* who are not deeply honest and reflexive about these "preferences." I will no longer hook up with straight or bi-curious women who want to fuck me in private but not hold my hand on the street. I will ignore and block every last cisgender straight man who slides into my DMs, asking about pegging them while they go and play macho man with their reserved girlfriends. Y'all, these messages are wild!

Fetishization, or seeking out romantic and sexual partners based on stereotypes and specific aspects of a person's embodiment and identity while disregarding the person's entire humanity, is now a common reality of modern dating and sexual life. And I want us to resist the urge, as I have observed in a lot of mainstream writing, to reduce fetishization to a personal kink divorced from its political connotations.

If someone has a specific sexual attraction to people with disabilities, called *devotism*, it is often described as a person's "kink." A kink describes non-normative desires and erotic practices. So, describing an attraction to people with disabilities as a kink, even if unintended, pathologizes attraction to disabled people, and it, without question, puts *sexual ableism* on display. Critical disability scholars and activists argue that in popular cultural imaginations, to be sexy *is* to be able-bodied.[34]

Stereotypes suggest disabled folks are not sexually attractive or desirable sexual partners, and racism and cissexism compound ableist sexual scripts for disabled people who are also people of color and transgender. The idea that people with disabilities are sexually undesirable and have little to no sexual capital is an ableist, dehumanizing, culturally created trope. So, fetishization is generally predicated on toxic stereotypes that reinforce broader systems of inequity.

New research, including my own, not only takes studying fetishization seriously, but also notes how critical it is to ask people how fetishization *feels*.[35] One study on racial fetishization showed how gay men of color who experienced it felt objectified and reduced to stereotypes, and that it thwarted their ability to connect with people who, through words or actions, fetishized them.[36] This is the response we might expect, but some people's answers regarding their experiences might also surprise you.

If we truly appreciate the social life of sexuality and the social functions of sex, then we must lean into the messiness of fetishization in all its complicated glory. For many people, there are indeed instances when fetishization can feel affirming and pleasurable, and, in fact, fetishization experiences are not always binary—bad or good, negative or positive—but rather, a complicated mix of the two that is also conditioned by the identities of the fetishizer and the context of where it happens. I told you it was messy!

My mixed feelings about the "exotic, powerful Amazonian woman" quip underscored that our experiences of fetishization can be a mixed bag of affirmation, anger, annoyance, disgust, and pleasure. It matters which component of our sexuality that fetishization shows up in. Like Xander, a.k.a. Mr. Lamborghini, in the context of a one-off sexual encounter, fetishization might be unbothersome, and some people indeed find it hot and pleasurable to play with social taboos in the context of sex. Whereas in the context of dating and relationships, fetishization might feel more problematic.

Consent is key here. Suppose someone wants to hook up or have a relationship with someone *precisely* because they are fat, Black, disabled, trans, a little person, and so forth. In that case, I believe they have an obligation to disclose those desires so the other person can make an informed choice regarding whether they want to engage with someone on these terms.

I have spent years thinking about my experiences of fetishization, and I invite others to do the same. For people who have experienced fetishization or frequently encounter it, I believe we need to communicate boundaries around fetishizing behaviors, if we need them, to people we date and hook up with.

Putting the shoe on the other foot, have you ever fetishized someone? And not just in fantasy. If you are an X person who only dates or fucks Y people, are you introspective about the politics of your desires and behaviors and, most importantly, do you own and share them openly with the people you date or hook up with? If you don't—and I mean this with love—I think you should.

In hindsight, when I look back at my first sex parties, these spaces, to my knowledge, were run by men. They were subcultures structured by heteropatriarchy and, thus, around men's desires and fantasies. But something cool happens when swinger clubs and parties are run by women who intentionally redesign these spaces to support a broader range of desires—who acknowledge and understand the importance of our identity kaleidoscopes and who prioritize the needs and desires of people who are often disadvantaged by systems of power. These spaces do exist—and I'm going to take us to one.

Today, sex party organizers in the lifestyle are actively challenging systems of power through intentional and thoughtful work in contemporary sex club scenes. One such venue is the Oasis Aqualounge in Toronto, Ontario, a women-run space.

Before visiting Oasis, I sat down with Fatima, the marketing director and a business partner at the Toronto hot spot. I had never been to a woman-run lifestyle sex club before, and I was intrigued, both personally and intellectually.

Fatima and I began talking about the club's origin story. Oasis was founded in 2010 by Judy Kaye and her husband, swingers with young children. The couple was struck by the lack of clubs in the area (outside of gay bathhouses) and the fact that, like most SOPVs, the ones that did exist only operated under the cover of darkness—not ideal for parents with young kids.

When a gay men's bathhouse in Toronto called The Club closed, the Kayes opened it as a club with new ideas about what a lifestyle venue and parties could look like. The new owners set out to create an inclusive space that was open during the day and evening.

Oasis's vision centered on two primary goals: women's sexual empowerment and couples' relationship enhancement. Fatima explained, "It was always from the standpoint of creating a safe space for women's sexuality, and then also to give a space for couples to take time away, to escape, to ignite passion—to spice up their intimacy. And that's why it is open day and night because it gives opportunities for people with different schedules to enjoy the club."

Today, the club hosts daily events designed to recognize how systems of inequality have often disempowered women and other marginalized people. Creating a welcoming space requires intentionality and a profound recognition that sexuality is political. Fatima talked me through the myriad ways she and her business partners actively do this, from staffing choices, such as hiring people of color and trans and genderqueer bartenders and personnel, to their thoughtful community rules and inclusive programming.

Scholars have come up with language and theories to describe how sexism, cissexism, and racism shape how institutions and organizations operate, from their rules and policies to their symbols and signals.[37] Feminist scholar Joan Acker coined *gendered organizational theory*, a framework specifically for analyzing how patriarchy and sexism are embedded within organizations and reproduce gender inequality. To challenge inequity within any organization, people must address each of these layers.

Applying this framework to an individual organization requires recognizing how the national, regional, and cultural context shapes an organization's structure. In Oasis's case, part of the context for its culture of inclusivity is the city of Toronto, Canada's most racially, ethnically, and nationally diverse city. As a global hub of immigration, with over 180 languages spoken in the city, Toronto is often touted as the most multicultural city in the world.[38]

Inside Oasis today, the women who run the club create and maintain rules and policies that recognize the critical role our identity kaleidoscope plays in our sex lives and our individual capacities for sexual empowerment. Fatima told me: "We very much strive to create a safe, judgment-free space that is not oppressive—free. I think there's a better word than safe . . . that's liberating, empowering."

I agree. The connotation of safety is often perceived as dull or tame, yet the term *safe space* actually means aiming to create and maintain spaces that are free from oppression. At the same time, I also believe that if cultures continue to use this phrase, we should use the term *safer spaces* because no space can really be 100 percent free from oppression—we can make that a goal, knowing that humans will continue to be human and that we will always exist within systems of power.

The erotic capabilities approach underscores that creating safer spaces that are genuinely empowering for everyone requires work and thoughtful action. Systems of power and people's identities within those systems of power inform who might feel safe or unsafe, seen or unseen, empowered or disempowered. Inclusivity isn't adding more people of color to a marketing ad, it is fundamentally reorganizing the architecture of the space to be inclusive.

The club's event programming is essential to how it flips the traditionally androcentric swinger script. Fatima and her partners intentionally created and managed a space that encouraged women to explore their sexuality. Here, women can discover and enjoy forms of eroticism they desire but are systemically discouraged from having and acting on, all in a nonjudgmental environment. This is the thinking behind

Down-to-Fuck Night, a night where women are in charge and can have sex with multiple men.

My mind raced as Fatima described a typical DTF night. When I thought about the women I met years back in the swingers' scene, I imagined how many would have benefited from a space like this. Instead of threesomes and orgies with women in whom they were uninterested, there was a space filled with men waiting to serve women in a club that created rules to support women.

Part of the DTF event involves a women's empowerment circle for women attendees. Early in the evening, club hosts meet with men to discuss safety and community rules. This approach again underscores that facilitating a women-centered place means giving men rules and holding them accountable for violating them.

Oasis offers a wide array of events that recognize that our identity kaleidoscope shapes our sexual experiences. The vision for Oasis drew inspiration from the previous venue, The Club. The Club was home to popular takeover nights, such as when the gay men's bathhouse became the Pussy Palace and Pleasure Palace, catering to women and trans-only parties.

Given my personal experiences, I was especially intrigued when Fatima told me about their Unicorn Night. I felt so seen as Fatima explained the lounge's vision for these nights. She said, "We really try to turn the focus more on the unicorn and her needs and her desires rather than couples hunting for a third."

Fatima went on to summarize how I, too, had felt in the past—that the erotic play in the lifestyle sometimes centers only the couple's fantasy and desires, and that, once satisfied, they exit stage left. As Fatima put it, "They got their fantasy, and then they kind of move on, and so there's sometimes a disregard for the woman in this scenario, and so in our programming . . . we always like to address how to care for a unicorn properly—how to make her feel heard and seen in the relationship . . . so that somebody doesn't necessarily feel objectified."

Oasis works to create a community. They host events that are not exclusively sexual but rather erotic, such as naked and partner yoga, comedy nights, erotic art nights, speed dating, open mic nights, and a wide range of educational workshops. None of these activities centers sex itself, but that's not the point. Eroticism is the nucleus of our sexual cells. When people feel like they are part of a community, they also happily follow many of its organizational rules and cultural norms.

How we design erotic spaces matters. Intentional design can circumvent and disrupt existing social power dynamics, opening up new opportunities for more empowering eroticism for individuals and helping us move toward more collective sexual liberation. Fatima underscored the intentionality of the space's curation. "I would say that our rules and our waiver are very extensive, more extensive than you would find in any other club that I've ever seen." For example, take one of the club rules concerning gender, sexuality, and body positivity: "Oasis Aqualounge is an inclusive facility, meaning that we are accepting of all genders and (sexual) orientations. All members must conduct themselves in a mature, courteous and responsible manner and be respectful of other members and club staff. No body shaming is permitted as we celebrate that bodies come in all shapes and sizes and all are welcome."

Oasis's approach to creating a culture of inclusion doesn't stop with programming and policies, but they take community safety measures and consent seriously. Fatima explained how the club is intentional about the language it uses in its community guidelines to focus on the importance of consent: "We are mindful about exercising active consent. We do a lot of workshops and are continuously talking about what active consent looks like."

Establishing community guidelines for consent is also critical. The club's policies are detailed and include rules and notes about accountability measures. "No means No. If a member's invitation to engage in consensual sexual activity with another club member is refused or declined, the member must accept the refusal. Unsolicited or unwanted touching of another member is prohibited. Be prepared to accept a 'No' graciously. If you reach out to another member over video or live chat and they are not responding, please don't be offended. Empowering someone to say 'No' and respecting their decision to not engage is a great way to reinforce someone feeling both sexy and in control."

Finally, their policies also address intoxication, which has critical implications for consent. "No prohibited drugs may be used at the club, and excessive drinking will not be permitted. If you are visibly impaired, you may be asked to leave the event, and no refund will be offered. If you are intoxicated, you are unable to consent, and you must be a consenting adult to attend our events."

People throughout the world notoriously use alcohol as a social lubricant, especially when it comes to sex—believe me, I know this well. And so, I promise we'll return to Oasis, but I want to ruminate on intoxication, sex, and empowerment for a hot second. Indulge me. This is critical for our sexual literacy skills and how we think about our bodies, identities, consent, and empowerment.

As I admitted already, when I first went to sex clubs, it was at a time in my life when I drank a lot. In hindsight, I understand how alcohol influenced those experiences. When we drink, our decision-making is impaired, and we may engage in sexual behavior we would not have if not drunk (or high). In my lifetime, I have had far more sex while somewhere on the intoxication spectrum than sober. I have spent A LOT of time processing this fact.

Today, I recognize that the most empowering sex I have is while sober because I am fully present and in control of my body and the erotic choices I am making. Years ago, a partner and I returned home from a dinner out, and as had become routine for me long before our relationship, I went to open a bottle of wine before we went to the bedroom. They stopped me with a soft hand on my shoulder, and then tenderly reached for my face. With their palm on my cheek, and looking deep into my eyes, as if to speak into the parts of me that needed to numb, they delicately said: "I want *you*, present." It took more time in my healing journey to appreciate not only what they meant, but how critical their trauma-informed response was.

When I am too sauced, I am not fully present and have a more challenging time communicating my desires and boundaries clearly. If I am drunk, I might not demand condom use—and nothing feels less empowering than waking up in the morning unable to remember the sex I had the previous night. And real talk, physiologically, while orgasms are not the be-all and end-all of sex, after even just a few glasses of wine, my capacity to cum is diminished.

For me, erotic empowerment is predicated on bodily autonomy, being in control of my body and what happens to it. Believe me, I understand that for many people (myself included), risk itself and feeling uninhibited can make sex feel exciting and pleasurable. So, I rely on other kinky approaches to introducing risk and work to play with submission in ways that do not deplete my ability to consent fully.

Given my sexual history, it has been critical for me to evaluate why I have had so much sex when intoxicated. This introspection has led me to numerous insights that I hope will be helpful to others. The big question for me was: If I am drinking or getting high when I hook up, why am I doing this?

First, somewhat defensively, I thought: I am drinking or getting high to enhance the experience! THC, for example, intensifies my orgasms—Mmm, they are so long and radiating. So, I understand the appeal of what some people call *chemsex* and of consensual agreements to use substances to increase sexual pleasure. This was valid, I contemplated. Still, I had to think long and hard about what it meant if I *needed* to be intoxicated to have sex.

I was clearly lowering my inhibitions, but I had to explore exactly why I needed to drop them. I considered how intoxication can make me feel less body-conscious, which is understandable in a world that makes so many of us constantly hyperscrutinize and loathe our bodies. Sharing our bodies, especially the bits we have hang-ups about—a jiggly belly, so-called bat wings, gynecomastia (a.k.a. man boobs), a large labia, a small penis, big balls, and so on—can feel really vulnerable. And until cultures dismantle their fatphobic, racist, transphobic, and sexist body-shaming systems as part of sexual liberation movements, intoxication during sex is a coping mechanism for our self-hatred and shame of our bodies.

Still—digging even deeper, through my work in therapy, reading about somatics and trauma, attending workshops, and spending a lot of time truly *with* myself, what I also discovered was that there are particular sex acts, with specific types of people, that, with alcohol-induced lowered inhibitions, have felt easier. I am attracted to masculine people, but I have spent a lot of my life feeling on high alert and unsafe around most cisgender men—it has felt instinctive. And it was. It was my nervous system at work, doing its job to protect me after many profoundly traumatizing experiences with men and due to my heteropatriarchal socialization.

For a period after these initial reflections years ago, I stopped hooking up with cisgender men altogether. I had more work to do on myself that alcohol could never fix, and in fact made worse. In my first sex club adventures, alcohol helped me feel looser, chattier, and more sociable—this has been true of *so* many spaces for me, since my neurodivergence and embodied traumas from years of violent childhood bullying often make loud, crowded spaces a sensory and social nightmare. But when it came to sex, I learned that alcohol was sometimes actually exacerbating my deeply learned and generalized freeze response. I accepted that until I healed further from systemic trauma, erotic empowerment would remain elusive, especially if I wanted eroticism with people across the gender spectrum.

After much work, ongoing healing, and some new embodied practices, I arrived in a place where, when I full-throatedly communicate boundaries and set the tone for how cisgender men are allowed to speak to me, approach me, and touch me—I—my body—feel safer and genuinely open to the deep pleasures of erotic connection and sex. My personal therapeutic and spiritual journeys, reckoning with my alcohol and substance problems, have been a critical part of my path toward more personal erotic empowerment. So, if alcohol or substances have played a noteworthy role in your erotic life, if it feels safe for you to do so, it is a worthwhile project to explore the reasons why you've relied on them and how they've shaped your communication and consent practices.

Currently, I practice mindfulness around alcohol consumption, and do not drink much, if at all, especially if sex is involved. My therapeutic and introspective work has also led me to put sex with cisgender men back on the table. Although, even as I am open to sex with cisgender men, I am typically not open to relationships with them, because I am still profoundly uninterested in straight culture, with all its patriarchal norms. In fact, I recently had the most mind-blowing, pleasurable sex with a cisgender sexually fluid man I met while traveling for this book. We met at a kinky play party. He was so gentle, responsive, and respectful in our somewhat vanilla rope scene—at my request, he just bound my chest in carefully knotted white ropes, but then softly and gently used his breath and fingers to caress my neck, collar, shoulders, and arms. I still fantasize about the sex, intimate conversations, and electric connection we shared all day, off and on, on my last day in the city, sober, where I communicated what I needed and he responded enthusiastically.

Point is: If and when a cis man shows me that he is not a long-taloned gnarling grizzly bear, I entertain his advances. But if he wants some of this good stuff, that burden of proof is on him.

In 2024, Screenshot HQ posted a TikTok that went viral. The host asked eight women on the streets of London: "Would you rather be stuck in the forest with a man or a bear?" Seven of the women, most immediately, chose the bear. In the initial post, women said things like:

> "Men are scary."
> "Bears don't always attack you, right, unless you fuck with them."
> "Depends on what man, but probably a bear."
> "One hundred percent the bear, which is terrifying to say."
> "Definitely the bear; some men are really scary out there."

Women across the Internet posted responses indicating why they, too, would unfortunately choose the bear.

Women even flipped the script and brought men into the conversation, asking if it was their daughter, #manorbear? Many men also agreed that the bear was safer for their mothers and daughters. On the other hand, some men protested, unsurprisingly suggesting that the comparison and the women's preference for the bear were ludicrous. And, of course, #NotAllMen.

Since some people seemed to have missed the message: Listen up. The point was that women have genuine reasons to fear men. Of course, #NotAllMen, but heteropatriarchal violence is real! According to the US National Park Service, the chances of a bear attack are 1 in 2.1 million. And to my knowledge, bears don't target women. And, in contrast, one in three women globally have experienced physical and/or sexual violence at the hands of a man.

One of my favorite responses in the viral kerfuffle came from a US Marine veteran. She posted a response about attending a captain's military training where a colonel gave a speech to hundreds of marines, addressing violence against women within the military. He acknowledged that, according to statistics, there were sexual predators in their ranks. Under his watch, he said, "they'd be done." The marine said it was the first time in thirty years that she felt safe and heard because it was the first time she saw a man stand in a room in front of a large group of men and speak out against the patriarchal violence women face. She said she would gladly choose that colonel over a bear any day.

To all men who *truly* love women (not just their bodies), I ask: How do you communicate that you are not a bear? How do you show, not just tell, a partner that you are no grizzly? How do the political realities of womanhood shape how you engage with women erotically? And ladies, do you put up with unwanted bearlike behavior? If so, why?

When people take seriously the fact that millions of women fear men more than a bear and that, statistically, most women will likely face sexual violence at some point in their lives, it means that romantic or erotic partners have a responsibility to acknowledge and address this empirical and political reality. Women are not a monolithic group, which means that individual women will have different needs. Still, suitors can and should inquire about how their partner's identity kaleidoscope shapes their needs.

Sometimes, when a man runs up on me, I just want to shake the shit out of him, and say: "Stop, man! Stop running up on women like you the POlice! I need you to approach me slowly so that my body doesn't immediately trigger the bear trap!" Sometimes, honestly, I think about what would happen if everyone, not just men approaching women, approached all humans like they were a survivor of sexual assault or have PTSD—with just a little extra care. Part of what I especially love about queer communities, and what I think many can learn from them, is precisely the ethos of care that sustains them.

Empowering eroticism often involves what feminists and disability justice advocates call *care work* and building intentional communities of care.[39] Recognizing the role that identity-based erotic needs play in sexual empowerment is critical. When we articulate our embodied erotic needs and our boundaries, and when our partners do work to respect and support our desires, we open up access to experiences of erotic empowerment.

Consider what Jane Ward has called *gender labor* in relationships.[40] The connotations of the term *labor*, though, obscure the erotic joys and pleasure of care work when it is a form of consensual intimacy and not a compulsory obligation. People often do work to support and validate their partner's gender. I believe women do this for men all the time—and not just for cisgender men. For example, I have had erotic encounters with trans men who have expressed particular needs around their bodies. They have asked me to use specific language to describe parts of their bodies. However, this was born of care and intimacy, not heteropatriarchal obligation.

In my research, too, I have interviewed transmasculine and nonbinary sex workers who talked with their clients about how to speak to them about their bodies, asking them, for example, to use the word "chest" and not "breasts," or "first hole" instead of "vagina." When a sex worker demands this from a client, and the customer respects the worker's boundaries and recognizes and validates them in their gender, it can feel empowering, even if the sex itself is a job. We don't have to be in long-term committed relationships to offer each other care.

So, here is the thing: We can do *all* the work on ourselves—we can read all the sex books, see all the therapists, and attend erotic workshops and seminars. But to fully understand our sexuality, a sociological lens demands that we recognize the vital role other people, organizations, and institutions play in our experiences of erotic empowerment.

Once again, we must appreciate how tightly our bodies and the social world are bound—we *feel* empowerment in our bodies. Still, others play a crucial role in thwarting, compromising, or supporting our sexualities and the joys and pleasures of them.

Our relationships and communities should make us feel good about our bodies—their shape, size, color, height, parts, disabilities, and all their beautiful imperfections. The multi-billion-dollar diet and beauty industries try to make us feel terrible about our natural bodies to line their owners' pockets. My wish for everyone is to have partners and communities that help counteract the work of these shame-producing industries.

My sincerest hope for everyone is that they can find relationships and spaces that make them feel seen, supported, and respected and that are intentionally designed to acknowledge the political and cultural realities of their identities, prioritizing consent. This, my friends, is where erotic empowerment lives in abundance.

Wait, let me show you.

My body pulsated with excitement the afternoon I first arrived at the front door of Toronto's Oasis Aqualounge. Since I was there for a tour, I asked for my Aqua Flirt host by name. The person at the front desk, who was behind the glass partition, told me they didn't give out information about their employees. Immediately impressed by the privacy, I corrected my wording and explained that Fatima had arranged a tour for me with this host. Then, with my poor syntax out of the way, I made my way through the door and into the club.

The person at the front desk reviewed all the community guidelines surrounding consent, safety, and club etiquette, to which I agreed before signing in at the computers at the entrance. Then, I stopped to consider whether to wear a colored bracelet from a selection of bins on the left wall beside the bar.

At Oasis, patrons can wear colored plastic bracelets to signal desires and consent. Different colors indicate whether you are open to, say, playing with other couples or seeking play partners of a specific gender. In a code familiar from both stoplights and the stoplight consent model, wearing a green bracelet signals that you are looking to meet new people; red indicates that you are not interested in meeting play partners. In practice, few members wear the bracelets, but their availability signals to all who attend, from the second they enter, that consent and communication, including nonverbal forms, are vital for empowering erotic experiences.

The club design was cool, strikingly different from the places I'd been to in the United States. It was part bathhouse (a space I'd never been in because I am not a gay man) and part sex club, with multiple floors and many unique playrooms, including a fully equipped BDSM play space and a Sybian, for those who enjoy that ride. They even had a closed-door bedroom upstairs for people who wanted privacy.

Contrary to the beliefs of pundits who push moral panics and wring their hands about safety at sex-on-premises venues, health is essential to Oasis community members. The second-floor hallway at Oasis features a large and popular condom dispenser. I have seen condom bowls galore at every sex party I've ever attended.

In the BDSM play space, clear rules are posted regarding risk-aware consensual kink. Staff regularly clean all spaces after each use, leaving a small laminated card with a green smiley face on all clean surfaces and equipment. Patrons take the cards off to use the spaces. The minute they finish, they put the card back, red face up, to signal to the staff to clean.

After my initial afternoon tour, I returned in the evening. It was only about 8 p.m., so the place was still not crowded. It was a traditional swinger Saturday night, yet everything about the event contrasted sharply with my experiences at swinger clubs over a decade ago.

As I approached the bar, I saw a genderqueer bartender—for me, a happy invitation to sit. I immediately remembered something Fatima had said: "Oasis attracts such a diverse group of people, who not only want to attend but also want to work there." Another of my bartenders was a gorgeous, tall Black woman. During my visits, I saw bartenders and other staff who were genderqueer and had they/them pronouns on their name tags, cleaning towels and play spaces. Hiring a diverse staff is not a challenge if your programming is inclusive and the locals know you as an accepting place.

On my first visit, I sat at the bar for some time, observing the scene. The ambient sounds of grunts and sounds of pleasure from porn on a screen behind me provided the score, filled out by human chatter and music.

This was my first time in a space with such a kaleidoscope of identities. Although, I would definitely say it skewed white, with an underrepresentation of Black folks, especially Black women. Still, outside of the club in Queens, I'd never seen this much ethnic, even if not racial, and other forms of diversity in a sex club. I'd been to a queer and trans sex party in New York, but I'd never been to a party with cisgender and transgender people together. And from my perch's view of the front door, I appreciated that almost nobody was arriving in clothing made for a ball—it didn't feel pretentious.

As I sat at the bar, I talked to my bubbly Aqua Flirt host again and struck up a conversation with another single person, this one a full-figured naked woman. One of the things I loved in my trips to Oasis was the true diversity in bodies. Feeling good about your body and leaving societal shame out on the curb lends itself to empowering eroticism. An online reviewer also noted, "You will see a surprising variety of body types." Still, this is by design, not accident.

Oasis has a clothing-optional policy, and they take body positivity seriously. Fatima remarked, "You just see so many different types of bodies in the space, and I feel like particularly for women who have been conditioned by mainstream society, this really opens their eyes to like what normal bodies look like, what normal forms of pleasure and sexuality look like, and just kind of really take it away from how it's being portrayed to us in the mainstream."

Policies without accountability are just statements. If you want people in your club or a person in your relationship to feel good in their body with you, then you have to do some work. "If someone is bad-mouthing another guest or making comments about their body, or any sort of thing, appearance, anything, you know the way that they sound when they're having sex, whatever it could be. That person is definitely pulled aside and spoken to, maybe asked to be removed, maybe banned," Fatima said.

When you are in a space that genuinely walks its body positivity talk, and you see members of the sex rabble of all body sizes walking around proud, it sustains a culture that can make everyone feel good about their bodies. As Sonya Renee Taylor explains in *The Body Is Not an Apology*, when your body is non-normative, institutions and people constantly make you apologize merely for existing in your skin. "Living in a female body, a Black body, an aging body, a fat body, a body with mental illness is to awaken daily to a planet that expects a certain set of apologies to already live on our tongues," she writes.[41] So, spaces that not only do not make us apologize, but celebrate our bodies just as they are, are vital to fostering a radical politics of self-love.

When I was there for a Saturday Unicorn Night, my IBS had been acting up all day—so much so that I had even resisted a poutine from a favorite downtown restaurant in preparation for my outing. With my chronic gastrointestinal issues coupled with the impending onset of menstruation, I was incredibly bloated and feeling uncomfortable in my body.

I knew about Oasis's body-positive culture, but I was still feeling pretty insecure about my body's appearance that night. As soon as I was back in the space, though, I felt much more at ease. On this crowded night, there was an even greater diversity of bodies than on my first visit—fat, thin, large penises, small penises, A cups, DD cups, giant asses, tiny asses, dark-skinned, light-skinned, shaved, hairy, and everywhere in between on all these spectrums. The range of bodies and gender diversity was especially pronounced on Sapphic Aquatic Night. Several people were using mobility devices—I saw two canes and a chair. I had often heard my transmasculine friends talking about feeling uncomfortable walking around with their shirts off and their top surgery scars exposed. Here, transmasculine folks walked around proudly with their shirts off. As feminist sociologists stef shuster and Laurel Westbrook argue in their 2022 study on transgender joy, when trans people have safer spaces to embrace their trans identities, their quality of life improves. So does their self-esteem, body positivity, peace, and access to joy.[42] Queer and trans folks of all body sizes were laughing—there was so much queer and trans joy everywhere. I talked with folks in the hot tub about how special this monthly event was, especially in the context of declining LGBTQ bars.[43]

In this regard, Oasis was extending the legacy of the Pussy Palace events back from when the club was still the gay bathhouse. In feminist researcher Corie Hammers's study of the Pussy Palace, attendees described finding affirmation in seeing so many people of diverse body sizes "flaunting their bodies." People discussed how seeing others exude confidence in their bodies made them feel good about their so-called imperfections. One participant said, "We are not all skinny, glamorous, conventionally pretty people. There are imperfect bodies, fat bodies, ambiguous bodies, but this is precisely what makes it so damn hot . . . and empowering."[44]

Feeling comfortable in your body contributes to bodily autonomy and, thus, enables your capacity to experience empowering eroticism. At Oasis, I felt seen and relaxed because the club had created a space that explicitly called out power dynamics and provided people with suggestions for navigating those power dynamics—even if no space can completely rid itself of any *-ism*.

On a Unicorn Night, I sat on a bench in the front of the second-floor ballroom area. A host stood on stage, conducting a workshop. In the packed room, people sat on yoga mats, on a row of bench seating, and all along the vast bed area that would later that evening have people fucking all over it.

In the interactive workshop, the host asked the audience to define "unicorn." People threw out definitions and asked questions. The host discussed how to approach and how not to approach a single woman in the club, underscoring that no couple should hover, follow around, or otherwise stalk a unicorn, like prey. The host explicitly said that people should never objectify a unicorn.

The workshop moved on to broader discussions of consent. The host told us that if someone says something like, "I am not interested" or "I am unsure I want to play," attendees should not respond with, "Are you sure?" If someone says anything but yes, move on.

The workshop leader acknowledged, with some humor, that most couples' threesome dreams would likely not come true that night. There would likely not be many single women looking to hook up with a couple—these women are called unicorns for a reason. Of those in attendance, none are obligated to hook up with anyone.

The host invited three couples and one unicorn up on stage and invited the unicorn to ask each couple erotic icebreaker questions. The short seminar was designed not just to *tell* people that communication and consent are crucial to empowering eroticism, but to *show* them examples of fun, yet straightforward ways to break the ice and communicate desire and consent. Setting these rules for engagement made me, a unicorn, feel at ease.

Later, I was in the outdoor heated pool and made small talk with another unicorn in the pool, who was there for the first time. She complimented my nipple piercings, and we talked a little. At this time, there were three of us unicorns in the pool. When I eventually got out of the pool and slowly walked naked to get my towel, I could feel eyes on my wet, naked body, but it felt erotic, exciting, and affirming—not creepy. This was one of those moments when I could *feel* erotic empowerment radiating throughout my tissues.

While I did not play with anyone on Unicorn Night, my body felt *really* good. My sexual history and socialization mean I have a heightened sense of physical insecurity. I have become entirely accustomed to dining alone and traveling alone, but going to a sex club alone is an altogether different ball game. I felt empowered when I was there because I felt in control of what would happen that night. If I wanted to talk to a couple or have any erotic encounter, I'd have to initiate. If I wanted to further explore the initial good vibe with a couple I had spoken with briefly in the locker room, I'd need to seek them out.

On Sapphic Night, I talked with a small group of queer women of color who all spoke positively and enthusiastically about the no-pressure vibe at Oasis across events. That same evening, I attended another workshop, this one on erotic intimacy. It reminded me so much of the feminist sex toy model, where education was incorporated into the business's mission to foster an empowering space for people with non-normative erotic desires and marginalized sexual identities.

The erotic intimacy workshop at Oasis focused on partner movement exercises, rotating partners with each activity. In one, we followed our partner's body movements. I leaned into all the awkwardness of sustained eye contact and vulnerability with a stranger. In my favorite exercises, we used our bodies and nonverbal movements to signal to our partners that we were providing or withdrawing consent. In our final exercise, we did some physical touch. Here, too, we communicated how we liked to be touched. We played with communicating seductively if we liked something and asking for consent.

In the closing circle, after the facilitator asked how we felt, one participant boisterously called out that they were filled with queer joy. I felt the same. There is so much joy and empowerment in bodily autonomy, in engaging in forms of erotic intimacy on our own terms, and in feeling reciprocal respect for our needs and boundaries—or exercising what feminist M. Jacqui Alexander calls *erotic autonomy*.[45]

As Corie Hammers argues, having sexual agency or being sexually empowered is not simply about being free to explore your desires. Sexual agency and empowerment have everything to do with being able to define boundaries for yourself and articulating them before, during, and after any sexual encounter.[46] Remember, our boundaries are for us and our self-care—they are about our limits and actions, not the rules or expectations we have for others.

When people, especially women, talk about safety being a prerequisite for empowering eroticism, they are not invoking patriarchal ideas that equate femininity with weakness and the need for protection. Remember, feminists for centuries have been telling us that heteropatriarchy is a violent political institution. Wanting to have sex in safer spaces is about freedom from the threat of violence in all its forms. Now, of course, depending on one's identity, safety may not be a prerequisite for empowering sex—and what a privilege that is!

Therapists often emphasize that only the individual is responsible for their somatic safety. This logic is born out of the pervasive idea that sexuality is a personal and private matter. However, if we understand the communal and political nature of sexuality, it also forces us to take responsibility for making others feel safer. For me, yes, it has been critical to understand what I need to feel safer, and to learn how to advocate for those conditions and set boundaries for myself in erotic contexts. Still, I believe our relationships and communities should prioritize making one another feel safer.

Erotic empowerment is not simply self-made. Too often, popular discussions of empowerment focus on our individual journeys as if they are divorced from other people and communities—ignoring the social life of sexuality. Yes, it is critical to connect with and understand what we do or do not desire, because as Audre Lorde so eloquently put it, "we have been raised to fear the *yes* within ourselves, our deepest cravings."[47] Still, once we do this internal work, we are ready to communicate those needs to others, because our sexualities are always also social and political.

Our relationships and communities are containers for our erotic lives, and we must ensure they are the right fit. Our friends, partners, and communities should affirm our identity-specific erotic needs. When they do, they facilitate erotic joy and empower us to be our authentic and genuine selves.

Chapter 5

RELATIONSHIPS

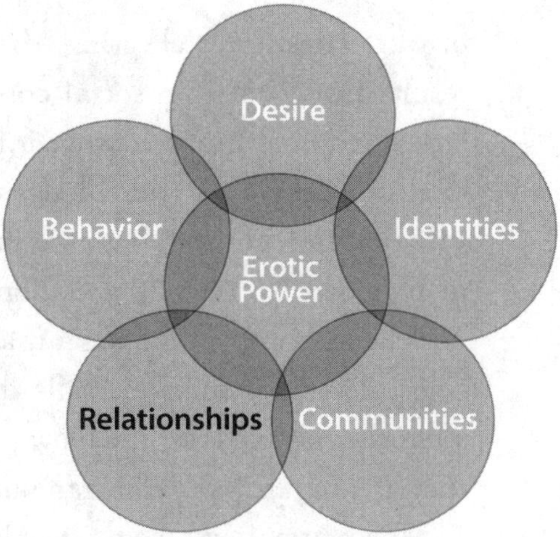

What if I told you that one reason relationships get stale is that people are using one-size-fits-all containers? Relationships, the next component of sexualities in the erotic power model, are like containers for our desires. Our identity-specific erotic needs mean we all require containers of different shapes and sizes. Yet, societies continually force people to reuse the same worn, ill-fitting Tupperware.

This chapter interrogates the cultural ideology that people are fundamentally better off in monogamous, romantic, long-term, coupled relationships and, critically, that everyone inherently desires them. This is what Elizabeth Brake calls *amatonormativity*.[1] As feminist sociologist Mimi Schippers argues, *compulsory monogamy*, the societal demand to turn away other lovers, is pervasive in many parts of the world. In many, if not most, societies, living the so-called good life means living in monogamous straight coupledom.[2]

Confession: I have never *actually* been in a monogamous relationship. I have been in relationships that were labeled as such, but in each, infidelities were painful prophets. I have cheated, and I have been cheated on. Muscle memory still burns from every swim through each rip current. And I know that I am not alone.

People regularly experience infidelity in so-called monogamous relationships. They underreport it due to dubious, discordant definitions of what constitutes cheating, the fear of stigma, and the shame that results from violating social conventions regarding monogamy. The lack of consensus about what infidelity is and the shame and stigma of acknowledging it goes a long way to explain why there is such wide variation in reporting, with various studies placing cheating occurring in anywhere between 20 and 90 percent of relationships.

When it comes to monogamy and cheating, people love to spin some colorful yarn. If someone calls themselves monogamous but furtively sees other people (yes, the blow job that one time on vacation counts), they are, in fact, not monogamous—just storytellers.

Mononormativity makes people feel like failures, like bad people, for not wanting monogamy or even fantasizing about experiences outside of it. One study found that a third of monogamous participants said that being in an open relationship was their top fantasy, and 80 percent of those people said they wanted to act on it at some point.[3] More people like these must be supported and told, as writer and philosophy professor Justin L. Clardy put it plainly in their 2023 book title, that it's OK to not be monogamous.[4] If you are unhappy *or* happy in your relationship and desire other sexual or romantic partners, and you live in a context where it is safe to do so—say it with your full chest!

And don't get it twisted, for people who love monogamy and find pleasure in connecting with and sharing intimacy with one partner only, that is cool, too. I am emphatically not coming for monogamous people. Instead, I want to prompt everyone to ask themselves: Did you choose monogamy, or was it chosen for you? Do you prefer monogamy because it is the most ideal relationship container for your desires and identity-specific needs? Have you set the terms and standards for your relationships, or has the society around you stripped you of the agency to do so for yourself?

So, monogamy itself, having a singular partner, is not inherently a problem—its compulsory nature and unrealistic standards are! Many monogamous people have not actually discussed how they want to organize their relationships with their partners, including whether the relationship is to be monogamous. In cultures where family and peers present monogamy as the expected standard and the media is saturated with endless depictions of monogamous love, it becomes an unquestioned default—even if it is not what people truly want.

Monogamist cultures are rife with impractical ideals that seem to stifle people's individual sense of freedom, cause incessant and unnecessary strife, and, frankly, make some people downright miserable. These are some of those core monogamist philosophies:

- Love is finite and scarce.
- People only have the capacity to romantically love one person fully. So, romantic relationships must be monogamous and dyadic.
- Love requires unconditional loyalty expressed as emotional and physical fidelity.
- Being in a relationship permits people to be possessive or to exert control over a partner.
- Being in a relationship requires relinquishing yourself and your autonomy to become a unit.
- Relationships must follow social scripts that organize partnerships according to existing power structures and shape every aspect of the relationship, from sex to who takes out the garbage.
- Everyone should fundamentally desire to be in romantic relationships and should actively work toward that goal.
- Relationships follow a linear path or ride the *relationship escalator* and should progress from dating to cohabitation, marriage, and, of course, to pushing a baby carriage.[5]
- Romantic relationships must take priority over platonic relationships.
- Romantic relationships must include sex, and other forms of eroticism and intimacy by themselves are not valid forms of connection in romantic relationships.[6]

I want everyone to understand that monogamy and these ideas are socially constructed and, for some people, actually thwart their capacity for healthy, happy relationships. This is why so many people globally are increasingly rejecting it, because it doesn't work for them.

In the modern world, our relationship options are fluid, not binary. In challenging compulsory monogamy, I am simply advocating for people's right to choose which *relationship container* is most suitable for them. As the Instagram influencer @PolyamorousBlackGirl, whom I had the privilege of interviewing, has noted on her popular page, polyamory is but one of many examples of ethical nonmonogamy.

There are plenty of relationship options for people to explore, and we keep seeing, over and over again, so many new identities, terms, and communities emerging. So, this is more good news. The point is, *we*, not the world around us, must decide what relationship style best suits our erotic and relationship needs—that is erotic empowerment. And, as the feminist slogan goes, the personal is political.

Globally, laws are beginning to recognize and grapple with the widespread return to nonmonogamies. In Colombia, in 2017, three gay men entered into the first legally recognized polyamorous marriage. In 2018, a Newfoundland court recognized the custodial rights of three unmarried polyamorous adults in a family. In 2022, New York Civil Court Judge Karen May Bacdayan defended polyamorous relationships in *West 49th St., LLC v. O'Neill*, arguing that polyamorous folks are entitled to the same legal protections given to people in dyadic relationships.

Also in 2022, a judge in Puebla's Eighth District Civil Court in Mexico argued in support of a polyamorous plaintiff, finding that local civil codes defining marriage as limited to two people were discriminatory in their refusal to recognize other intimate relationship structures.

When more people en masse choose relationships that align with their desires, the erotic power produced shifts norms and laws regarding sexuality, especially marriage laws and others that govern intimacy. As erotic power abounds, it inevitably broadens relational norms and prompts changes in how relationships are organized in society.

There is so much for everyone to learn from nonmonogamous people. As Kevin Patterson, author of *Love's Not Color Blind* and creator of Poly Role Models on Tumblr, told me: "Even if you have zero desire to engage in nonmonogamy, you should study nonmonogamous relationships and nonmonogamous people because even if that's not what you want to do, we prioritize communication and emotional literacy in a way that every relationship can and should benefit from."[7]

Monogamy is not natural! *Mononormativity*, or the idea that monogamy is natural and the ideal relationship structure, is socially constructed—not evolutionary destiny. Evolutionary biologists, dating back to Charles Darwin, have long since argued that humans fundamentally adhere to *sexual dimorphism*. As a species, we have two sexes and are designed to pair off to reproduce and raise offspring, ensuring the continuation of the species. This narrative is ahistorical and wildly reductive. Using the language of biology and naturalizing monogamy, some scientists erase the numerous counterhistories and examples across time and space that clearly show how humans form relationships in all sorts of different ways and that existing systems of power shape those relationships.

The norms wherever, and whenever, a person lives govern their possibilities and choices. If someone was born and raised in the Tibetan Himalayas, where everyone in the community practices *polyandry* and women have multiple husbands (often brothers, *fraternal polyandry*), that is their normal. If someone else was raised in Mali and grew up in and around other *polygynist* families, where men have more than one wife, this is their normal. And if someone is raised in the United Kingdom and their communities practice *monogamy*, in which people have one exclusive partner, that's their normal. There is no universal, inherently normal, or natural way to structure relationships; standards are constantly in flux and culturally determined.

And while these cultural standards for relationships are pervasive and compulsory, when we tune into erotic dialectics, we can observe that there have always been people who resist them. Some working-class Afro-Surinamese women have engaged in a long-standing practice called *mati work*. They create their own kinship and relationship systems in which they build intimate and sexual relationships with other women for emotional support and pleasure, often all while maintaining connections to men, with whom they have children. As Gloria Wekker argues in *The Politics of Passion*, there are benefits to subversion: "Mati, with their 'unruly,' 'unrespectable' behavior, have a more autonomous, 'alternative' understanding of their own sexuality."[8] And this case is not an anomaly.

Did you know that polygamy, the practice of being married to more than one person at a time, was once the global standard? Monogamy emerged as a normative relationship structure in agrarian societies and became idealized as heteropatriarchal property rights developed under capitalism in the Global North. In their best-selling, controversial 2010 book *Sex at Dawn*, Christopher Ryan and Cacilda Jethá examine prehistoric collectivist societies, upending conventional cultural wisdom that monogamy is innate and a historical constant.[9]

Hunter-gatherer societies, which existed from two million years ago until approximately twelve thousand years ago, were egalitarian. They shared resources, including partners, as a survival strategy. Given early humans' constant migration, they did not form long-term monogamous partnerships, but they still had libidinal needs—so, in short, they were promiscuous. Children were raised in the collective, so there weren't any concerns about paternity or the treatment of kids as property as we see today.

Monogamy, like heteropatriarchy, is also a product of colonialism.[10] Historically, monogamy has been a part of a settler-colonial project. Colonists have frequently justified their presence through their *civilizing missions*, which hold that it was and is white people's duty to help non-whites become more civilized, to convince or force them to adopt white people's so-called superior values and ways of life. Monogamy, in other words, was part of *the white man's burden*. What queer feminist anthropologist Scott Morgensen has called *settler sexuality* is a fundamental part of the histories of colonialism and conquest.[11]

Take the United States of America, where I am from. In the seventeenth and eighteenth centuries, British Christian settler colonists held monogamous marriage to be the ideal relationship form.[12] At that time, however, monogamy was not the common practice of the Catawba, Cherokee, Powhatan, or the vast majority of the over one thousand Indigenous tribes already here, nor of cultures worldwide, who valued extended kinship systems and practiced forms of polygamy. It took centuries of court battles, legislation, and social sanctions criminalizing and marginalizing nonmonogamy to make monogamy the dominant relationship standard in the late nineteenth century.[13]

Even today, ongoing government regulations against and prohibitions of polygamy are part of what sociologists have called *racial projects*.[14] Prohibiting polygamy is rooted in the pervasive white colonial idea that monogamy is divine, progressive, and normal, and polygamy, in any form, is sinful, backward, uncivilized, and aberrant. But as with all prohibitions, sanctions against polygamy, and polygyny in particular, only push it underground. They do not eliminate it.

Regulating polygamy in the Global North is a racial project that has allowed nations to position themselves as civilized and unlike supposedly backward Black and Brown people from "other" places in the Global South. Feminist sociologist Melanie Heath evidenced this in her book *Forbidden Intimacies*. She examined governmental regulations regarding families and marriage in Canada, France, French colonial Mayotte, and the United States of America.[15] Laws governing polygamy also affect other policies, such as immigration. So, they come to define citizenship and belonging. When countries pass policies rooted in the idea that polygamist relational practices are less civilized or barbaric, they reify racism and xenophobia on a grander scale.

Polygamy, specifically polygyny, is illegal throughout much of the world. In most cases, it is unlawful because governments believe, as the United Nations Human Rights Committee has strongly opined, it violates the dignity and rights of women and should be banned everywhere.[16] This argument, however sympathetic I am to it, glosses over other interdependent systems of power that shape the governance and regulation of intimate relationship forms.

I agree that all relationships should be consensual, rooted in justice, and based on equality between all partners. However, the systematic deprivation of women's dignity and rights is not specific to any relationship form. It is endemic across relationship structures in any heteropatriarchal society—including monogamous relationships and marriages. If we point out patriarchal violence and gender inequity "over there," we best be ready to call that shit out in our own houses. Because from here—it just looks like folks' racist slips are showing!

Monogamy, too, has been rooted in heteropatriarchy, and, too often, these relationships, especially straight ones, are characterized by various forms of violence, inequities, and injustices for women. Consider legalized spousal rape, dowries, women's unfair share of domestic labor, the never-ending masculine validation that straight women do for men, the prioritizing of men's sexual pleasure, the practice of "giving away" a bride and asking a woman's father for her hand in marriage (as if she is his property, and it's his decision), and so on. These gendered scripts are woven into monogamous heteropatriarchal relationships and are all rooted in men's supremacy. They exemplify forms of intimate injustice.

So, if patriarchal values shape the relationship, it doesn't matter if it is monogamous, polygynist, or any form of nonmonogamy; it produces what we can call *intimate sexism*. In Rachel Krantz's memoir *Open*, she exposes how patriarchal ideas can seep into all forms of relationships, vulnerably sharing how the man who introduced her to nonmonogamy dismissed her feelings, gaslit her, and behaved abusively.[17]

Here is my point: Humans aren't inherently monogamous *or* nonmonogamous, and societal ideas about which relationships are most ideal are socially constructed. We must relinquish all ideas that humans are biologically or naturally inclined toward monogamy.

In recent years, a number of scholars and activists have pointed to examples throughout history to suggest that humans are inherently nonmonogamous. I understand the impulse! Yet, as Angela Willey astutely asserts in *Undoing Monogamy*, as people rightfully contest the dominance of monogamy, they run the risk of naturalizing nonmonogamies and, in turn, reinforcing amatonormativity.[18] People are also entitled not to want to form any romantic relationships!

These days, people involved in nonmonogamous relationships often use the term *ethical* nonmonogamy, or *consensual* nonmonogamy, as a shield to soften the blows of stigma, distancing themselves from ideas about polygamy. If we must speak in the register of ethics, then the principles of consent, harm reduction, and social justice must guide our moral compass. So-called ethical relationships are intentionally designed to combat inequity and function through active communication built on empathy, trust, and a deep commitment to care.

So, I am not arguing for a nonmonogamous utopia that will never be. I am profoundly uninterested in joining what psychologist Jorge Ferrer calls the *mono–poly wars*, in which one relationship form is portrayed as inherently more ethical or ideal.[19] People can be shitty and abusive across relationship forms. I simply want everyone to have the agency to envision, create, and live out the relationships that best support their consensual desires, including the right not to want one at all. I want everyone to understand the political nature of their relationship choices and call out injustice, especially intimate sexism, racism, and ableism across relationship forms. Now, that's the stuff sexual liberation is made of!

My first serious adult relationship was with a woman twelve years my senior. I met Grace when I was nineteen, going on twenty. I vividly remember standing behind my receptionist's desk next to the stairs on the lower level of the salon when I saw her. I was captivated by this person seductively floating up and down the stairs in a long billowing brightly colored garment. She was the most beautiful woman I'd ever seen in real life.

When Grace and I met in 1997, I had already dropped out of college and was living with roommates in a three-bedroom third-floor walk-up in Queens, New York. Our apartment was a popular, joy-filled neighborhood hangout. We did not sell drugs, per se, but it *was*, in today's terms, a trap house. With the turnstile of gray economy hustlers hanging out and coming and going, someone with weed, ecstasy, MDMA, angel dust (dips), ketamine, or cocaine was always sitting on the couch or a blanket up on what we called black tar beach (a.k.a. the tar-floored roof). Loud music was a staple as guests and I spun vinyl on my Technics turntables, sitting around laughing, talking, and smoking Newports—break beats inevitably producing dancing.

In addition to the day job that paid my share of the rent, which was $350 a month, I was self-employed as a full-time partygoer. My crew and I went to nightclubs and raves almost every weekend and did promotions in the New York tristate area. On off-days, we lived like vampires. We slept all day and debauched ourselves at night, with drugs as our lifeblood.

By societal standards, I was a pretty naughty girl, but I had *a lot* of fun failing.[20] My chosen family and I developed unconventional modes of kinship and a community of care that I desperately needed at that time. We rejected heteropatriarchal, capitalist, and ableist obsessions with productivity and normative forms of time, eroticism, family, and love. I learned a lot about my erotic desires through this type of exploration, but I also learned what type of partner I wanted to be—regrettably, at Grace's expense.

Grace was unhappily "married" to a woman with whom she had an ostensibly perfect suburban life, including a young child. Looking back, I suppose my party life, fueled by the gluttonous pleasures of shirking responsibility, was a space where she could escape the monotony of her homonormative life. She likely felt trapped and bored. She, too, was enticed by the redolent smells emanating from failure's kitchen.

Our relationship provided the catalyst Grace had been looking for to split from her wife. When they sold their co-owned town house, they called that their divorce. I say "called" because gay marriage was not legally recognized at the time in the United States. Still, queer folks always find ways to resist prohibitions and live authentically and joyfully and with dignity—even if, in this case, getting married ended in divorce.

Grace's desire for freedom is part of how I have reconciled, then and now, why a thirty-two-year-old woman was dating an impetuous and mercurial twenty-year-old in dire need of a therapist. Only Grace truly knows why she was interested in me and what functions our relationship had for her. I can only speculate. So, from here, I'll only speak for myself.

I loved Grace. I *truly* did. Everyone around us, with their necks giraffed and noses north, disapproved for one reason or another—the sapphic stuff—the adultery stuff—her so-called cradle-robbing. All of it caused people to rip, not clutch, their pearls. Don't worry. I never tripped over those fallen pearls.

Honestly, the prohibitions only made it feel more exciting. It reminds me of cheating. Even if adulterers don't say it out loud, many find it thrilling precisely because of the rule-breaking and stealthy maneuvering. But what if I told you we can experience those same types of excitements consensually and without stomping on someone else's heart?

When it came to Grace, I also struggled with how immersed she became in my cultural world. She adopted our aesthetics, when part of what I fell in love with was how different she looked and acted from the people I hung out with. She also struggled with my need for space alone with my friends.

Retaining a solid sense of self is critical to a healthy relationship. We do not have to, and probably should not, change the core attributes of who we are for our partners. As the prolific writer and psychotherapist Esther Perel tells us, relationships ideally balance two core human needs: connection and freedom.[21]

With Grace, I felt like I was on one end of a seesaw, smothered and weighed down in connection, while I watched my freedom propelled upward, lost in the playground sky. Our relationship's fulcrum was corroded, held together by trauma bonding, and neither of us had the emotional literacy tools to fix it. None of this legitimized my own cheating.

I cheated on Grace a lot. I did not know how to communicate that I needed space and that, while I loved her, I did not want to be monogamous. I needed her to respect these boundaries, but I did not articulate what they were.

I am not proud of this behavior. It was immature, unkind, and disrespectful. I was also young, scared, and in the throes of a trauma-induced love affair with self-destruction that had nothing to do with Grace. However selfish, I needed the affirmation and the overflow of her undying love, even as I felt smothered by it.

Explanations are not excuses. Justice is fundamentally about people standing on business and taking accountability for their actions when they cause harm to others. So, restitution for my past behavior involves doing better by my partners today. Looking back at my relationship with Grace and others that followed, I have learned that I do not want to lie to my partners. I don't want my partner to think we will marry when I don't desire the same. I do not want to hurt people because I can't communicate my feelings and needs.

Anyone who has been cheated on knows that erotic betrayal cuts like an obsidian knife. I have those scars, too. The person I married and had a child with cheated on me and lied profusely about it. Oh, that man gaslit me to the point that it made me unhinged. I was gutted—dismembered by his dishonesty.

On top of this, I felt like I had already sacrificed a lot being with him. Marrying a cisgender man and moving to the suburbs had left me feeling like a treasonous queer. All I wanted was realness from him. I can work with honesty, but I struggle to come back from deception. I ended that relationship not long after our confrontations over his cheating, but as you might know, the lacerations of a despoiled heart can take a long time to heal.

Having been on both sides of the cheating coin, I have spent years since my divorce exploring different forms of nonmonogamy. As you already know from the previous chapter, not all available options have worked for me. Still, I have had so much fun exploring. I also know that what works for me today could change tomorrow, because sexualities are fluid, not static.

Today, I am a relationship anarchist. This term, which challenges many popular assumptions and ideas about monogamous relationships, comes from Swedish activist and queer feminist Andie Nordgren.[22] For me, relationship anarchy means that when I am in a relationship, my partners and I set and craft our own rules together. We don't make assumptions about what we want from the relationship or what it will look like, and we never base how it functions on gendered, racialized, or other predefined cultural scripts. Unless, of course, we are intentionally erotically role-playing—but more on that soon.

What people need and want from a relationship will shift and change because, as humans, we grow and change as our social locations change. People worldwide migrate in and out of cultural contexts with varying norms, which shape our sexualities and needs, and our sexualities can also inform why and where we migrate.[23] So, whatever we design will need updating, and sometimes, over time, we will find our relationship needs are no longer compatible. Rather than wringing our hands over how to force ourselves back into alignment, I try to find peace, accept when a relationship has run its course, and lean into gratitude for the joyful times spent in sync.

"Polyamory is having its moment in the sun," Evita Sawyers declaratively remarked during our interview.[24] *Polyamory* is one form of nonmonogamy in which people consent to relationships with multiple people simultaneously.[25] We've already spent some time examining another form of nonmonogamy—swinging. Swingers are generally interested in sexual escapes that take place around the edges of a dyadic romantic relationship. Still, some swingers are also polyamorous or, more often, they became polyamorous after starting out as swingers. Another form of nonmonogamy is the open relationship, where people consensually have sex outside of a singular or primary relationship.[26]

Polyamory varies widely across geographical, cultural, and historical contexts, but what all polyamorous people have in common is that they form many romantic relationships. The term *polyamory* is derived from the Greek word *polús*, many, and the Latin word *amor*, love—so it literally means many loves.[27] In what follows, I describe polyamory in its broadest terms, with the caveat that people's cultural locations, race, gender, age, and sexuality, among other factors, will shape how people understand, practice, and talk about polyamory.

Today, more people globally are accepting of polyamory than was common a generation ago. Psychologists, using what they call the Attitudes Towards Polyamory scale, have showed that younger generations have more positive views of polyamory than older ones.[28] Unsurprisingly, this same study found that politically conservative and religious people were more likely than liberal and nonreligious people to hold favorable opinions of monogamy and unfavorable views of polyamory. For example, a study in Greece showed that women with high levels of religiosity were more likely to oppose polyamory.[29]

Polyamorous people are often labeled perverts. They face myriad forms of discrimination, a situation that is compounded for racially marginalized and poor people.[30] One Canadian study, for example, revealed the rampant stigma and discrimination that polyamorous people face in having and raising children, particularly in medical and legal contexts.[31] Another study focused on Spanish law showed how mononormativity influenced economic and legal benefits, including access to a partner's pensions, taxes, and even immigration rights. Mononormativity, in other words, even shapes who is and can be a citizen.[32]

At an interpersonal level, people who harbor prejudice against nonmonogamy adhere to what scholars call *zero-sum romantic beliefs*—the belief that people can only love one person and do not have the capacity to meet more than one partner's needs.[33] Studies show people tend to equate monogamy with commitment, more lasting relationships, and better environments for raising children.[34] Yet, such perceptions are not grounded in empirical realities.[35]

These unfounded beliefs, in turn, shape how some monogamous people see and treat polyamorous people. In a study on polyamorous people in Norway, participants noted that living in a mononormative culture means constantly having people dismiss and question your relationships as "not real" and abnormal.[36] Many polyamorous people report being rejected by family and friends. They are forced into secrecy, especially about their relationships with people perceived as non-primary partners.[37]

Polyamorous people everywhere are cultivating and sustaining healthy, supportive, and joyful relationships. These positive outcomes of polyamorous relationships have been documented around the world. In another study on polyamorous people in Canada, participants said that nonmonogamy provided them with autonomy and allowed them to be their authentic selves. Respondents said having more partners leads to more fulfillment in long-term relationships; enhances their interpersonal, friendship, and community ties; allows for sexual exploration; and fosters personal and relational growth.[38]

Participants in a Spanish study similarly reported that their relationships were free from possessiveness and were based on deep care, trust, respect, and friendship. Because participants did not subscribe to traditional gender roles, their relationships were profoundly equitable.[39] When it comes to sex, a study in the United States of nonmonogamous people showed that, across genders and marital status, polyamorous people had more sex and experienced higher rates of sexual satisfaction than monogamous people.[40]

Critically, none of this data means that polyamory is inherently better than or more equitable than monogamy. It just shows that, for one, most monogamous people could learn a thing or two from nonmonogamous people, and that for some people, nonmonogamy is a much better fitting container for their erotic needs than monogamy.

Kevin was excited about his yearly trip to Toronto with friends, and then—they canceled. What he didn't anticipate was how this initial disappointment would change his life. Once he learned his usual crew couldn't go, he invited his girlfriend of a few months, who'd later become his wife. They also asked her best friend to join them. Before leaving, Kevin joked with his then-girlfriend: "Ya know, something might pop off!" Kevin was genuinely kidding around, but his girlfriend raised an excited eyebrow, and they lightheartedly talked about what those logistics might look like.

Fast-forward. After nights of partying and living their best lives on vacation, Kevin leaned over to his girlfriend and seductively said, "I'm gonna kiss your friend."

"Go for it!" she excitedly responded.

They all enjoyed each other for a bit, and even though the three of them did not ride into some rom-com-style throuple sunset, Kevin's wife and her bestie remain incredibly tight more than two decades later. According to Kevin, the experience changed his life. He explained, "Not just in that it changed my relationship, it changed my viewpoint on how much I can customize my own experiences."

Kevin reminds us that monogamy itself is not inherently a problem. The issue is the compulsory nature of monogamous cultures. Like Kevin and his wife, we can customize our relationships. There is power and pleasure in realizing that we have the agency to choose and design relationships that best fit our erotic needs.

People come to polyamory and nonmonogamy for myriad reasons. The most common is the most obvious: A person acknowledges their desires for more than one sexual and romantic partner, but doesn't want to cheat. Others are "introduced" to polyamory by meeting and dating a polyamorous partner, someone Evita Sawyers has termed an *entry partner*. Still, others have read, listened to, or watched positive media representations about polyamory and want to try it out. And yet others are interested in building different types of family relationships, including sharing the responsibilities and costs of parenting with multiple people. The list could go on, but the point is that there are as many reasons for exploring polyamory as there are for anything else.

Critically, many people do not describe their stories of entry into polyamory in black-and-white ways. Chaneé Jackson Kendall's story exemplifies this.[41] When explaining how she first arrived at polyamory, Chaneé emphasized the importance of her family background. She described her parents as bastions of their community—stable parents to her and her siblings. They were about to celebrate their forty-ninth wedding anniversary at the time of our interview.

Still, she underscored that, like many Black folks, she did not grow up with just a nuclear family. "My parents were always taking people in who needed help," she said. She grew up surrounded by the warmth and love of family friends, women she called her aunties. She animatedly told me, "My parents taught me that family is defined by you, not by blood."

So, when Chaneé and her then-boyfriend started exploring nonmonogamies in her early twenties, nearly twenty years ago, she was already sold on designing her own relationships. She wanted to find her own way of embracing the extended and fluid kinship systems that have been a staple of many communities of color for centuries.

On the "Let's Talk Hierarchy" episode of *Monogamish Pod*, then-guest Chaneé joked with host Jhen, who also spoke to me for this book, that "the swinging to polyamory pipeline is real." Some people who begin with swinging find that, over time, they want more intimacy and connection with additional partners instead of just one-and-done escapades. Some others, like me, have trouble finding couples in which they are attracted to both people. What are the chances that each person in two (or more) dyadic couples will be attracted to each person? Polyamory resolves these issues.

Once people choose polyamory, there are many different forms, providing many different container options for everyone to try out. In *hierarchical polyamory*, there is a primary or *anchor relationship*, frequently among *nesting partners*, who live together or are otherwise in a committed relationship. Each partner prioritizes this relationship. Any secondary (or tertiary, and so on) relationships play second fiddle to the primary one.

Increasingly, some polyamorous people are rejecting hierarchical polyamory in favor of *nonhierarchical polyamory*, in which no relationship is prioritized over another. To call this a contentious subject in polyamorous communities would be an understatement. Some critics argue that people will inevitably allocate their time and care in ways that signal one relationship is prioritized over another. Therefore, according to some polyamorous folks, nonhierarchical polyamory is an unobtainable goal at best, and disingenuous virtue signaling at worst.

But still, many people say the spirit of nonhierarchical polyamory is to reject compulsory cultural ideas suggesting that one single person, our soulmate, is entitled to all our attention and our bodies, minds, and care. It seems as though many who embrace nonhierarchical polyamory are also reacting to the connotation of the word *hierarchy* or *hierarchical*, which by definition refers to a ranking system, and hierarchical systems generally sustain inequities and power imbalances. And the point of polyamory for many people is to circumvent and reject inequality in relationships.

Chaneé explained how she applies the principles of relationship anarchy and nonhierarchical polyamory in her life: "I practice nonhierarchical polyamory, which for me means that anyone with whom I enter into a relationship has access to the same ability to grow and build a life with me as anyone else."

She continued, "The nature of our relationship does not dictate the weight and importance of our relationship. We live in a society where romantic relationships, no matter how long they have been in our lives or how much time we devote to them, are supposed to be more important to us than any other relationship. That is not my life."

A key lesson from polyamorous people is that everyone, regardless of the broader structure of their relationships, can and should choose how they want those relationships to look—including aromantic people designing platonic relationships and people practicing solo polyamory. In *solo polyamory*, people have multiple intimate relationships with no desire for a nesting partner. Instead, many people who practice solo polyamory characterize *themselves* as their primary partner.

Calico Roman, a participant in Manijeh Badiee and Evita Sawyers's study on Black queer femme and nonbinary polyamorists, defined solo polyamory this way: "My personal definition of solo polyamory holds self-love and self-responsibility at its center, leaving room for love to bloom outside of relationship escalator–prescribed enmeshment, familial conditions or social pressures. In a society where the very idea of love and its imagery has been warped to suit a dyadic model, solo polyamory reasserts that freedom and autonomy are not at odds with love and commitment."[42]

One critical decision in nonmonogamous relationships is whether people want to know their partner's (or partners') other partners, called *metamours* (metas). When partners regularly interact and hang out, it's colloquially referred to as *kitchen table polyamory*—think of sitting around the table together and sharing a meal, which in some households might just look like conversations. In others, it might include all the forms of dessert.

Chaneé explained, "My partners can all sit around the kitchen table and have a cup of coffee. I like that with my partners, we can decide to have a movie night, order takeout, and just relax and chill. . . . I prefer to have, at the very least, cordial and loving interactions with my metamours." In my research, some people noted that they felt that kitchen table polyamory doesn't force people to navigate *hinging*, or figuring out how to divide time and energy between the partners of one person—*the hinge.*

Maybe someone wants to know their metamours in a limited and less intimate capacity—that's *garden party polyamory.* In this case, think of a birthday party, where a person attends only once a year, catching up with people they otherwise don't regularly interact with or communicate with. Well, that's like garden party polyamory.

Or perhaps they prefer not to have any contact with their metas at all. This is called *parallel polyamory.* Still, even in parallel polyamory, people might run into other metas at the local *munch*, a social meet-up in public places for food and socializing, or other community spaces.

These are not all-or-nothing options. Polyamorous people don't always have a fixed preference for relationship styles, and the type of relationships they have with metas are often determined by those specific people. Polyamorous folks sometimes prefer parallel polyamory until their partner and metas have been seeing each other for a while. Then, they sometimes organically find themselves at the kitchen table over time.

Evita Sawyers explained that her relationships had run the gamut. She's done the kitchen table and has adored some of her now ex-husband's partners, and then there have been people she can't stand. Evita quipped with a wry smile, "We ain't doing that with that one. Okayyy!"

Kevin, too, said he has used the language of the kitchen table, but he generally resonates with relationship anarchy because he does not decide the structure beforehand—the people in the relationship choose the dynamics. He gave me a few examples. "If I've got a partner that's like, 'Hey, Kev, I love you, but I'm not interested in being around your kids,' okay, cool. We'll see if we can make that work."

But he went on to unpack how people who strictly only want parallel relationships won't work for him. He explained, "I'm not gonna force my partners to interact. But if you can't even exist in the same space as other people that I love, that's a hard no for me. You know, no harm, no foul [but] we're incompatible." Kevin spoke cheerily about his relationships with his wife, partners, and metas, how much he enjoys spending time together, and how, at minimum, he desires everyone to be on friendly terms.

Here is the salient point when considering these different forms of polyamory: There is no right way to have consensual relationships! The only so-called right way, or the most ethical way, to do polyamory or any form of relationship, including monogamy, is if everyone consents and folks have chosen and communicated clearly about the best relationship style for their needs at that time.

Whatever the labels we use—polyamorous, open, nonmonogamous, monogamish, monogamous—the point is that we must define boundaries for ourselves in our relationships and communicate clearly and often about what we want and how we want our relationship to function. Most importantly, nobody should face persecution, discrimination, or stigma for choosing a relationship structure that best supports their desires, especially when it is profoundly consensual and rooted in care and intimate justice. Fighting the systems responsible for these forms of systemic discrimination is what sexual liberation is all about.

Relationships are like gardens. They require care, time, space, nourishment, and the proper conditions to bloom and thrive. As in our previous lessons, polyamory is not just an identity category; like all sexual identities, it reflects sets of cultural practices.

If our relationships are a critical component of our sexualities and we want them to flourish, we must make deliberate and thoughtful choices and recommit to them every day. Chaneé has termed this *intentional polyamory.* The intentional polyamory model Chaneé created consists of four pillars: self-work, relational culture, information sharing, and community. And indeed, these themes ran through all my conversations with polyamorous people in my research for this book.

Chaneé educates people on the four pillars in her Intentional Polyamory cohort workshops. Everyone, regardless of their type of relationship container, can find value in the insights derived from converting these pillars into effective relationship practices. While I discuss each insight separately, they are, of course, all intertwined—just like all the dimensions of our sexuality.

Chaneé's workshops start with the pillar of self-work. Polyamory is not just a relationship style; it is a journey of self-discovery and introspection. As Chaneé emphatically put it, in polyamory, "you will have to face your own shit! Polyamory will really test your emotional intelligence." When people have cultivated a deep understanding of their sexual socialization, they become more in touch with their feelings and needs. This not only fosters individual emotional intelligence and growth but, in turn, makes them better partners.

Perhaps I have just watched too many seasons and episodes of the *Love Is Blind* and *Love Island* global television franchises, but I truly believe so many of the issues we face in relationships are rooted in our insecurities, past traumas, and a lack of deep understanding of our sexualities and what we need from partners. I believe so many people are missing the sexual and media literacy tools to understand how systems of power and cultural mores shape our ability to speak our truths to partners full-throatedly. In other words, sometimes our relationship problems reflect issues within ourselves, not our partners.

Polyamorous people prioritize self-care, and not in the hollow bourgeois ways that the term is trotted out in consumerist societies. Polyamorous people often note that self-discovery and individual growth are significant benefits of their relationships compared to their experiences in monogamous ones, which generally emphasize relinquishing the self to become one unit.

Evita emphasized the same point, telling me passionately, "It was so fascinating, all these things that I'm learning about myself. That, to me, is the biggest benefit of polyamory—the self-discovery." She and I talked about how when relationships provide people with the freedom for autonomy and space for individual growth and pleasure, they become better humans, more thoughtful partners, and better parents.

She explained, "Because of polyamory, I'm a much more self-aware person. I'm a much more self-contained person. I'm a much more [emotionally] regulated person." In our conversation, she mentioned that individual growth comes from ongoing introspective work, similar to the work people often do in therapy, which has made her a better global citizen—a better human.

This is not to say that self-work in polyamory is a replacement for therapy. For some, having a sex-positive and culturally competent personal therapist is essential for navigating their nonmonogamous relationships. Personally, I believe everyone should be in therapy at some point, and, like all health care, therapy should be free and available to everyone.

Chenée, Evita, Kevin, and others I spoke to all talked about the self-work they have done to ensure they can communicate well with their partners, understand their needs and behaviors, and show up for themselves and their partners. This has also made them better friends, parents, and humans. Personally, I think the world could use so much more of this.

Polyamory demands that people design relationship architectures for themselves. When Chaneé talks about relational culture, then, she asks people to consider the following: What are the values, ethics, and principles guiding your relationships? Having done self-work, what boundaries do you need? What boundaries does your partner need? Establishing a relational culture not only sets standards that work for partners, but it also creates commitments for which people hold themselves and one another accountable in loving and empathetic ways.

Think of relationships like a board game, except we make up our own rules rather than following the existing printed ones. There is pleasure in creativity and imaginative eroticism. And what's exciting is that we can create new rules each time we play with new people. We must establish new relational cultures in each new relationship because, as Chaneé remarked, "We are different. Our connection is different. The place where we meet each other in our lives and on our journeys are different."

Kevin and I similarly talked about how monogamous cultures come with prescribed rules for engagement that many people do not question or discuss with their partners. These assumptions can stifle and foreclose opportunities for eroticism, human intimacy, and connection. For example, in relationships, we must communicate and agree on how we will interact with other humans—especially those to whom we find ourselves attracted.

Kevin posed a few scenarios in our conversation: "I meet somebody at an event, and we have a flirty energy." We went on to chat about how, in monogamous cultures, people will often shut down such interactions outright and feel guilty if they do entertain flirtatious banter. Some partners would chastise the other for engaging in flirting if they found out. Kevin explained that, for many, "this is a violation." And, à la disciplinary power, they think, "Let me go and do penance, or let me make an abrupt exit from a conversation that I'm enjoying."

It is pretty understandable that some monogamous people consider this behavior a no-no, but to others, it is not a big deal and part of what they see as human nature. Without meaningful conversations between partners and establishing clear expectations and boundaries, conflict over these types of everyday interactions is inevitable. Let's turn to one more of Kevin's scenarios.

Kevin gave the example of a coworker. If you are friendly with a coworker and regularly go to lunch together, Kevin rhetorically asked, "Are you having an emotional affair?" He raised an excellent point. It is essential that people discuss the idea that humans can only share physical and emotional intimacy with one person, and whether they believe this is realistic or ideal for their relationship.

A critical part of creating relational cultures is setting up both expectations and accountability systems. What happens if someone violates a partner's boundary or a co-created "rule"? In our conversation, Chaneé emphasized that much self-work and communication must focus on *rupture* and *repair.* When an issue arises, we must decide, in consultation with our partners, how we will respond, what actions we will take, and how we will repair the situation.

The point is that we have the agency to create our own rules and standards for accountability. Still, if we set unrealistic standards for anyone in the relationship, we create a self-fulfilling prophecy. Putting the work into designing and upholding these cultures leads to pleasure. Chaneé said, "My biggest pleasure that I gained from polyamory is the feeling of being consistently and intentionally chosen."

Once people have created a relational culture that works for all parties, they can build agreements through ongoing communication practices that support that culture. Open, honest, and transparent communication supports a healthy and joyful relationship. This is never one and done; our agreements and self-determined relational culture will always need updating because our lives and needs are always changing.

Our partners don't have telepathy! If I'm early into dating someone, and I suspect they are upset, and I get the dreaded "I'm fine" response to a compassionate query about how they're doing—I know we're headed for trouble.

Anyone with even one toe in the relationship industrial complex has heard experts and writers from across all walks of life telling us how vital communication is to our relationships. But if communicating were easy, everyone would do it well, and couples' therapists would need new gigs. Talking about our feelings, knowing why we have them, and setting and maintaining boundaries is inherently challenging, especially if our relationships don't provide intentional space for ongoing self-work.

Communication always requires practice. In our romantic relationships, the first thing we must communicate about is what style of relationships we desire. Kevin said, "This should be part of the conversation on your first or second date, like, 'Hey, how do you feel about monogamy?' Are you strictly monogamous, or are you doing another thing? How does that work for you? That should be a standard question." When monogamy is the norm, people do not always discuss this component of their sexuality right off the bat. Yet, it is just as critical as letting a partner know "I'm bisexual" or "I'm into feet."

The people I spoke with emphasized that the more you do polyamory, the better you will get at articulating your feelings and, most importantly, knowing why you are having them. To successfully navigate polyamory, or any relationship style, for that matter, people must commit to finding ways to stare down and talk through their vulnerabilities and fears with their partners, in ways that take seriously how external systems of power mute and empower.

Take jealousy as an example.

People often see jealousy as an agent of chaos inimical to healthy relationships. Even in polyamorous communities, people don't always experience *compersion*, or joy in knowing their partner was enriched in another relationship. The emotion of jealousy is particularly fraught for people in polyamorous relationships because so many of them have opted for polyamory precisely because they reject the norms associated with compulsory monogamy. If you're not expecting monogamy, the thinking goes, why are you jealous?

Despite toxic messaging to the contrary, experiencing jealousy does not mean you are doing polyamory wrong. Kevin underscored this point. He said authoritatively, "Jealousy is information. If a partner does something, and it makes me feel jealous, maybe I have a problem with them doing this thing, *or* maybe I have a problem within myself."

Evita also brilliantly crystallized this point about introspection and jealousy in our discussions. "I've come to know that my jealousy is not here to hurt me. It is a friend. It is an information bringer and brings a lot of information." She animatedly said that when jealousy shows up, she talks directly to it: "I go, alright. Come on, sit down, have a cup of coffee. What do you got to say? What's your message? And so, I listen to it. That's what I do with jealousy. I listen to it. I speak to it. I sit with it. I talk to it, and I glean its message."

I chimed in and told Evita how much I agreed with her. I, too, believe that jealousy and shame are productive emotions, even if they make us feel shitty. They always show up to teach us something about ourselves. So, when they appear, I check in with my body, become curious, and ask questions. She explained that, after introspection and with a better understanding of why she feels triggered, she sometimes needs to share this with a partner. Maybe she needs reassurance, or she needs them to change something. Sometimes it becomes a beautiful opportunity for, in her words, her partners to "get a deeper understanding of how I tick."

As writer, sex educator, and sex worker Tina Horn argued, jealousy reflects a fear of loss.[43] People worry that if their partner finds emotional or physical comfort with another human, it means they will leave them, or that they must not be good enough. Otherwise, why would their partner be looking at, talking to, or sleeping with anyone else? This is a hard one. I get it. My abandonment issues run deep. But my fear of loss doesn't mean my partner doesn't love me and is going anywhere.

Sometimes, our feelings of inadequacy lie beneath the smothering covers of jealousy. Our fight-or-flight responses might step in to protect us from perceived emotional warfare, but if we have cultivated emotional literacy, we can talk with our mind's ninjas and tell them: "I am good. Thank you, but I want to confront these feelings with my partner and discuss why I am agitated."

Like with any embodied emotional state, how we react to jealousy is what matters most. Critically, how our partners respond to our emotional disclosures also matters—no partner should gaslight, shame, or judge their partners for their feelings. As Evita and I went on to discuss, sometimes when someone reacts negatively to a partner talking about their feelings of jealousy, it is precisely because the disclosure triggered something about themselves that they aren't ready to confront.

Communicating not just what we feel jealous about but *why* we feel jealous is hard. As scary as it can feel, though, leaning into that vulnerability is critical to sustaining a healthy relationship. As Evita emphasized, sharing these vulnerabilities builds intimacy. It deepens connections. When necessary, jealousy can lead to changes in the relationship that, when addressed, make partners feel seen, heard, supported, loved, cared for, and safe.

Relationships, especially non-normative ones, do not thrive in isolation. In Chaneé's words, "relationships of all kinds need infrastructure to support them." Community involvement is one such form of infrastructure that gives people access to vital information and education, advisors, role models, friends, and, quite critically—joy.

As we segue into our final chapter, let's hear from Black polyamorous folks on the importance of erotic communities. Black people and other people of color often feel marginalized in white-dominated polyamorous spaces. They have responded by creating alternative community spaces and resources specific to the identity kaleidoscope, many of which have emerged in thriving online polyamorous communities.

For years, these folks have been doing an enormous amount of work in educating and building polyamorous communities, both online and offline. Over time, some have found ways to monetize their work. However, especially for social media content creators, many are doing uncompensated labor on corporate-owned social media sites. As Moya Bailey in *Misogynoir Transformed* and Catherine Knight Steele in *Digital Black Feminism* have both adroitly demonstrated, Black women's digital alchemy and resistance, in particular, have been too often overlooked.[44]

From Facebook to Instagram and in podcasts galore, Black polyamorous people create spaces to connect and provide peer-to-peer education and affirmation. In 2013 in the United States, Ron Young started the blog Black and Poly. The blog soon turned into a Facebook group with almost thirty thousand members, and, later, a dating site. Black and Poly also hosted monthly global online meetings. Spaces like these are essential. As Kevin said emphatically of community, "it plays an important role, not just so that we can find each other, but so that we get validation! That our lives are not a mistake."

People often look to social media platforms to connect with and learn from others. On Instagram, PolyamorousBlackGirl has been sharing experiences to affirm and help others for years. When PolyamorousBlackGirl began posting on Instagram, she told me she was "just a girl trying to figure out how to do polyamory while being a Black woman in Canada." Over time, she has built a sizable following. As she has shared her pains, joys, and knowledge, she has become a *possibility model* for others in the polyamorous community, especially for Black women.

Today, countless podcasts about polyamory provide critical community-based education. On *Monogamish Pod*, Jhen discusses non-monogamies and polyamory through a Black Caribbean lens. When I spoke to Jhen, she explained how uplifting it has been to receive messages from people thanking her for the podcast. She gave an example of a message she received, which went like this: "Hey, I'm from this small country in the Caribbean. It's so great to see another Caribbean person talking about this stuff because I'm the only one I know doing this here."

Jhen said that while *Monogamish*'s primary listeners have been from the United States, Canada, and the UK, people have even tuned in from Uganda. Accessible forms of this work are so important for people living in conservative cultural contexts, who may struggle to find vibrant and accessible erotic communities to support their desires.

People also turn to polyamorous communities for examples of affirming role models and education. That's precisely why Kevin created Poly Role Models on Tumblr. As Kevin explained, people can make many predictable, yet unnecessary, mistakes when they first begin exploring polyamory. Connecting with community can help minimize this. Kevin shared with me that he and his wife made many of what he called "rookie mistakes" initially, but they avoided other newbie pitfalls because they got networked quickly.

Chaneé shared a similar perspective. About two years into her relationship with her husband, the two of them got into their first polyamorous relationship with another woman. She explained, "It wasn't very intentional . . . that's when I started studying and learning. I'm the kind of person who if I'm going to do something, I want to do it well. So, I began studying how best to do it. I began seeking community, which I think is something that people often do when they're learning a new thing."

Further, people often have no role models for polyamory in their immediate families and broader cultural environments, and are frequently rejected by those communities. Kevin told me his relationships with family had improved, but in his words, "I missed a lot of my cousins growing up because my family wasn't trying to hear any weird shit I was talking about." So, finding erotic communities that support people is critical. We need people to talk about our weird shit with.

When polyamorous people try to talk about their relationships with monogamous people in their immediate communities, as Kevin told me, people often dismiss their issues. Too frequently, the listener attributes any problems in a polyamorous relationship to nonmonogamy itself. But as folks pointed out in our conversations, monogamous people can cheat and get divorced, and they don't attribute their divorce or fighting to monogamy—although perhaps they should be connecting them to specific ideological characteristics of monogamous cultures. Challenging and dismantling the oppressive and inequitable ideologies that sustain monogamy are vital parts of sexual liberation.

This is not to say that polyamorous communities are perfect. Again, no erotic community I've ever heard of is a utopia. I talked to people who left groups like Black and Poly due to heteropatriarchal norms within the community. Still, as Evita explained, she has generally remained friends with people from groups she is no longer formally a part of, sometimes nearly a decade later. She said earnestly, "I always tell people that the relationships of substance that I've made since becoming polyamorous have been my friends. Partners have come and gone, but my friends are still here."

Erotic communities are not only sources of affirmational and educational support. They are spaces for friendship, intimacy, human connection, and joy. Chaneé spoke ardently about this when discussing Black Poly Pride, a weekend conference filled with education, conversation, socializing, and pleasure that she cofounded with Cheri' Calico Roman in 2019. She said, "There is alchemy and magic that happens when people share space, especially Black people. It is deep in our tradition—there is healing that happens when we share space."

While Chaneé radiated joy throughout our conversation, she shined even brighter when she spoke about the 2019 event. She excitedly explained, "We had the party, but we also just communed with one another. We talked, and we spent time together. We worked through things, we cried, and it was just the most beautiful, life-changing experience for me. It was deeply impactful because it showed me that my feelings about community and its importance were true—and not just for me. There was so much Black joy!"

Chaneé's comments are instructive. If those around you do not erotically support you, it might be time to find communities that do.

Black Poly Pride, 2019, photo courtesy of Chaneé Jackson Kendall.

I want everyone to more deeply consider whether the communities around them—that have raised them, that they spend time immersed in—support them erotically.

Finding supportive erotic communities does not necessarily mean we must leave our existing friends, families, and communities in the dust. Still, we might find that some of the issues we have faced with our sexuality and relationships have nothing to do with an inner struggle or some deficiency within us. The problem, instead, might be that we do not have an encouraging erotic community. We thrive erotically when we have communities that support us on our own terms!

Chapter 6

COMMUNITIES

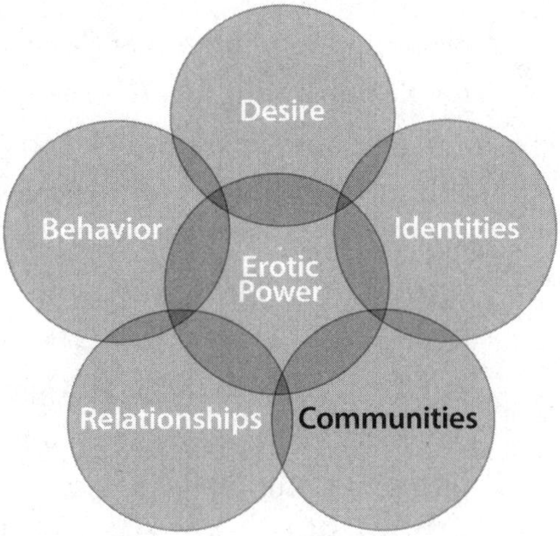

Eroticism binds. It is *the* ne plus ultra social adhesive. The human desire for social belonging and acceptance drives people to form communities and cultural spaces where they can bathe in the warmth and soul-nurturing rays of human connection and affirmation. Ace people, sex doll owners, swingers, sex club enthusiasts, and poly and nonmonogamous folks have already shown us this in their own unique ways.

Communities, the final component of our sexualities in the erotic power model, are vital to our sexual well-being. They are spaces, be they IRL or some virtual place, where people find social connection, support, wisdom, and pleasure. People often understand their sexuality through a physiological lens, instead of a social one. When we do this, we fail to recognize fully how the communities and people around us shape how we embody our sexualities—how we feel them and how we live them.

The various communities we inhabit socialize us. Every community has its own unique languages, customs, values, and norms, as well as accountability systems to enforce these parameters and punish those who transgress. This means that when people are shamed, isolated, marginalized, and harmed for disobedience, they must find alternative spaces for support. Scholars have documented, for example, how queer people build communities for survival, support, and care, and as spaces for pleasure in the face of persecution.[1]

Grace introduced me to Cherry Grove, Fire Island—the first gay and lesbian town in the United States.[2] I still remember the joy and freedom I felt when I arrived at the small beach town filled with unapologetic gayness for the first time—being in a space just for queer folks, feeling safe, feeling at home. In the years since, I have spent much time in Cherry Grove, and it still gives me these feelings. Unfortunately, not everyone has access to community spaces where they feel free to be themselves. But they should.

What exactly do I mean by this elusive term, *community*? Sociologists rely on three primary definitions of communities: groups of people with shared identities, shared ecological or physical spaces, and shared social networks.[3] These three forms of community are often intertwined and can be challenging to study separately, especially today.

The idea of community reminds me of Russian Matryoshka dolls. Within each community, there are often seemingly endless smaller communities. Take, for example, the BDSM community. At a macro level, people in the BDSM community are members of a loosely knit global community of people with shared identities who might meet each other on a global platform like FetLife. But they also might be part of a specific community in one particular location, say, regularly attending a munch (a social gathering for kinky people) and rope and play parties in Berlin, Germany.

Other smaller groupings of people in the broader BDSM community might form intentional organizations built around specific identity-based needs. Leather communities, for example, highlight how LGBTQ people have created their own communities, often apart from the straight BDSM community. The Lesbian Sex Mafia, for instance, is the oldest continuously running women's leather BDSM support and education group in the United States. And due to racism and exclusion within queer leather communities, people of color, and Black folks in particular, have created their own organizations, such as ONYX and

ONYX Pearls, which are leading organizations for men and women of color in the US leather community.

The many and varied types of BDSM groups highlight the ever-changing definitions of community. I treat these kinky communities as a case study that shows how all the components of our sexualities bind together in erotic action. The scenes we'll saunter into and the people we'll meet will show us the importance of supportive communities to our sexualities, particularly for those of us with non-normative sexualities. And people who belong to such erotic communities don't just rely on their peers for support where their sex lives are concerned.

Life can be hard! People around the world live under varying degrees of governmental persecution and states of settler occupation. People face merciless forms of economic, social, and political injustice. Many of us have found ourselves standing at the nadir—financially broke, ill, sad, and brokenhearted. But as James Baldwin once famously said, "suffering is your bridge."[4] When we experience struggle, it connects us to others who are also struggling. Once in community and connected to others who understand our suffering, we share knowledge and hope, which is the source of light and joy. Hopefully, we have all communities to lean on for so many forms of support, from mutual aid to emotional care. So, erotic communities aren't just important for us perverts and deviants.

And, as critical as supportive erotic communities are for our well-being, I've already shown that they are never, ever utopias. Communities are often exclusionary, and members frequently engage in boundary policing for many reasons—sometimes for their own safety, and sometimes for outright bigoted reasons. Even as organizers, leaders, and members aim to create safer spaces, members are still sometimes harmed within them. There is no perfect community! Still, for most, when we find "our people," the benefits far outweigh the drawbacks.

Despite whatever limitations exist in any space, overall, people benefit from having supportive communities. We just have to find them, and when they don't exist, we must create them. When it comes to sexuality, we especially thrive when we have ones that provide rigorous, scientifically informed, and inclusive sex education and affirmational spaces that combat shame and create a context for joy and empowerment.

The specific terminology varies across the world, but generally, *BDSM* is an umbrella term that reflects a wide range of erotic desires, behaviors, identities, relationships, and communities related to *bondage* and *discipline*, *dominance* and *submission (D/s)*, and *sadism* and *masochism.*

BDSM involves consensual exchanges of power, but keep in mind that power shapes all erotic and sexual encounters. Most sexual relationships involve social scripts around who is the so-called top, or dominant partner, and who is the bottom, or submissive partner. These assumptions reflect positions of power. People who practice BDSM are just more intentional and imaginative than non-kinky folks about how they play with power in erotic encounters.

Like our sexualities, BDSM contains multitudes. It does not just reflect a set of practices performed in a dungeon by a black latex–wearing, spike leather–booted, whip-holding dominatrix with a menacing smile—as enticing as she sounds.[5] BDSM also reflects each component of our sexualities. *D/s* could refer to specific erotic role-playing desires, actual behaviors or practices, identities (e.g., people identifying as a Dom or a sub), or a specific relationship (e.g., a collared or committed relationship between a sub and Dom). It can also refer to a community of Doms and subs.

As part of my research to understand how the various identities of BDSM intertwine in the community, I visited many kinky spaces in different countries. On one such trip, I went to the Happy Kitten Portal at the Prive in New Orleans, in the United States. The Prive is a members-only lifestyle community. The space itself is gorgeous, with an inviting outdoor private courtyard space with a pool and hot tub—reminiscent of a high-class boutique resort. Inside are a bar, spaces for erotic play, and the BDSM portal, where I spent most of my time. I hung out with the owner one evening and booked a rope session, an erotic practice that combines aspects of bondage, dominance and submission, and masochism.

Before my rope top started tying any knots, we talked. We talked about this book. We discussed the members-only space, the sex parties they host, the features of the BDSM playroom space, the various BDSM and nonmonogamous communities in the area, and local strip clubs. Somewhere in between all this chatter about sex, we shared a few personal stories. This rapport building was important.

And before we even had these conversations, we had already discussed stylizing the space, since the session would be photographed. *Shibari*, or Japanese rope bondage, is a beautiful art form, blending technique and creativity, where knots are carefully designed, and the

Author, the Prive in New Orleans, Louisiana, photo by JonGunnar Gylfason.

bounded body is the canvas. I firmly believe co-curated fantasies are a form of artistic expression.

My rope top and I talked about my past experiences with BDSM, especially since I'd never been suspended before. We talked about my tolerance for pain and corporeal discomfort. He explained possible sensations, and we discussed how I would articulate when and if I was nearing my limits or felt unenjoyable pain. Finally, he confirmed that I had not been drinking or taking any drugs. With all of this necessary conversation out of the way, it was time to begin.

He laid out a copious pile of yellow, green, and red ropes on a set of black pads on top of the long puppy kennel on the far side of the room. He took his time, making creative choices about which colors to use and how to design them. With a yellow rope in his hand, he asked if I was ready. Once I had offered my eager affirmation, he began attending to my right thigh.

Rustle, crackle—he pulled the rope. At first, the friction of the fibers was all I heard. Then, a baritone voice. As he wrapped and knotted: "Are you okay?"

"Yes!"

"How are you doing?"

"Great!" Rustle—crackle.

"Too tight?"

"No, it feels like a hug."

Hoist—clank—clang. "Too much?"

"No, just right."

Given my sexual history and socialization, entrusting another person with my body isn't something I do capriciously. Allowing another human, especially a cisgender man, to have control over my body, tying me up—this is difficult. Relinquishing power to a Dom and trusting that they will care for my body feels vulnerable, but doing so with consent feels cathartic. It turns out that this kind of exchange also builds human connection. Engaging in what sociologist Staci Newmahr calls *edgework*, or risky behavior that transgresses social boundaries with another human, produces intimacy.[6]

During my flight, as each lithe limb was bound and hoisted, my unflappable captain checked in. I reiterated consent. In this scene, my relation to my own body was restored through my rearticulation of consent and this man's respect for my boundaries. I felt in control of my body and, thus, empowered. I know I am not alone in this experience.

Research has shown that BDSM practitioners who are survivors of sexual assault often find the practices healing, particularly so for bondage.[7] As Ariane Cruz notes in *The Color of Kink*, many people find pleasures and healing in kink. This is especially the case for Black women, given the global legacies of violence against us. Acknowledging the relationship between past trauma and present pleasure, however, opens up critiques of BDSM as psychopathology.[8] A political reluctance to explore how trauma is imbricated in our sexualities, especially non-normative sexualities, is understandable, but silence harms just the same. Silence can reinforce shame and hinder healing.

I understand the incredulous reactions I sometimes get when I tell someone that being bound feels like tasting freedom: "Free? You are quite literally shackled!" How can someone feel in control when they're in such a vulnerable and subservient position? Legitimate question. Yes, the *rigger*, or *rope top*, is seemingly in control, and I am the submissive as the *rope bottom*. Throughout the process, however, I continually reauthorized the rigger's dominance and control. I, too, derived much power and pleasure from this erotic exchange of consent.

The rope around my left thigh pinched and clawed at the butterflies inked on my skin. Still, no pressure, no diamonds! Once I was suspended, endorphins exploded like fireworks. My body felt euphoric and light—transported and suspended in a temporal plane.

As researcher and journalist Leigh Cowart explored in their book *Hurts So Good*, people across time and cultures deliberately choose "to feel bad, to feel better" and "to feel pain on purpose" to hack and enjoy the body's physiological responses to pain.[9] When I hike twelve miles up a mountain's brutal course and my quadriceps burn like hellfire, I also know the pleasures of an apex view, the grounded feeling when

I am connected to the Earth, and what the feeling of strength in my body does for my self-esteem.

I also loved the quieting of my mind when I focused on the sensations of the ropes. As Amber Jamilla Musser argues in *Sensational Flesh*, in masochism, "sensation resides at the border of reality and consciousness."[10] My garrulous inner narrator never stops, and my body can't keep still. I am part manta ray: If I stop moving, I'm not breathing. Or at least that's how it has sometimes felt to live in my skin. Still, in this ephemeral bound moment, I did not have to worry, knowing I was cared for and safe, which was freeing.

Each feeling of restricted skin was a pleasurable reminder of my safety. Being bound tightly, anchored to a pole, my chest immovable, ropes forcing me to hug myself—it felt like I was in a chrysalis. I was almost naked, but my body felt like womb warmth. Safety felt like home.

Once I told my rigger I'd reached my limits, he took me down. Then, we slowly unraveled my body. He asked me how I felt, and I responded truthfully. Wonderful, but tired. We ventured downstairs to the outdoor pool and hot tub, decompressing, drinking water, and talking as the bubble jets soothed and replenished my body. All of this formed part of our aftercare.

In BDSM, aftercare is a ritual of caring for a partner after a scene. But while the practice comes from the BDSM community, it can be helpful to everyone, even in so-called vanilla forms of eroticism. The more ways we find to communicate about our erotic needs and experiences with our partners, and the more we do to ensure our partners feel supported and seen, the better. How do you communicate consent, needs, pleasures, and displeasures with partners before, during, and after erotic play beyond the cliché "Was that good for you?" or "Did you cum?"

Now, people are bound to have different embodied experiences of kinky play. Our sexual socialization and our identity kaleidoscopes shape how each of us feels when we transgress boundaries through BDSM practices.[11] Still, research shows that many people, across demographics, share similar experiences.

First and foremost, the erotic interactions involved in BDSM play and the intentional rescripting of power provide much of the pleasure.[12] Researchers have documented positive mental health outcomes associated with participating in BDSM play, including decreasing levels of cortisol, often called our stress hormone. Some participants even characterize their experiences as transcendental, ecstatic, or spiritual.[13]

BDSM increases bodily awareness and strengthens people's relationships with their bodies, positively impacting various social experiences. The vulnerability and communication skills involved in BDSM play and relationships strengthen human intimacy and emotional literacy. BDSM involves learning specialized information and techniques that increase people's sexual education. All of these outcomes have a favorable impact on overall sexual health.

Even if people have no interest in exploring BDSM practices themselves, there is so much to be learned about sexuality from these erotic communities. Look, we don't have to choreograph every sexual encounter, but I suspect lots of folks' erotic and sex lives would benefit from more open communication about their desires and more intentional eroticism with their partners. Even if people have zero interest in joining any BDSM communities, from them we learn that there is much pleasure in playing with power, and, for example, flipping gendered and racialized sexual scripts in the bedroom. Consider role-playing, even of the cheesiest variety. I get it; this might even feel a little goofy, but roll with it—sex is supposed to be fun!

Despite the efforts of conservative pundits to depict queer and kinky eroticism, identities, and communities as recent sinful phenomena, they have a really long history. And over time, as politicians and religious leaders have pushed for the regulation and public condemnation of those who practice BDSM, people have formed communities to support one another and create spaces for pleasure. BDSM communities illuminate the essential role of cultures in shaping our sexuality, the necessity of having supportive communities, and the pleasures of finding new communities when the ones we were raised in and live in reject and shame us and force us into dark closets.

The Cully Flaug'd © The Trustees of the British Museum.

The artistic and historical record is rife with evidence of people spanking, binding, flogging, or engaging in any number of practices we have come to associate with BDSM for centuries.[14] For example, in the eighteenth and nineteenth centuries, flagellation brothels, where men hired sex workers to engage in whipping and spanking, flourished in London's famous Holywell Street, known for its sex and smut.

BDSM-specific identities, however, and a language to mark specific kinds of relationships and communities, have a relatively shorter history. And, of course, it once again begins with those sex-negative sexologists and the people who, in turn, said, "Fuck that noise!"

As the visibility of brothels and pornography increased in Europe, they drew the attention of the world's first sexologists. In the late nineteenth century, psychologists, the new sexologists, began publishing work naming and pathologizing such behaviors as bondage, spanking, and whipping. Now, take a moment to harken back to Chapter 1. Remember Richard von Krafft-Ebing? Well, in 1886, in his book *Psychopathia Sexualis*, he coined the terms *sadism* (after the Marquis de Sade) and *masochism* (after Leopold von Sacher-Masoch) as abnormal perversities.

In 1905, Sigmund Freud, too, discussed what he called *sadomasochism* in *Three Contributions to the Theory of Sex*. With these two works as their guide, early sexologists in the United States began producing a wave of psychological texts that named such behaviors as aberrant.

Fast-forward several decades to the publication of the first *Diagnostic and Statistical Manual of Mental Disorders (DSM)* in 1952, and it is no wonder that the American Psychiatric Association saw fit to add homosexuality and sexual sadism as "sexual deviations" to its list of 128 mental illnesses. Homosexuality was removed as a mental disorder in 1973, but other "sexual deviations" stayed put. In 1980, the third edition and revision to the *DSM* renamed them as "psychosexual dysfunctions."

It was not until the release of the fifth edition of the *DSM* in 2013 that the American Psychiatric Association changed the diagnostic codes on "psychosexual dysfunctions" and recognized consensual BDSM practices as simply "other sexual interests." This change resulted from campaigns and efforts by the National Coalition for Sexual Freedom (NCSF), an advocacy group founded in 1997, and its coalition work with the Eulenspiegel Society, the first BDSM organization founded in the United States. Sexologists had created enduring harmful language dressed up as science, and the sex rabble, as usual, resisted. This is an example of sexual liberation work.

While the sexologists were busy discursively creating systems of social control, exacerbating stigma, shame, and discrimination, BDSM subcultures focused on fetishism flourished. These communities started to become visible in England, France, and Germany in the 1890s, but presumably existed more quietly in other locations as well. It is no coincidence that we can trace the origins of the scientific ideas pathologizing kinky erotic behaviors to German sexologists. Today, Berlin remains home to a large, vocal, and visible BDSM subculture.

Those who couldn't get themselves to a nineteenth-century flagellation brothel had other options to get their freak on. Over time, a sex industry fed by global capitalism provided distribution channels for BDSM-related pornography and other sex education materials. Those with the funds to do so could purchase sex products, clothing, and equipment tailored to their interests. In Europe, in the early 1900s, the growth of this sex industry coincided with people establishing private spaces for BDSM play.

The growth of these erotic communities in Europe and the circulation of their cultural products across national borders meant that BDSM materials eventually found their way to the United States. The first self-identifying BDSM communities seem to have appeared in the United States sometime in the 1930s or 1940s.[15] However, there is still so much we do not know about past underground communities, especially among marginalized racial, gender, and class groups.

By the 1950s, a distinct gay BDSM culture, often simply referred to as "leather," emerged. There were growing numbers of gay men's motorcycle clubs, gay leather bars, and community spaces and events for leatherfolk in such major US cities as Chicago, Los Angeles, New York, and San Francisco.[16] Given the growing visibility of gay men's leather culture, it is also no wonder that these cultural shifts shaped what the psychologists added to the first edition of the *DSM* in 1952.

Today, the global reach of BDSM communities includes political organizations, social clubs, educational spaces, conferences, and conventions; cultural products such as magazines and other educational resources; online spaces and informal social gatherings called munches and sloshes; and museums, archives, and international events. Some of these, within queer leather communities, underscore their political nature, as seen in events like the Folsom Street Fair and the International Ms. and Mr. Leather contests, which donate portions of their proceeds to LGBTQ community organizations and charities.

Today, you can attend regular BDSM events on every continent except Antarctica. The Internet is full of forums for engagement and educational resources. As BDSM communities have become more visible, both online and off, researchers and media outlets have begun to check their urge to pathologize the practices associated with it.[17]

BDSM communities today are not monolithic. They vary across geographical and cultural contexts. Gender, nation, age, class, and race influence people's access to and experiences in these communities. A study in Sweden showed that the pervasive antipatriarchal and gender-egalitarian political discourse in that country profoundly shaped its BDSM cultural spaces.[18] Another study in Czechia examined how the post-Communist political backdrop drove intergenerational fissures among the people in its relatively new BDSM communities.[19]

In the book *Techniques of Pleasure*, the anthropologist Margot Weiss studied BDSM as a commodity-driven erotic community.[20] BDSM communities, and people's desires within them, have contributed to a flourishing global market for BDSM-related sex products. As costs go up, and members of BDSM communities feel increased social pressure to purchase endless equipment and to pay the exorbitant costs of club entrance fees, workshops, and sessions with pro-dommes, BDSM communities can prove difficult for the nonaffluent to access.

Race also shapes people's experiences in BDSM in communities, especially in nations with long histories of institutionalized racism. One study found that 45.8 percent of the people of color in their sample felt discriminated against at a BDSM event, and 63 percent had felt fetishized at an event.[21] Put another way, people of color were sixteen times more likely than white people to feel discriminated against at BDSM events, and seventeen times more likely than white people to feel fetishized. While only 2.5 percent of the people of color in the study reported experiencing overt racism, many reported regular microaggressions and feelings of isolation. They frequently felt dismissed, especially when raising issues related to racism.

Despite the differences in subcultural norms and the political factors shaping access to BDSM communities, research shows that participation in BDSM communities has numerous benefits. They provide spaces for people to enjoy themselves, socialize, make friends, find acceptance and belonging, explore their desires safely, and gain access to a wealth of education.[22]

For kinky people experiencing rampant discrimination and harassment, the sense of belonging to a BDSM community can act as a shield.[23] This discrimination can feel omnipresent, as even other so-called sexual minorities have excluded, harassed, and put them down in the name of respectability politics. Lesbian and gay communities, for instance, have often excluded leatherfolk and kinky people from their movements and community events.[24]

In the mid- to late 1980s, one notorious example involved a clash between three feminist groups in New York City. Feminists Fighting Pornography (FFP) and Women Against Pornography (WAP), both of which described themselves as radical feminist political groups, constantly targeted and harassed the Lesbian Sex Mafia (LSM), a feminist leather organization I'll have more to say about shortly. During NYC Gay Pride marches, originally called Christopher Street Liberation Day to commemorate the Stonewall Riots, members of FFP spat on and verbally harassed LSM members. On another occasion, two women from WAP piled trash outside the door of an LSM event space and lit it on fire!

Despite the threats of harm from outside groups and individuals, people participate in non-normative erotic communities because they benefit from the experience. At the personal level, engagement facilitates erotic empowerment and personal and spiritual growth. It has therapeutic benefits. Getting involved with a sexual community also fosters educational opportunities, mentoring, sharing of material resources, various forms of support, political and community action opportunities, and safety. These BDSM communities and spaces have been vital to supporting the erotic literacy, well-being, and pleasure of so many people throughout the world. Everyone can use supportive erotic communities!

FetLife is the Facebook of BDSM, which, in some ways, signals signs of social change and the normalization and assimilation of kinky lifestyles in many mainstream cultures—for better or worse. Headquartered in Vancouver, British Columbia, FetLife is a global platform that, at the time of this writing, boasts over a whopping eleven and a half million users. The social networking site for people who desire, practice, identify with, and seek BDSM relationships was created by John "Baku" Kopanas in 2008.

Baku created FetLife because he wanted to create a space that supported people's consensual, non-normative erotic desires. Growing up, his father was a hairdresser, and he spent a lot of time in the salon with his father's gay colleagues and friends. Back then, in the late 1980s, many of the gay men he grew up around were joyful, yet they frequently said that they wished they weren't gay—a response to the profound homophobia, especially during the early AIDS epidemic, that made it hard to live an authentic life and feel safe. These experiences influenced Baku's desire to see more people feel comfortable and supported in who they are.

Today, he gets so much joy when he receives emails from people telling him some version of "Hey, I thought I was all by myself in this world, and then I came onto FetLife and found out there's other people just like me, and now I know I'm not alone in this world anymore."[25]

Without its almost twelve million users, FetLife is just a website. As Dan "Apus Monoceros," a kinky coach and event organizer from Berlin, emphasized, spaces for interaction are not communities in and of themselves. In his words, "people make communities." Human engagement is the life force that powers them.

On FetLife, members curate individual profiles. As with other social media platforms, they then interact with other people's posts. Users can explore other people's profiles, join groups, engage in discussion, and share and find information on events worldwide.

FetLife has over one hundred and eighty thousand groups dedicated to specific desires, practices, and identities. Let's say, for example, that you are new to BDSM and interested in getting your feet wet. First, you can join the novice and newbie group, where you can find a wealth of information from diverse perspectives. Then, suppose you want more specific information on spanking. In a spanking-designated group, you can engage with other people, ask questions, read existing posts, and access educational resources, including information about offline workshops, community events, and play parties.

One user named Blake said, "Overall, it is such a fantastic place to express yourself. It has resources into different kinks and ways to learn more. You can join groups tailored to your specific kinks, and you can find events near where you live for education and practice. When I joined, it was because I wanted to learn more about the lifestyle. And it has taught me so much."

People made it very clear that FetLife is not a dating site. Especially for women, being on FetLife means constantly swatting off catfish, trolls, and men who love to send unsolicited dick pics—there are Jimmies everywhere!

Still, some people have successfully met play partners on FetLife, and others have started connections that turned into long-term relationships. At the same time, the people I spoke to overwhelmingly indicated that FetLife works best as an online community space for education and locating information about local, non-play meet-up events, such as munches at restaurants and sloshes at bars. They have more success meeting people for play at these events than on the website itself.

One FetLife member, Reily, noted: "I prefer using it to locate and sign up for local events, things like weekly kinky hiking, and monthly kinky karaoke. There are tons of educational events—the occasional play party—and I keep in touch with all the friends I've made."

Because our identity kaleidoscopes and regional contexts shape our access to offline communities, FetLife can be especially useful for people who feel isolated in their localities. Ingrid, a user from Norway, remarked, "FetLife has been nice for me. I live in a small town, and I'm trans. FetLife is an outlet and space I wouldn't otherwise have here." Another FetLife user, Alex, noted, "I am a disabled person, and I am in a small town, and having no car makes it impossible for me to get to events and munches. Online contact has been my only way to meet new people." Once again, we are reminded that having online spaces for community engagement is critical.

Like all communities made up of messy humans, FetLife is imperfect, and the site has often failed to intervene around important issues. Here is the CliffsNotes version: Users, not site employees, moderate the groups—so these spaces can get *really* unruly. Over the years, people have called out FetLife for its moderation practices, with some arguing that it has been way too passive in regulating gender-based harassment, racism, and other abusive behavior on the site, even though its policies explicitly condemn such behaviors. As we saw in various sex clubs, the people who organize community spaces are responsible for running them in ways that promote safety *and* empowerment.

FetLife has been the source of much controversy over its management of the online community space. As has been captured in the press, users have repeatedly called out the platform for failing to protect users from harm, and have accused FetLife of contributing to harm by protecting abusers.[26] FetLife used to have a callout page, which was a space where users anonymously reported abuse occurring both online and in person. However, in 2011, setting the cats among the pigeons, FetLife took down the page, simply stating that it was against its terms of use policies to make "criminal accusations against another member in a public forum."[27]

Its failures to protect members, especially women, are no surprise to many, who see the platform as an incredibly heteropatriarchal space. Pro-dommes have criticized FetLife for taking down their personal accounts with algorithms that scour the site for users with so-called commercial platforms. When dominatrices have reported these issues and harassment, especially from nonprofessional Doms who are men, the site has done nothing.[28]

People of color have complained for a long time about racism on the platform. Reaching a fever pitch after the rise of the Black Lives Matter movement, and especially after the 2020 George Floyd and Breonna Taylor protests worldwide, people reported a significant uptick in far-right white supremacist FetLife users posting racist comments and imagery—often under the guise of consensual race play. FetLife's failures to act have driven Black users and others off the platform.[29] While all of the above is inexcusable, FetLife's laissez-faire approach reflects broader cultural norms and practices in many BDSM spaces, especially straight ones, that intentionally leave regulation to community members.

In the BDSM community, boundary violations and abuses, whether on- or offline, are generally handled internally by community caretakers and people designated to enforce community rules.[30] Given that BDSM is a stigmatized form of eroticism, their communities typically refrain from involving outside parties, like law enforcement, in their disputes. Calling in the cops would likely compound harm for many reasons, especially in jurisdictions where various forms of play are illegal.[31] Community accountability systems can lead to abusers having their memberships revoked or being blacklisted.

Today, online spaces have become critical components of subcultural communities, especially for people with limited financial resources and mobility constraints. From FetLife to Fetish.com, The Cage to Kink Talk, and Reddit, there are so many places for kinky people to connect online. Apps like Discord, Telegram, Signal, and WhatsApp also help people stay in contact and organize meet-ups offline.

For so many, finding community spaces is about gaining access to belonging, dignity, and safety, essential for taking refuge and healing from the systems of power and people that harm and punish sexual rule breakers.

As popular and expansive as online spaces have become, for people with access, offline community spaces are where the magic happens. And what better place than Germany to explore sex-positive communities? As Dan, a kinky coach and event organizer from Berlin, said to me with animation, "Berlin is the number one hot spot for kink." I had a fantastic time speaking with so many people about kinky communities in Berlin, especially their histories and the importance they hold in people's lives today.

Jeff Mannes and I walked around the Berlin gayborhood of Schöneberg and sat in a café, where we got lost in conversation for hours. Jeff is a social scientist, writer, certified sex educator, and sex workers' rights advocate who does tours on kinky Berlin and the history of sexuality in Berlin.

Our walks took us by historical sites such as The Eldorado, which was home to infamous drag shows in the 1920s. We discussed the histories and decline of lesbian bars and other queer spaces that thrived before the Nazis took power and closed them. As Robert Beachy documents in *Gay Berlin*, in the nearly five decades before the Nazis, Berlin was a gay mecca.[32] It was indeed a haven for white gay and lesbian individuals. It was the site of the first gay journal, the first gay rights organization, the first Institute for Sexual Science, and the origin of groundbreaking gender-affirming health care.

My emotions oscillated, pendulum-like, over our coffee, tea, and light fare. We belly laughed about a local nudist who went viral after chasing a boar who stole his bag in Teufelssee Park in West Berlin in 2020, and my eyes welled as Jeff told me stories of Nazi persecution and the killing of LGBTQ people. We wandered through the history of sexuality in Germany, from Freikörperkultur, a free-body nudist cultural movement, to histories of sex work, to the life and legacy of

Magnus Hirschfeld, a sexual scientist, LGBTQ advocate, and founder of the Institute for Sexology—whom you may remember back from Chapter 1.

Jeff and I spent much time talking about Berlin's rich history of erotic resistance and its notoriety as a sex-positive global city. Berlin has a thriving sex-positive nightlife scene. People often stand in line for over two hours just hoping to get into places like the world-famous Berghain. I'd tell you more, but the number one rule of Berghain is, as with Vegas, what happens at Berghain stays at Berghain. The famed KitKatClub is known as a hedonistic playground. When there, I longed for more racial and ethnic diversity in the club, but the whiteness of so many renowned clubs around the world is nothing new. So, I got lost in the music, and I danced on a bar in the handmade rainbow harness I found on Etsy for hours, watching humans delight in erotic joy. Berlin's history and broader culture are critical to the kinky communities that thrive there today.

Berlin also has numerous studios where people can spend time with a professional dominatrix. Even in Berlin, it has become harder for these studios to survive amid gentrification, regulation, conservative political shifts, and the ongoing effects of the COVID-19 pandemic, which led to the closure of the beloved Studio Avalon in 2020.[33] I was interested in seeing these endangered spaces. Still, given my interest in community, I spent most of my time in the city exploring kinky spaces for education, socializing, and focusing on noncommercial erotic encounters.

Local BDSM scenes in global cities aim to welcome diverse crowds, in part because they recognize that people may have previously connected online in vastly different places. At the Friday International munch in Berlin, organizers asked local attendees to use English so that everyone felt included. The munch is a cornerstone of BDSM communities around the globe. In a study sample of FetLife users, 62 percent said attending a slosh or munch was important to their involvement in the lifestyle.[34]

The popularity of sloshes, munches, and other non-play gatherings in BDSM communities underscores a core lesson of this book: Sex and sexuality are not synonymous, and our sexualities have a distinct cultural life. At a weekly educational and social "rope jam," participants socialized and shared information about technique and safety. These events did include some play, typically rope tying and suspension, but never what people typically understand as sex. It was, nevertheless, profoundly erotic.

The kinky scene in Berlin highlights how messy it can be to define community. In Berlin, the various scenes overlap, making it difficult to draw hard lines between, say, the BDSM folks and the swingers. Insomnia, for example, is a nightclub that caters to swingers and other nonmonogamous people and also hosts many events for primarily straight BDSM communities. This is where the broader term "kinky" comes in handy as an umbrella big enough to cover the larger community of people with a wide range of non-normative sexualities. Even people whose specific desires and identities differ from one another often experience the benefits of erotic community together.

Insomnia touts this big-tent approach to sexual identity on its website, which describes it as "a temple for all non-conformist, free-spirited forms of life and love of any inclination: whether vanilla, swinger, genderfluid, queer, bizarre, fetish or BDSM." As Dominique, Insomnia's fabulous owner, said to me jokingly, "You know, the kinksters can show the swingers that there's a little bit more than just fucking, and the swingers bring the fucking back to the hardcore BDSMers who only hit and don't fuck anymore."

When I spoke to Dominique, she described how her vision for the club emerged from her years working and organizing in Berlin's kinky community. In the 1990s, she'd been working as a dominatrix in a studio co-owned with her mother in Berlin. As sex-positive cultural movements gained more visibility after the fall of the Berlin Wall, Dominique began doing more kinky educational workshops. At the same time, Berlin's techno music and club scene exploded. When Simon Thaur and Kirsten Krüger opened KitKatClub in 1994, they brought techno and sex together.

After ten years of organizing parties at KitKat and within the local kinky scene, Dominique wanted to open a venue unlike anything in

Berlin at the time. She opened Insomnia in 2006. She explained, "It is common and totally normal that men have a sexual infrastructure, and in this infrastructure, mostly, women have a serving position. So, Insomnia is made to have a sexual infrastructure for couples and women."

Cisgender men have entire erotic industries built around their presumed desires. Under heteropatriarchy, women are givers of pleasure, and men are receivers. When we think about consumers of sex, most will envision cisgender men—from porn to bathhouses to brothels. Does this mean women, or anyone else on the gender spectrum, do not desire access to various erotic and sex industries and commerce? It damn sure doesn't. What this means is that heteropatriarchy and other systems, such as racial capitalism, build sexual commerce and, as Dominique said, "an infrastructure" around men's desires. So, in turn, just as we saw back at Oasis and as we'll observe at Karada House shortly, all of us excluded from cisgender men–focused industries must build our own spaces. For anyone who is not a cisgender man and has felt a desire to explore sex industries, but hasn't because they are built for men, I've got more excellent news. Thanks to the sex rabble, things are changing!

Dominique's comments reinforced what should by now be a familiar point about how erotic communities and spaces work: Erotic communities are vital to our sexual well-being because they provide nonjudgmental spaces for exploration and learning. She went on to describe Insomnia as a space for human sexual growth. "It's like a private sex laboratory that you find all the ingredients you need to grow, and it's not just a place where you party," she said. Dominique explained that the club provides a safer and clean space for sexual exploration, regularly hosting workshops, seminars, and tutorials for community members.

I had a blast at Insomnia! I attended both a traditional swingers night and a kink party with a kick-ass DJ, a dungeon with BDSM equipment, and performances, including burlesque and an interactive BDSM rope show. While I couldn't be certain of the genders and sexualities of the people at Insomnia, the swingers night was notably straight and cisgender-centered—although some might very well identify as bisexual or queer. The kinky night felt less so. While I saw a bit of presumably same-gender play, it was primarily people whom I assumed were women and men engaged in erotic play.

Dan, a kinky coach and event organizer, who in the local scene goes by Dan Apus Monoceros, helped explain these gendered dynamics, explaining that factors such as people's gender and sexual identities shape how the wider community self-organizes in Berlin, even amid the broader kink scene. And because sexuality has a cultural life, each space has its own specific norms regarding everything from dress to language to accountability systems. While a head-to-toe black rubber suit might win points in the fetish community, it might not be the best thing to wear at a rope jam.

In Berlin, for example, you can attend events that are specifically designed for LGBTQ+ people that exclude cisgender men for safety. In Germany, this grouping is typically referred to as "FLINTA," for female, lesbian, intersex, nonbinary, trans, and agender. Other events, like the exclusive and men-only Snax party at Lab.oratory and those hosted by Quälgeist or Böse Buben, cater to gay and queer men. Queer spaces like Karada House are intentionally designed for LGBTQ+ people, who are often marginalized from kinky spaces dominated by straight and cisgender people.

Karada House is a nonprofit queer community art space that centers marginalized people. It takes seriously how people's identity kaleidoscopes inform who feels safe and comfortable exploring their desires and sexualities. The space hosts a wide range of events, from social gatherings like Crafty Queers Hangouts and Dungeons and Dragons nights, to rope jams and play parties. Karada House also hosts erotic workshops and other sexual educational events.

I attended an event at Karada House and also spoke with Ceci, a member of the queer collective that runs this extraordinary venue. Ceci is a queer nonbinary sexologist. They have been teaching bondage and BDSM for over ten years, with a special interest in *shibari*. At Karada House, Ceci does sex and couples therapy, facilitates workshops, and supports the team's strategic and day-to-day administrative work.

It was interesting to me that Ceci described Karada House not as "a sex-positive space," but as "a sex-possible space." With so many venues focused on sex and play, Karada House's focus on eroticism and respecting people's boundaries felt special.

Ceci and I also talked about the critical issue of making space for people who feel "not queer enough." Karada House is a space where baby queers, people who may just be beginning to figure things out, are just as welcome as the person who has been out as queer and/or kinky for decades. "It's welcoming to people who have a hard time even accessing other spaces," Ceci said. I observed this from the minute I arrived at the organization's new venue, from the wheelchair ramp to the dedicated quiet space upstairs for people needing a sensory break from the action.

As Ceci explained, Karada House uses the ritual of the opening circle to introduce folks to the community. The organizers emphasized the importance of arriving on time so that people would not miss the orientation. When I was there, we all introduced ourselves, including our pronouns, and we shared what forms of play we might be interested in pursuing. Critically, the host emphasized that this was a safer space for LGBTQ people and provided a detailed overview of the venue's consent and abuse policies.

Ceci explained, "It's important to know that everybody has heard the same code of conduct, to know that everybody knows how this space is operating. I think that creates a lot of feelings of safety, and that's also something I hear from people who come here for the first time. Some of them get very touched by it and feel like, 'Wow, okay, that makes a huge difference for me.'"

Ceci described my experience to a tee. I felt safer and comfortable, creating the conditions for deeply consensual, intimate, and pleasurable play. Brandon Robinson writes, "Comfort is central to how people experience and navigate dating, sex, hooking up, desire, pleasure, joy, and euphoria. One might even say comfort is foundational to the types of pleasure and joy that do not hurt, harm, and oppress. . . . [It] is a mode of relation that is crucial for care, communication, consent, and community."[35] Karada House's prioritizing of this type of politicized comfort was a profoundly unique experience, and I feel privileged to have been there and shared space with the humans attending that evening. For me, they intentionally designed a space that not only recognized the importance of people's kaleidoscope of identities and potential needs, but centered a trauma-informed approach to sexuality.

In our conversation, Ceci repeatedly emphasized how intentional Karada House is about its politics. For example, they told me about some of Karada House's classes that specifically focus on tying up fat people. Ceci explained, "Every time I teach it, people get angry, and they realize that they should expect more of other teachers and of other spaces, and it should be included, that knowledge shouldn't be something you just figure out on your own."

Institutionalized fatphobia, just like ableism, white supremacy, capitalism, heteronormativity, cisgenderism, and heteropatriarchy, are all dehumanizing and traumatizing to those who are marginalized by those respective systems. So, having organizers who understand how trauma affects our sexuality is critical, which is especially important in spaces that cater to queer folks, people of color, disabled folks, and members of other marginalized groups. Still, sometimes I think about what it would be like if every space were committed to a trauma-informed approach to community rules and design. Shit, I wish that trauma-informed sex education were available to everyone!

Building a community space rooted in an ethos of care and sexual justice requires intentionality and a commitment to collaboration. Ceci and I discussed how Karada House's community guidelines, abuse policies, and the content and types of events and workshops are all developed in response to ongoing communication with and input from those who come there. Organizations like Karada House exemplify the forms of care that go into designing and maintaining erotic communities and the effort it takes to create spaces that are affirming, supportive, and facilitate erotic joy and pleasure.

Having a clear understanding of what is and isn't acceptable community behavior is essential to make people feel safer. There isn't necessarily consensus on what those rules might be; the point is that participants should be aware of the rules, whatever they are. Organizers have vastly different approaches to what people refer to as their *awareness culture*. For example, some people and organizers, including Karada House, prohibit alcohol and substance use. In contrast, others might provide suggestions for watching intake. Other spaces take a more laissez-faire attitude, deferring entirely to individuals to decide what is best for them.

Organizers also set rules for what erotic acts are allowed at parties. For instance, scenes involving race play, especially slave markets, or any blood play or consensual nonconsent (e.g., rape play) may be offensive or triggering to community members. Accordingly, such behaviors are generally reserved for private spaces. In some cases, when such practices happen publicly, organizers may provide trigger warnings and make sure that attendees know what to expect.

All the parties and events I attended had clear policies emphasizing the importance of consent. At Insomnia, an enormous illuminated sign hanging above the dance floor reads: Consent is Sexy. Still, how a specific part of the community creates consent rules and holds people accountable for violations varies based on their approach to awareness.

To further ensure safety and reduce harm, community organizers often rely on blacklists. Their practices for how and if they use blacklists depends on their awareness approach to safety and accountability. Many organizers will not let someone known to be an abuser or an exploiter into their spaces. Others might maintain more skepticism about information gained through whisper networks, merely putting people on notice (and watching them closely). No matter what approach organizers or any community leaders take, this discussion is a reminder that communities can aim to promote safety and harm reduction and to craft spaces for empowering eroticism. Still, this intention doesn't inherently make those spaces free from bigotry, exclusion, or any form of violence.

As Dan Apus Monoceros reminded me in our conversation, a club is "just a room." He emphasized, "The people who go there regularly are the community." People's eroticism and the cultures, norms, and choices they make are what give erotic communities a social life. When erotic communities are structured in thoughtful ways that promote harm reduction, center pleasure, and prioritize bodily autonomy, they can be integral to our sexual well-being.

Please allow me to introduce the Lesbian Sex Mafia, our final example of a BDSM community. To learn more about the feminist leather organization, I spent much time in the archives.

Archives are erotic. When you sit in the archives, you are sitting in silence with the ghosts of ancestors who have entrusted you with their secrets. There is an intimacy in engaging with old documents. I am reminded of this each time I touch them—care and tenderness are required when we handle their delicate bodies of knowledge. The history I present here is distilled from my time connecting *with* the archives.

The Lesbian Sex Mafia (LSM) was founded in 1981 by Dorothy Allison and Jo Arnone. It is the oldest continuously running women's BDSM support and education group in the United States.[36] Their current statement of purpose reads: "The Lesbian Sex Mafia is a social and educational organization for women who have a positive personal interest in BDSM with other women. Our tenets are safety, consensuality, confidentiality, and the right of women to explore their sexuality as they choose."

LSM is currently gender inclusive; like FLINTA communities in Germany, the organization only excludes cisgender men from its membership. However, this has not always been the case. The archive reveals vitriolic debates over trans exclusionary and transmisogynistic policies. For example, the 1984 bylaws indicate that trans women had to undergo special membership evaluation by the orientation committee on a case-by-case basis: "Failure to disclose transsexualism constitutes misrepresentation, which is grounds for refusing or revoking membership."[37] For some time, LSM also did not allow transfeminine people with penises to expose them at play parties.

Carrie D. Efrain J. Gonzalez Photography Collection, Lesbian Sex Mafia photograph, New York City LGBT Pride March 1996, Leather Archives and Museum.

LSM emerged alongside its West Coast contemporary, SAMOIS, which was the first lesbian BDSM leather organization in the United States. Unlike LSM, SAMOIS folded in 1983, but the two organizations led the way for emerging lesbian sadomasochist leather communities. Before LSM and SAMOIS, all the leather and kinky bars and community spaces were for gay men. Jo Arnone has talked about how she had to go to leather spaces, pass as a man, and engage in eroticism with men in the absence of lesbian spaces. In an interview, she noted how fantastic and affirming it was once lesbians finally created their own community spaces for exploring BDSM.[38]

LSM gave people a place to address their internalized shame surrounding their kinky desires, a consequence of having been socialized in heteropatriarchal spaces and living in nonsupportive communities. Feminist scholar Sarah Heying noted about LSM that "S/M offered pathways for lesbians to connect with their sexuality under patriarchy."[39] Dorothy Allison explained: "If you have not created your own sense of legitimacy and you're out of your own community, you are vulnerable to their redefinition. That's hegemony. You've got to fight it. That's what we were doing in the Lesbian Sex Mafia that I still think is important and powerful and saved people's lives."[40]

A primary function of LSM, then, is to provide a space for affirmation and achieving self-love. A 1982 letter to prospective members explained, "To be queer in this society is to be constantly subjected to a barrage of hatred and emotional battering—particularly if you are a queer queer. One of our primary functions therefore is to give each other support—to help each other to a positive self-image." Too often, mainstream self-help and self-care talk neglect the social life of sexuality. In contrast, erotic communities start by acknowledging that our ability to feel good about ourselves is maximized when we have support from others.

The informational letter to prospective members went on to emphasize the vital education that erotic communities and formal organizations like LSM can provide for their members. "But equally important is the goal of community education. We want to make it possible for lesbian sadomasochists, fetish queens, and women who find themselves anywhere within the range of practices now labeled 'politically incorrect' to live openly and comfortably with their own sexuality."[41]

As an educational group, much of LSM's work has focused on helping folks learn safer ways to explore erotic exchanges of power in S/M. In the 1980s, new members had to attend orientation and safety workshops. The Winter/Spring newsletter of 1984 discussed this policy, noting, "We have always prided ourselves on the fact that LSM women are the most safety-conscious and best-informed members of the women's S/M world."[42]

In the years since, LSM has continued to do a lot of kink education and has hosted many workshops at local community spaces, such as the NYC LGBT Center. Allison noted, "The whole premise of the Lesbian Sex Mafia [was] what if we really just tried to make it a little safer and saner? Some of it was just about getting information. 'How Not to Get Killed' was one of our early workshops."[43]

In addition to promoting the safety of individuals and people engaged in erotic play, LSM has also been committed to the collective safety of the group. The 1984 bylaws stated that LSM would revoke the membership of anyone violating community rules regarding safety, consensuality, confidentiality, legitimate interest (women who have no personal interest but are attending for journalism or research), illegal activities, or age of consent.

LSM also helped create and promote community spaces for erotic play and pleasure. A 1987 member survey indicated that the activities that members most wanted to see from the organization were play parties, spaces for "fantasy enactment," educational forums, and other day, overnight, and weekend social events.[44] Many noted that meetings, while necessary, were boring; they craved more social activities. One member wrote to LSM leaders to say that meetings left her

Flyer, LSM event at Paddles, available in Box 34, Dorothy Allison Papers, David M. Rubenstein Rare Book & Manuscript Library, Duke University.

feeling isolated; the organization was cliquish and not geared toward socializing. What new members needed most, the letter writer said, was "something almost everyone in LSM already has—somebody to talk to."[45]

Dorothy Allison recalled that when LSM first organized parties in New York's Meatpacking District, they ran a weekly party at a gay men's leather bar. In her words, they put a "feminist spin" on the traditional play party. But because most bars restricted sex and play, many of LSM's play parties were held in private homes. One flyer for a party explicitly noted that a private party at Dorothy Allison's Brooklyn apartment was to "provide an alternative to the bars and clubs where the boys outnumber the women so outrageously."[46]

Even later, when LSM no longer facilitated its own parties, the organization provided information about play parties and other spaces for connection. One such event was the long-running Submit party for women and trans and nonbinary people. Submit was founded in 1998 by Red Robinson, a kink personality, BDSM consultant, community leader, and former coordinator for the International Ms. Leather conference. Submit remains a staple of the queer leather community in New York today.

Finally, like all communities, LSM has been part of a much broader network of BDSM and other leather groups, cohosting events like Leather Pride Night with organizations like the Eulenspiegel Society and the Gay Male S/M Activists (GMSMA), among others.[47] These Pride events foster affirmation, help people understand the political origins of shame, and make it feel safer to be unapologetically authentic.

Our sexualities are communal. This doesn't mean our bodies are buffets—we don't have to share our bodies with anyone. It just means that our communities shape how we understand and show up in our desires, behaviors, identities, and relationships. Ideally, the people around us should help us access scientifically accurate, inclusive, and sex-positive information about our bodies and desires and affirm and support our consensual, sexuality-related choices. Critically, our communities should help us feel safer.

I believe that so many of us are born into or inhabit communities that don't adequately support us. And I get it; we can feel beholden and deeply connected to these communities, even when, in some ways, they harm us. Yet, when we do not get the care, love, and understanding we need and are instead met with shame and judgment, we must seek alternatives. We must find erotic communities that sustain us. People can and do design caring communities built around respect for bodily autonomy, consent, and justice. The world could use so much more of this erotic resistance.

Having our sexualities supported by the people around us is essential. As humans, we desire belonging and crave dignity in a world that, especially for marginalized people, seems committed to taking it away. People can find safety in communities. Still, no matter how safe our community spaces feel, we must feel safe in our own bodies. The pleasures and agency of erotic empowerment live in this synergistic space. When people find it, they are in a position to challenge harmful, misguided, and oppressive measures regulating erotic life—to realize sexual liberation.

CONCLUSION

Sexual literacy is a human right! And yet so many nations have systematically kept their people sexually illiterate by insisting that sexuality is a private matter. I'd argue that for the nation-state, people who lack bodily autonomy and who are deprived of the profound pleasures of self-knowledge and erotic empowerment are easier to control and keep fettered to their work—our bodies only used in ways deemed productive and appropriate to those with institutionalized power. If you've read this far in this book, you know how wrong that is. These final pages are about what we should do with that knowledge.

The battle to liberate ourselves and each other can only be won with the right weapons. And to transform ourselves and the systems that constrain us, I believe we need a range of sexual literacy tools. This encompasses the knowledge and skills that promote our sexual well-being and enhance our capacity to make well-informed, ethical, deeply consensual decisions, promoting our own and our partners' care, pleasure, and experiences of erotic empowerment.

Like the ones offered in these pages, sexual literacy tools can help us take control of our bodies and gain a deeper understanding of ourselves and how the world around us seeks to control our bodies and sexualities. This knowledge is the foundation and a prerequisite for moving toward sexual liberation and building a world that strengthens, cares, nurtures, empowers, and pleasures us. Full sexual literacy is in the best interest of public health and, frankly, in the pursuit of a world that is happier and more caring, joyful, humane, equitable, and just.

Sexual literacy *starts* with us! We must decode our own individual experience of sexuality's five core dimensions. To understand our sexuality fully, we need to think like a cartographer, tracing the social roads on which ours developed. We need to identify precisely what our desires are now, how they have changed over time, and how they feel in our bodies. If we do not experience sexual desire, or we do not experience it anymore, we can identify other forms of intimacy that we find pleasurable.

Now that we have a map, or at least a set of coordinates, that locates us on the spectrum of desire, we can go further to discern how society has influenced or overwritten our desires. This can help us interrogate the ways we communicate or express our desires to partners—or not—and why. To communicate our needs to our partners, we must know what conditions and forms of care we require to feel empowered in sex—however we define sex. We must dig deep through the hot mantle to the inner core to determine how our identities and the social positions they reflect shape our erotic lives. Armed with these insights, we can draw closer to the feeling of empowerment that eroticism can fuel if we are attentive to the interplay between our bodies, the systems that shape us, and the desires and needs of others.

The tools in this book have innumerable applications to relationships. We can choose the correct-fitting container for our sexuality. We must take back control of our relationships, designing and programming them in ways that serve our erotic needs, rather than defaulting to the culture's factory settings. We need to use *our* erotic imaginations here—let's get creative and design them in ways that are rooted in care and equity, and that respect people's needs for both connection and autonomy.[1]

To know our sexuality fully and cultivate self-knowledge that improves our sexual literacy, we need to first identify the role of sexual cultures in our socialization. And if the sexual cultures and communities around you have not made you feel safe, seen, welcomed, and empowered to let your freak flag fly, it is time for some new ones. Everyone deserves access to sexual cultures and communities that respect bodily autonomy, that provide affirmation and support, and that are rooted in commitments to justice and an ethos of care.

Now, I've said it over and over again: Sex isn't solitary! Any understanding of sexuality as purely individual completely misunderstands the assignment. And yet, the paradox we all live with is being an individual in a collective system. Therefore, even if we have a better understanding of our erotic selves internally, there is still much work to be done externally.

Sexual literacy tools should be available to everyone. But they are not. Sure, some people, depending on where they live in the world, have received rudimentary free sex education in schools. Typically, this includes surface-level information about genitals, heterosexual reproductive mechanics, and disease, but not a robust understanding of human sexuality. It generally won't include the expansive definition of sexuality and inclusive, non-normative eroticism we've explored together or detailed scientific information about our bodies—in all their glorious diversity. Most nations are not Denmark. There, since 1970, sex education has been mandatory for students six to fifteen years old; the curriculum is imperfect, but well-funded, comprehensive, inclusive, science-based, and pleasure-centered. I want this *and* more for everyone!

I believe sexual literacy is as fundamental as any other basic form of literacy and should be taught in all schools. However, increasingly, in the absence of rigorous school-based sex education, the sex rabble are showing out, educating people on social media and across the Internet and in documentaries, books, and IRL workshops for those with access. At the same time, the rise of sexperts and public-driven sex education has followed neoliberal logics, and sexual literacy has too often become just another commodity for sale. That means that one of our goals must be to undermine society's tendency to treat sexuality like a private and personal matter.

Sex is social, sexual literacy is a fundamental human right, and real sexual education has incredible power to destabilize, to heal, to empower, and to promote sexual justice.

So, what can we do to make it happen?

In this book, I have been dedicated to demystifying sexuality's social reality and undermining the systems of power that constrain sexuality on a personal level and repress sexual expression on a social level. But the sex education contained within this book's pages is just the beginning. I want *all* sex education always to be accessible, science-based, pleasure-centered, focused on harm reduction—not prohibition—and inclusive of the diversity of human life, encompassing all spectrums of gender, sexuality, abilities, race, ethnicity, ages, and body types.

What is more, I also want sex education to be trauma-informed, recognizing the implications of systemic trauma caused by political systems on our bodies and sexualities. People living with trauma, especially sexual trauma, who want sexual relationships do not necessarily have to forgo them. However, the somatic experience of simultaneously desiring sex in a triggered body is complicated and requires specific tools to process. This is vital work, from which I have personally benefited, and I believe every survivor who wants it should have free access to it. Still, I want sexual trauma literacy for everyone.

However, because psychologists, among so many others, see sex as private and not social, they downplay the role that others play in our healing from trauma. Sure, as I've heard therapists tell me and others, our trauma and feelings are our individual responsibility. Still, I firmly believe that downplaying the role that systems play in causing harm, as well as the role our partners and communities play in healing, does everyone a great disservice. I long for a world that understands and appreciates the erotic power of collective healing.[2]

I believe *sexual trauma literacy*, a term I use to refer to the skills to understand and recognize how trauma affects and manifests in all the dimensions of human sexuality, can help us to know ourselves better. But if we take the public nature of sex seriously, we can recognize how sexual trauma literacy can help everyone. These tools can help people become more aware, caring, and supportive, both as partners and community members. They can help us deepen our risk-aware consent practices and design and build erotic communities committed to making our spaces safer for everyone to enjoy the embodied pleasures of erotic empowerment.

Being able to recognize potential dissociation, appeasement, or a fight, flight, or freeze response is useful, especially in navigating consent and sexual encounters. While we can never know for sure what is happening for our partners somatically, sexual trauma literacy can help us tap into potential cues. For example, if a partner looks checked out, or I notice their jaw is clenched and their body is visibly tense, I will check in: "Are you okay?" or "You wanna hit pause for a second? We can stop." Or maybe even a declarative "Let's stop." Sometimes, I wonder how often one person's dissociation or freeze response, for example, is misrecognized as passive consent. And this, by the way, is how we get to calls for enthusiastic consent, which, while I appreciate the impulse, is problematic and unrealistic.

Crucially, having a deep understanding of the scars that systematic trauma leaves on people and how it shows up in our erotic lives can help us approach and treat others with more empathy and care. This work advances and deepens our *emotional literacy skills*, or our ability to understand our own emotions deeply and respond effectively and compassionately to the feelings of others. Sexual trauma literacy skills bring the entire body into conversation with our emotional literacy skills. Combined, these two skills lend themselves to the intentional care work that I believe is critical for how we show up for ourselves, our partners, and our communities.

At the same time, we also need to fight for better *consent literacy*. We need a politics of consent that is rooted in the somatic, of which verbal communication is only one part and for which sexual trauma literacy skills are invaluable. We need to be able to equip people everywhere with the skills necessary to understand how risk and power shape all erotic encounters, how to interpret somatic communications (verbal *and* nonverbal cues), and how to determine and supply essential information about desired eroticism and boundaries needed to consent, as well as how to give and receive permission to any activity in any context.

We also need to dispense with well-meaning consent campaigns that have oversimplified the concept of consent. One-size-fits-all models of consent are as helpful as a chocolate teapot. Speaking of, consent is not as fucking simple as tea, and as "no means no," or "yes means yes." Every person has different risk thresholds, different identity kaleidoscopes and relationships to power, different motivations for arriving at an encounter, different levels of desire, and different relationships to systemic trauma. And all of these factors shape the ongoing process of giving and receiving consent.

In a world where the Internet pipes never-ending images of sex, trauma, and horror to us whenever we glance at our phones, tablets, and gadgets, we also need to equip people, especially young people, with a set of *sexual media literacy* tools to understand the images that saturate their lives. Case in point: pornography.

I am vehemently opposed to the censorship of any consensually made pornography. Porn work is a form of labor that provides a decent income to millions. For many more, porn offers a healthy source of entertainment and pleasure. A lot of the queer porn I consume is also quite educational—I've picked up an interesting trick or two. Even in straight genres, there is porn dedicated to showing men how to be more generous and attentive lovers to women.

But not all porn is created equal. Porn is still a capitalist commodity and, as such, often replicates sexist, transmisogynistic, and racist tropes for profit. I share some people's concerns about the online saturation of porn sites, many of which are free and sometimes feature unrealistic depictions of sex that center on men's pleasure, degrade and dehumanize women's bodies, and replicate toxic tropes of transfeminine people and men of color as predators. I do worry about how these forms of porn socialize young people in real life as they reach sexual maturity.

But let's be real, what we don't need is prohibition driven by hysterical *porn panics*.[3] People have some nerve, spewing vitriol and hurling moralistic condemnations at the consumers of porn, especially young people, while refusing to support or provide comprehensive, inclusive, and medically accurate sex education. Instead of prohibiting porn, we need comprehensive porn literacy programs so people of all ages have critical tools for understanding fantasy, power, and pleasure.[4]

Few of us were raised with the critical tools of intersectional feminism and sociology that give us frameworks for analyzing the media we consume. It's why I believe conservative politicians in places like the United States are so hell-bent on taking away access to these ideas in universities. These tools wake us up, give us new lenses from which to understand power, and invite us to leave the sheep pen and join the resistance. All that remains is to make them accessible to everyone.

Increased sexual literacy in all its myriad forms can be an antidote to the erotic ills so many people face, but to make erotic empowerment a reality, we need sexual liberation. Erotic empowerment, while often involving the respect and care of others, is a personal journey. Community-level projects are the incubators and playgrounds for what is possible on a grander scale, the spaces in which we experiment, fail, and, hopefully, meet ourselves and our chosen kin with care and compassion when we do. Sexual liberation is the endgame—the collective political project aimed at dismantling the unjust systems that control and regulate our bodies and sexualities, causing harm, shame, and trauma.

I worry that the emphasis on pleasure-centered sex education and individual erotic empowerment, as crucial as they are, sometimes misses the entire point of this book—our sexualities do not exist outside of systems of power, and are inherently political. If we only focus on pleasure and personal empowerment, the resulting pockets of pleasure will be perennial and will not open to everyone until we achieve sexual liberation. As feminist Breanne Fahs argues, sexual liberation and justice are predicated not just on a *freedom to* do what we please erotically, but also on the *freedom from* oppressive structures.[5]

Erotic empowerment and sexual liberation are co-constitutive projects. Just look at the way we relate to our bodies. If we want more erotic pleasure and empowerment, redefining our relationships to our bodies is essential. In *The Body Is Not an Apology*, Sonya Renee Taylor explains, "Radical self-love is indeed our inherent natural state, but social, political, and economic systems of oppression have distanced us from that knowing."[6]

Learning to feel comfortable, safe, and at home in our bodies is key—learning to love them is paramount. It's great when we find partners or community spaces that make us feel this way. But cultures must destroy the capitalist-driven industries that make us hate ourselves, and we need to refuse and boycott media that only depict beauty and hotness as young, thin, able-bodied, super fit people with white features. And, of course, the sex rabble are indeed already doing this work. FYI, it's why I love feminist and queer porn.[7] We must continue to build alternatives to shame-producing cultural industries.

Sexual liberation is inherently intersectional work devoted to "freedom from" oppressive structures—from heteropatriarchy, white supremacy, cisgenderism, ableism, capitalism, and fatphobia. For example, addressing sexual violence is not simply about catching rapists *or* dismantling heteropatriarchy. Angela Davis astutely made the need for an intersectional politics of sexual freedom plain in her classic essay "Rape, Racism, and the Myth of the Black Rapist," which interrogated the historical political weaponization of rape, often involving the criminal legal system and all its arms to maintain social control, subjugate Black women, and lynch Black men.[8]

Sexual violence is a tool of heteropatriarchal dominance, but it is also a tool of empire and the state, and all its apparatuses often play roles in its ongoing existence. In *Violent Differences*, Doug Meyer's groundbreaking book about sexual assault among queer men, he foregrounded the experiences of Black men who have survived sexual violence.[9] What this often-ignored vantage point showed was how deeply entangled white supremacy is with heteronormativity and how the law enforcement systems are too often of little help and frequently contribute to and exacerbate the harm that survivors across the gender and sexual spectrum face.

Sex workers and queer, trans, nonbinary, disabled, and undocumented people have been at the forefront of antiviolence movements and have long advocated for intersectional politics of sexual freedom—especially freedom from sexual violence. They have challenged the whitewashed, cis women–centered focus of anti-sexual violence movements and campaigns, forcing us to contend with the overlapping systems of power that erase the violence and systemic trauma they face in schools, families, detention centers, the criminal legal system, and beyond. The voices that powerfully animated the pages of the remarkable anthology *Queering Sexual Violence* showcased that marginalized people fight for sexual freedoms every single day, even as mainstream cultures, institutions, and systems of power ignore them, harm them, persecute them, and try to suffocate their joy.[10] And even still, they resist and generate erotic power that changes the world.

Sexual liberation is rooted in economic and social justice. Sexual liberation is inextricably linked to disability justice, trans liberation, sex workers' rights, immigrant rights, and racial, gender, and economic justice. Once we achieve "freedom from," it opens up flourishing opportunities for "freedom to" outside of the margins of societies. When we understand that sexuality is a public, not a private, matter, we recognize that true erotic empowerment for all hinges upon liberation work. Sexual liberation work involves chipping away at and eliminating oppression and exploitation, allowing people to experience greater empowerment, joy, pleasure, camaraderie, and freedom.

As I pen this conclusion, right-wing conservative authoritarian regimes are gaining frightening levels of power all around the world. With all the usual trappings of fascism, we are witnessing global attacks on science, higher education, feminism, and marginalized people, as well as the political weaponization of fear and resentment. This has profound implications for our sexualities and sexual liberation.

One of the first agenda items for these politicians and their ilk is to gain further control over our bodies and erotic lives—precisely because they are fundamental, yet often taken-for-granted, components of human freedom. With the world literally and figuratively on fire all around us, it's all the more urgent that I spend the very last pages of this book driving home the connections between our sexualities and the governance systems around us.

Erotic power is a commanding social force. Our expansive sexualities—our desires, behaviors, identities, relationships, and communities—affect law, medicine, economies, families, media, and so much more. No institution is untouched by human eroticism. Prohibitions will never stop eroticism from shaping our social, political, and economic lives—no matter how much politicians try!

Fear is one of the greatest threats to sexual liberation and justice. When it comes to regulating the erotic, too often, nations and cultures build policies around exceptions, fear, emotions, and people's religious sensibilities. When it comes to regulating sex, too often, politicians are reactionary and take their cues from everyone but stakeholders—the very people impacted by legislating sex.

Instead of a well-measured, empirically informed policy rooted in harm reduction, protection of bodily autonomy, and justice, we will inevitably see even more politically weaponized moral and sex panics, which in turn will lead to ineffective and harmful prohibition and carceral policies.[11] Such laws and regulations further ossify existing systems of power, exacerbating sexual injustice and its harms, especially for the world's most marginalized.

Moral panics around sex reflect what Gilbert Herdt calls *cultural anger*. Having tapped into existing social, economic, and political anxieties and frustrations, politicians offer the public a monstrous scapegoat. But folks, don't be afraid to pull back the curtain on their theatrics. I promise you, there are no monsters under the bed—just red herrings.

Governments are paternalistic entities. One of their favorite excuses for exercising control over sexualities is the protection of children's welfare. As Lee Edelman argues, *the figure of the child* is a pervasive trope in moral panics.[12] Reactionary politicians invoke the innocence of children, children who are, as José Esteban Muñoz reminds us, "indeed always already white" to demand punishment or exile for the supposedly antisocial, pleasure-seeking queers who refuse to stop producing erotic power.[13] In so many of the case studies discussed in this book—sex work, sexual technologies and toys, sex clubs and parties, polyamorous relationships, and BDSM practices and spaces, governmental restrictions on erotic freedom, whether they take the form of governmental regulations, policing, or other carceral approaches, are frequently made in the name of children.

Today, we can witness the political weaponization of the figure of the child all around the world—from prohibitions on drag queens to restrictions on polyamorous people raising children to curtailing and eliminating trans rights. Politicians, unsupported by any reliable social science, scream about how non-heteropatriarchal forms of gender and sexuality are a clear and present danger to children. After all, what kind of deplorable person wouldn't want to protect children?

Politicians demand these types of sexual prohibitions even when they themselves are caught with their pants down. Just ask Larry Craig, a conservative US lawmaker who had a well-documented history of supporting anti-LGBTQ legislation. In 2007, an infamous scandal broke when he was arrested for seeking sex acts with other men in a public bathroom—a practice called *tea-rooming* in the United States and *cottaging* in the UK.

And wait for this one, because you can't make this shit up. József Szájer, a conservative anti-LGBTQ Hungarian politician and former Member of the European Parliament, was caught after he attempted to evade police by jumping out of a first-floor window during a gay sex party in the midst of the COVID-19 lockdown in Brussels. The married politician was also carrying drugs. Talk about do as I say, not as I do!

It's tempting to write an entire book about the sex scandals perpetrated by hypocritical politicians who believe that sexual regulations are for everyone else but them. But for now, I merely note that the existence of a laundry list of legislators who fit this bill underscores that politicians' support for repressive sexual policies, more often than not, comes from a desire to seize and maintain political positions, political expedience, and fear, not out of a deep commitment to reducing harm or promoting sexual justice.

As humans' desires shift alongside technologies, and as erotic power causes new sexual cultures and erotic options to emerge, I am worried that nations, cultures, and people are woefully unprepared to adapt to these shifts in ways that simultaneously prioritize bodily autonomy and justice and take public harm and danger seriously. Throughout history, governments and cultures have established systems that attempt to regulate people's sexualities in fiercely oppressive ways. Societal leaders and institutions treat sexuality like an apex predator that must be kept tamed and caged. As members of SAMOIS, a lesbian feminist S/M organization, wrote, "what we fear we try to keep contained."[14]

Yet laws can never fully tame people's erotic behavior. In *The Boundaries of Desire*, human rights lawyer Eric Berkowitz reminds us that, throughout history, sexual behaviors have shaped laws, but because people are horndogs, the law can never keep up.[15]

It is true that the erotic realm brings some real dangers, but those dangers should be met with harm reduction programs, not full-blown prohibition. Harm reduction techniques focus on minimizing risk and improving safety, not prevention. Trying to get people to stop buying and selling sex, for example, is the ultimate fool's errand. It's called the oldest profession for a reason! Instead of trying to eliminate sex work and punishing people who participate, harm reduction focuses on making those industries safer for everyone involved.

Drawing from the feminist model of pleasure and danger, we know that the realm of sexuality contains danger, exploitation, and injustice, *as well as* pleasure, joy, ecstasy, and empowerment. Efforts to address the former generally come at the expense of the latter—but it doesn't have to be this way. Sexual freedoms don't have to be the sacrificial lambs on the altar of social order, or worse, political expedience and theater.

Our sexualities do not exist in a vacuum. Understanding that our sexualities are political means connecting them to government policies. When governments pass policies that restrict erotic and bodily freedoms, they produce sexual injustice that affects everyone. We can push the boundaries of these restrictions, we can enlarge our understanding of sexuality's social workings, we can seek erotic empowerment—but true sexual liberation requires a collective fight against political repression.

For the sex rabble, that fight is already underway—join us!

ACKNOWLEDGMENTS

Over the years, I have given considerable thought to the politics of acknowledgments, especially in academia—the power structures they perpetuate and how they can evoke memories of high school cafeterias all over again. At the same time, I would like to genuinely acknowledge, celebrate, and express my profound gratitude to the people who supported the project, as well as those who nurtured and cared for my mind, body, and soul during the research and writing process.

I hope the people in my life know how grateful I am to them, as I strive to express it in the context of our relationships. But, if I have *ever* missed a beat—hear me now—gratitude, my friend! The people who have shaped my mind and practices and helped me grow as a thinker and writer, or who are no longer with us, are celebrated in my citational practice and prose. Thank you for making me better!

Thank you to all my people. To those whose texts cheer me up, to those on whose shoulders I cry, and to those on whose shoulders I stand, to those who tirelessly fight for our rights, freedom, and justice at all costs, and to those whose ideas and brilliance continue to educate and inspire me—a heartfelt thank-you!

NOTES

Introduction

1. Westbrook, Laurel, Jamie Budnick, and Aliya Saperstein. 2021. "Dangerous Data: Seeing Social Surveys Through the Sexuality Prism." *Sexualities* 25 (5–6): 717–49.

2. For an excellent and potentially surprising account of the sex lives of religious conservatives, see Burke, Kelsy. 2016. *Christians Under Covers: Evangelicals and Sexual Pleasure on the Internet.* University of California Press.

3. For a critical review of the studies on hookup culture, see Pham, J. M. 2017. "Beyond Hookup Culture: Current Trends in the Study of College Student Sex and Where to Next." *Sociology Compass* 11 (8): e12499.

4. Wade, Lisa. 2017. *American Hookup: The New Culture of Sex on Campus.* W. W. Norton.

5. Terminology varies globally, but generally, BDSM is an umbrella term reflecting a wide range of erotic desires, practices, identities, relationships, and communities related to bondage and discipline, dominance and submission, and sadism and masochism.

6. Lorde, Audre. 1984. "Uses of the Erotic." In *Sister Outsider: Essays and Speeches by Audre Lorde.* Crossing Press, 54, 58.

7. Price, Devon. 2024. *Unlearning Shame: How We Can Reject Self-Blame Culture and Reclaim Our Power.* Penguin Random House.

8. Taylor, Sonya Renee. 2018. *The Body Is Not an Apology: The Power of Radical Self-Love.* Berrett-Koehler Publishers.

9. Beck, Koa. 2021. *White Feminism: From the Suffragettes to Influencers and Who They Leave Behind.* Atria Books, 104.

10. Otálvaro-Hormillosa, Gigi. 2024. *Erotic Resistance: The Struggle for the Soul of San Francisco.* University of California Press.

11. Lorde, Audre. 1978. *The Black Unicorn: Poems.* Norton and Norton, 31–2.

12. Jones, Angela. 2025. "The Black Feminist Erotic Imagination." *Sex & Sexualities* 1 (1): 10.1177/3033371251324187.

13. Cooper, Brittney. 2018. *Eloquent Rage: A Black Feminist Discovers Her Superpower.* Picador, 34.

14. Miles, Brittney. 2019. "Theorizing Conscious Black Asexuality Through Claire Kann's *Let's Talk About Love.*" *Humanities* 8 (4): 165.

15. Lugones, María Cristina. 2010. "Toward a Decolonial Feminism." *Hypatia* 25 (4): 742–59.

Chapter 1. The Social Life of Sexuality

1. Berkowitz, Eric. 2015. *The Boundaries of Desire: A Century of Bad Laws, Good Sex, and Changing Identities.* Counterpoint.

2. Horn, Tina. 2024. *Why Are People into That? A Cultural Investigation of Kink.* Hachette.

3. Autoethnography allows the researcher to constructively use personal narratives as data, revealing insights about social institutions and interactions. Black feminists have long embraced autoethnography for exploring how systems of domination function and disrupting the erasure of Black women's lives and knowledge production. For excellent examples, check out Zora Neale Hurston's pioneering work in anthropology. For more recent work, see Christina Sharpe's book *In the Wake* for a remarkable use of the personal to build theory. Robin Boylorn is a leader in the field, advancing what she calls Blackgirl autoethnography.

4. Ellis, Havelock. 1900 [1897]. *Studies in the Psychology of Sex, Vol. II: Sexual Inversion.* F. A. Davis Company, 91.

5. Somerville, Siobhan. 1994. "Scientific Racism and the Emergence of the Homosexual Body." *Journal of the History of Sexuality* 5 (2): 243–66.

6. Katz, Jonathan Ned. 1990. "The Invention of Heterosexuality." *Socialist Review* 20 (1): 7–34; Foucault, Michel. 1976. *The History of Sexuality Vol. I: An Introduction.* Vintage Books.

7. Johnson, Kevin R. 2006. "The Legacy of Jim Crow: The Enduring Taboo of Black-White Romance." *Texas Law Review* 84 (3): 739–66. Siobhan B. Somerville. 2000. *Queering the Color Line: Race and the Invention of Homosexuality in American Culture.* Duke University Press.

8. McWhorter, Ladelle. 2009. *Racism and Sexual Oppression in Anglo-America: A Genealogy.* Indiana University Press; Somerville, "Scientific Racism and the Emergence of the Homosexual Body."

9. Chauncey, George. 1995. *Gay New York: Gender, Urban Culture, and the Making of the Gay Male World, 1890–1940.* Basic Books.

10. For accessible accounts of the history of heterosexuality, see Katz, Jonathan Ned. 2007. *The Invention of Heterosexuality.* University of Chicago Press; Blank, Hanne. 2012. *Straight: The Surprisingly Short History of Heterosexuality.* Beacon Press; Ambrosino, Brandon. March 16, 2017. "The Invention of 'Heterosexuality.'" www.bbc.com/future/article/20170315-the-invention-of-heterosexuality.

11. Fuechtner, Veronika, Douglas E. Haynes, and Ryan M. Jones, eds. 2018. *A Global History of Sexual Science, 1880–1960.* University of California Press.

12. McLelland, Mark. 2018. "Takahashi Tetsu and Popular Sexology in Early Postwar Japan." In Fuechtner, Veronika, Douglas E. Haynes, and Ryan M. Jones, eds. 2018. *A Global History of Sexual Science, 1880–1960.* University of California Press, 211–32.

13. For a much more detailed and nuanced account of Masters and Johnson, Kinsey, and the history of sexual physiology and laboratory experiments and studies, see Roach, Mary. 2022 [2008]. *Bonk: The Curious Coupling of Science and Sex.* W. W. Norton.

14. Kaplan, Helen Singer. 1979. *Disorders of Sexual Desire and Other New Concepts and Techniques in Sex Therapy.* Brunner/Hazel Publications.

15. Epstein, Steven. 2022. *The Quest for Sexual Health: How an Elusive Ideal Has Transformed Science, Politics, and Everyday Life.* University of Chicago Press, 5.

16. Millett, Kate. 2000 [1970]. *Sexual Politics.* University of Illinois Press.

17. Koedt, Anne. 1970. *The Myth of the Vaginal Orgasm.* New England Free Press.

18. The Boston Women's Health Book Collective. 1973. *Our Bodies, Ourselves: A Book by and for Women.* Simon and Schuster.

19. For an excellent review of this science, see Meirmans, Stephanie, and Roger Strand. "Why Are There So Many Theories for Sex, and What Do We Do with Them?" *Journal of Heredity* 101 (March–April 2010): S3–12.

20. Ridley, Matt. 1993. *The Red Queen: Sex and the Evolution of Human Nature.* Harper Perennial, 4.

21. Ferguson, Roderick. 2005. "Race-ing Homonormativity: Citizenship, Sociology, and Gay Identity." In E. Patrick Johnson and Mae G. Henderson, eds. *Black Queer Studies.* Duke University Press, 52–67.

22. Cruz, Ariane. 2016. *The Color of Kink: Black Women, BDSM, and Pornography.* NYU Press, 33.

23. Kimberlé Crenshaw, a legal and critical race scholar, coined the term *intersectionality* in 1989. However, as Jennifer C. Nash (2019) has argued, while Crenshaw gave this perspective a name, Black feminists have been thinking, practicing, and advocating for intersectional understandings of oppression and injustice for centuries. For example, in 1892, Anna Julia Cooper published *A Voice from the South by a Black Woman of the South,* connecting race, gender, and class in her scathing analyses and critiques of systemic inequity in the US South. So, even long before the term *intersectionality* became in vogue, Black feminists have highlighted how systems of power overlap and the importance of race, gender, class, and sexual orientation in conditioning individuals' experiences. In the 1970s and '80s, there was a proliferation of Black feminist intersectional theorizing that sociologists could have drawn from. While this is not an exhaustive list, see Beal, Frances. 1970. "Double Jeopardy: To Be Black and Female." In Toni Cade Bambara, ed. *The Black Woman.* New American Library, 90–100; Combahee River Collective. "A Black Feminist Statement." In Cherríe Moraga and Gloria E. Anzaldúa, eds. 2015 [1981]. *This Bridge Called My Back: Writings by Radical Women of Color*, 4th ed. SUNY Press, 210–18; Davis, Angela Y. 1981. *Women, Race, and Class.* Vintage Books; hooks, bell. 1984. *Feminist Theory: From Margin to Center.* South End Press; hooks, bell. 1981. *Ain't I a Woman: Black Women and Feminism.* South End Press.

24. Combahee River Collective, 212–13.

25. Firestone, Shulamith. 1970. *The Dialectic of Sex: The Case for Feminist Revolution.* Bantam Books; Snitow, Ann, Christine Stansell, and Sharon Thompson, eds. 1983. *Powers of Desire: The Politics of Sexuality.* Monthly Review Press; Vance, Carol, ed. 1984. *Pleasure and Danger: Exploring Female Sexuality.* Routledge and Kegan Paul; Millett, *Sexual Politics*; Koedt, *Myth of the Vaginal Orgasm*; The Boston Women's Health Book Collective, *Our Bodies, Ourselves.*

26. Queen, Carol. 1997a. "Sex Radical Politics, Sex-Positive Feminist Thought, and Whore Stigma." In Jill Nagle, ed. *Whores and Other Feminists.* Routledge, 125–35; Queen, Carol. 1997b. *Real, Live, Nude Girl: Chronicles of Sex-Positive Culture.* Cleis Press.

27. Duggan, Lisa, and Nan D. Hunter. 1995. *Sex Wars: Sexual Dissent and Political Culture.* Routledge.

28. Dworkin, Andrea. 1981. *Pornography: Men Possessing Women.* Perigee; Dworkin, Andrea, and Catharine MacKinnon. 1988. *Pornography*

and Civil Rights: A New Day for Women's Equality. Organizing Against Pornography.

29. Rubin, Gayle. 1984. "Thinking Sex: Notes for a Radical Theory of the Politics of Sexuality." In Carole S. Vance, ed., *Pleasure and Danger: Exploring Female Sexuality.* Routledge & Kegan Paul, 267–319; Willis, Ellen. [1992] 2012. "Feminism, Moralism, and Pornography." In *Beginning to See the Light: Sex, Hope, and Rock-and-Roll.* University of Minnesota Press, 219–27; Willis, Ellen. [1992] 2012. "Lust Horizons: Is the Women's Movement Pro-Sex?" In *No More Nice Girls: Countercultural Essays.* University of Minnesota Press, 3–14.

30. Vance, *Pleasure and Danger*; Snitow et al., *Powers of Desire.*

31. Lorde, Audre. 1978. *Uses of the Erotic.* Fourth Berkshire Conference on the History of Women, Mount Holyoke College, August 25, 1978; Holland, Sharon P. 2012. *The Erotic Life of Racism.* Duke University Press; Miller-Young, Mireille. 2014. *A Taste for Brown Sugar: Black Women in Pornography.* Duke University Press; Morgan, Joan. 2015. "Why We Get Off: Moving Towards a Black Feminist Politics of Pleasure." *The Black Scholar* 45 (4): 36–46; McMillan, Uri. 2015. *Embodied Avatars: Genealogies of Black Feminist Art and Performance.* NYU Press; Musser, Amber Jamilla. 2018. *Sexual Excess: Queer Femininity and Brown Jouissance.* NYU Press; Musser, Amber Jamilla. 2014. *Sensational Flesh: Race, Power, and Masochism.* NYU Press; Nash, Jennifer C. 2014. *The Black Body in Ecstasy: Reading Race, Reading Pornography.* Duke University Press; Nash, Jennifer. 2017. "Pleasurable Blackness." In Louisa Allen and Mary Lou Rasmussen, eds. *The Palgrave Handbook of Sexuality Education.* Palgrave Macmillan; Nash, Jennifer C. 2018. "Black Sexualities." *Feminist Theory* 19 (1): 3–5; Cruz, Ariane. 2016. *The Color of Kink: Black Women, BDSM, and Pornography.* NYU Press; Cruz, Ariane. 2015. "Beyond Black and Blue: BDSM, Internet Pornography, and Black Female Sexuality." *Feminist Studies* 41 (2): 409–36; Stallings, L. H. 2015. *Funk the Erotic: Transaesthetics and Black Sexual Cultures.* University of Chicago Press; Jones, Angela. 2020. *Camming: Money, Power, and Pleasure in the Sex Work Industry.* NYU Press.

32. Lorde, Audre. 1984. "Uses of the Erotic," in *Sister Outsider: Essays and Speeches by Audre Lorde.* Crossing Press, 56.

33. brown, adrienne maree. 2019. *Pleasure Activism: The Politics of Feeling Good.* AK Press.

34. For a fantastic account of the science and social history of masturbation, see Sprankle, Eric. 2024. *DIY: The Wonderfully Weird History and Science of Masturbation.* Union Square and Co.

35. Warner, Michael. 1993. *Fear of a Queer Planet: Queer Politics and Social Theory.* University of Minnesota Press, xvi.

36. hooks, bell. "Are You Still a Slave? Liberating the Black Female Body." Panel at The New School, May 6, 2014. YouTube, www.youtube.com/watch?v=rJk0hNROvzs.

37. Ward, Jane. 2020. *The Tragedy of Heterosexuality.* NYU Press.

38. Rubin, "Thinking Sex."

39. As feminist scholars have well noted, the 1984 depiction of the charmed circle focuses on white women from the Global North. It does not capture how intersectional lived realities such as race, caste, gender, ability, age, nationality, and culture shape prevailing sexual norms and taboos. See the symposium: Love, Heather, ed. 2011. "Rethinking Sex." *Journal of Lesbian and Gay Studies* 17 (1); Jones, Rebecca L. 2020. "Later Life Sex and Rubin's 'Charmed Circle.'" *Sexuality & Culture* 24: 1480–98.

40. Martin, Karin A. 2009. "Normalizing Heterosexuality: Mothers' Assumptions, Talk, and Strategies with Young Children." *American Sociological Review* 74 (2): 190–207.

41. Ndinda, Catherine, Chiweni Chimbwete, Nuala McGrath, and Robert Pool. 2008. "Perceptions of Anal Sex in Rural South Africa." *Culture, Health & Sexuality* 10 (2): 205–12.

42. See sociologist and postcolonial feminist Jyoti Puri's work on the relationship between sexuality and the state. In *Sexual States: Governance and the Struggle over the Anti-Sodomy Law in India*, she argues that the regulation of sex is central to state formation and the persistence of states in an increasingly postcolonial and transnational global landscape. Also see Mitra, Durba. 2020. *Indian Sex Life: Sexuality and the Colonial Origins of Modern Social Thought.* Princeton University Press.

43. McClintock, Anne. 1995. *Imperial Leather: Race, Gender, and Sexuality in the Colonial Contest.* Routledge, 63.

44. Patil, Vrushali, and Jyoti Puri. 2020. "Postcolonial Sexualities." In N. A. Naples, ed., *Companion to Sexuality Studies.* John Wiley and Sons, 61–74.

45. Puri, Jyoti. 2016. *Sexual States: Governance and the Struggle over the Anti-Sodomy Law in India.* Duke University Press; Jeong-Mi, Park. 2024. *The State's Sexuality: Prostitution and Postcolonial Nation Building in South Korea.* University of California Press.

46. Puri, *Sexual States.*

47. Gaudio, Rudolf Pell. 2009. *Allah Made Us: Sexual Outlaws in an Islamic African City.* Wiley-Blackwell, 3.

48. Sekyiamah, Nana Darkoa. 2022. *The Sex Lives of African Women: Self-Discovery, Freedom, and Healing.* Astra House.

49. Al Jazerah, Madian. 2021. *Are You This? Or Are You This?: A Story of Identity and Worth.* Hurst and Company, 246.

50. Rose, Tricia. 2003. *Longing to Tell: Black Women Talk About Sexuality and Intimacy.* Picador, 390.

51. Foucault, *History of Sexuality*, 95.

52. For excellent accounts of rethinking enthusiastic consent, see Fischel, Joseph. 2019. *Screw Consent: A Better Politics of Sexual Justice.* University of California Press; Buggs, Shantel, and Trevor Hoppe, eds. 2022. *Unsafe Words: Queering Consent in the #MeToo Era.* Rutgers University Press.

53. Leigh, B. C. 1989. "Reasons for Having and Avoiding Sex: Gender, Sexual Orientation, and Relationship to Sexual Behavior." *Journal of Sex Research* 26: 199–209; Hill, C. A., and L. K. Preston. 1996. "Individual Differences in the Experience of Sexual Motivation: Theory and Measurement of Dispositional Sexual Motives." *Journal of Sex Research* 33: 27–45; Meston, Cindy M., and David M. Buss. 2007. "Why Humans Have Sex." *Archives of Sexual Behavior* 36 (4): 477–507.

54. Jones, *Camming.*

55. Viviana Zelizer. 2005. *The Purchase of Intimacy.* Princeton University Press, 1.

56. Dale, Laura Kate, ed. 2022. *Gender Euphoria: Stories of Joy from Trans, Non-Binary and Intersex Writers.* Unbound.

57. For excellent books written by sex workers that cover the complexities of contemporary sex work (not an exhaustive list), see Lee, Jiz, ed. 2015. *Coming Out Like a Porn Star: Essays on Pornography, Protection, and Privacy.* ThreeL Media; Smith, Molly, and Juno Mac. 2018. *Revolting Prostitutes: The Fight for Sex Workers' Rights.* Verso; suprihmbé. 2019. *HeauxThots: On Terminology, and Other [Un]Important Things.* BBYDoll Press; West, Natalie, and Tina Horn, eds. 2021. *We Too: Essays on Sex Work and Survival.* Feminist Press; Bickers, Matilda, peech breshears, and Janis Luna, eds. 2023. *Working It: Sex Workers on the Work of Sex.* PM Press; COYOTE, RI. 2024. *Sex Work Policy: Participatory Action Research by and for Sex Workers and Sex Trafficking Survivors*; Simmons, Molly B., and Emily Marie Passos Duffy, eds. 2024. *The Holy Hour: An Anthology on Sex Work, Magic, and the Divine.* Working Girls Press; Moira, Amara.

2025. *So What if I'm a Puta: Diaries of Transness, Sex Work, and Desire.* Feminist Press.

Chapter 2. Desire

1. See Emily Nagoski's *Come as You Are: The Surprising New Science That Will Transform Your Sex Life* for an excellent and deeply scientifically grounded discussion of desire, bodies, orgasms, and pleasure.

2. Green, Adam Isaiah. 2008. "Erotic Habitus: Toward a Sociology of Desire." *Theory and Society* 37 (6): 597–626; Green, Adam Isaiah. 2014. *Sexual Fields: Toward a Sociology of Collective Sexual Life.* University of Chicago Press.

3. Carpenter, Laura. 2010. "Gendered Sexuality Over the Life Course: A Conceptual Framework." *Sociological Perspectives* 53 (2): 155–178.

4. Levine, Stephen B. 2003. "The Nature of Sexual Desire: A Clinician's Perspective." *Archives of Sexual Behavior* 32 (3): 279–85, 280.

5. Toates, Frederick. 2014. *How Sexual Desire Works: The Enigmatic Urge.* Cambridge University Press, 23–24.

6. Lewis, Marc. 2015. *The Biology of Desire: Why Addiction Is Not a Disease.* PublicAffairs, 30.

7. Green, Adam Isaiah, "Erotic Habitus"; Green, Adam Isaiah, *Sexual Fields*; Han, C. Winter. 2021. *Racial Erotics: Gay Men of Color, Sexual Racism, and the Politics of Desire.* University of Washington Press.

8. For its original conceptualization, see Connell, R. W. 1987. *Gender and Power: Society, the Person, and Sexual Politics.* Stanford University Press, and Connell, R. W., and James W. Messerschmidt. 2005. "Hegemonic Masculinity: Rethinking the Concept." *Gender & Society* 19 (6): 829–59. For excellent developments in theorizing masculinities, see Pascoe, C. J., and Tristan Bridges. 2015. *Exploring Masculinities: Identity, Inequality, Continuity and Change.* Oxford University Press.

9. Angel, Katherine. 2021. *Tomorrow Sex Will Be Good Again: Women and Desire in the Age of Consent.* Verso, 66–67.

10. Serano, Julia. 2022. *Sexed Up: How Society Sexualizes Us, and How We Can Fight Back.* Seal Press.

11. In 1990, 2 Live Crew's platinum-selling album *As Nasty as They Want to Be* was the first music in the United States labeled legally obscene. Subsequently, it led Uncle Luke through a set of legal battles, setting some of the most important First Amendment (freedom of speech) legal precedents in the country's history. In 1992, the US Court of Appeals for the Eleventh Circuit found in *Luke Records v. Navarro*, under the (1973)

Miller test principle, that even 2 Live Crew's vulgar, misogynistic music had serious artistic value and was not legally obscene. Then again, in 1994, in *Campbell v. Acuff-Rose Music, Inc.*, Luke once again defended eroticism in a SCOTUS copyright law case, establishing that parody qualifies as fair use.

12. Beyond Luke and 2 Live Crew, similar moments would later emerge, such as the case of Black women's writing and Take Back the Music protests surrounding rapper Nelly's infamous "Tip Drill" video in 2004. For an excellent Black feminist analysis of these themes, see Crenshaw, Kimberlé W. 1991. "Beyond Racism and Misogyny: Black Feminism and the 2 Live Crew." *Boston Review* 16 (6): 6–33; Peterson-Lewis, Sonja. 1991. "A Feminist Analysis of the Defenses of Obscene Rap Lyrics." *Black Sacred Music* 5 (1): 68–79; Rose, Tricia. 1994. *Black Noise: Rap Music and Black Culture in Contemporary America.* Wesleyan University Press; Miller-Young, Mireille. 2008. "Hip-Hop Honeys and Da Hustlaz: Black Sexualities in the New Hip-Hop Pornography." *Meridians* 8 (1): 261–92.

13. Bederman, Gail. 1995. *Manliness & Civilization: A Cultural History of Gender and Race in the United States, 1880–1917.* University of Chicago Press; Collins, Patricia Hill. 2004. *Black Sexual Politics: African Americans, Gender, and the New Racism.* Routledge; Partridge, D. J. 2008. "We Were Dancing in the Club, Not on the Berlin Wall: Black Bodies, Street Bureaucrats, and Exclusionary Incorporation into the New Europe." *Cultural Anthropology* 23: 660–87; Meszaros, Julia, and Christina Bazzaroni. 2014. "From Taboo to Tourist Industry: The Construction of Interracial Intimacies Between Black Men and White Women in Colonial and Contemporary Times." *Sociology Compass* 8: 1256–68.

14. Bederman, *Manliness & Civilization*; Staples, Robert. 2006. *Exploring Black Sexuality.* Roman and Littlefield; Scott, Darieck. 2010. *Extravagant Abjection: Blackness, Power, and Sexuality in the African American Literary Imagination.* NYU Press; Foster, Thomas. 2019. *Rethinking Rufus: Sexual Violations of Enslaved Men.* University of Georgia Press.

15. Patricia Hill Collins, a famous Black feminist sociologist, defined controlling images as images "designed to make racism, sexism, poverty, and other forms of social injustice appear to be natural, normal, and inevitable parts of everyday life" (*Black Sexual Politics,* 69). Pierce, Alexandra (Sandi). 2015. "'Sexual Savages': Christian Stereotypes and Violence Against North America's Native Women." In A. J. Johnson, ed., *Religion and Men's Violence Against Women.* Springer.

16. For more on this social construction of sexualization, see Serano, Julia. *Sexed Up*.

17. Hoppe, Trevor. 2017. *Punishing Disease: HIV and the Criminalization of Sickness*. University of California Press; Thrasher, Steven. 2022. *The Viral Underclass: The Human Toll When Inequality and Disease Collide*. Celadon Books.

18. Roberts, Dorothy. 1998. *Killing the Black Body: Race, Reproduction, and the Meaning of Liberty*. Penguin Random House; Threadcraft, Shatema. 2016. *Intimate Justice: The Black Female Body and the Body Politic*. Oxford University Press.

19. Croisy, Sophie. 2017. "Fighting Colonial Violence in 'Indian Country': Deconstructing Racist Sexual Stereotypes of Native American Women in American Popular Culture and History." *Angles. New Perspectives on the Anglophone World*: 5; Merskin, Debra. 2010. "The S-Word: Discourse, Stereotypes, and the American Indian Woman." *Howard Journal of Communications* 21 (4): 345–66; NCAI Policy Research Center. 2021. "Research Policy Update: State of the Data on Violence Against American Indian Women and Girls." *National Congress of American Indians*, October 2021.

20. Cerankowski, Karli June, and Megan Milks, eds. 2014. *Asexualities: Feminist and Queer Perspectives*. Routledge; Przybylo, Ela. 2019. *Asexual Erotics: Intimate Readings of Compulsory Sexuality*. Ohio State University Press; Chen, Angela. 2020. *Ace: What Asexuality Reveals About Desire, Society, and the Meaning of Sex*. Beacon Press; Brown, Sherronda J. 2022. *Refusing Compulsory Sexuality: A Black Asexual Lens on Our Sex-Obsessed Culture*. North Atlantic Books; Young, Eris. 2023. *Ace Voices: What It Means to Be Asexual, Aromantic, Demi or Grey-Ace*. Jessica Kingsley.

21. "General FAQ." The Asexual Visibility and Education Network. www.asexuality.org/?q=general.html#def, accessed November 24, 2023.

22. Stonewall. 2023. *Ace in the UK Report*, 7, www.stonewall.org.uk/resources/ace-report.

23. Brown, *Refusing Compulsory Sexuality*, 2.

24. Miles, Brittney. 2019. "Theorizing Conscious Black Asexuality Through Claire Kann's *Let's Talk About Love*." *Humanities* 8 (4): 165.

25. Jo. 2016. "Is 'Lack of Sexual Attraction' the Best Way of Describing Asexuality?" A Life Unexamined (blog). May 26, 2016. https://alifeunexamined.wordpress.com/2016/05/26/is-lack-of-sexual-attraction-the-best-way-of-describing-asexuality.

26. For those interested, there are webinars from David Jay, the founder of AVEN, talking about this history and how and why definitions of asexuality have changed for AVEN. One such webinar is here: www.youtube.com/watch?v=EouWUIU5FnM.

27. Stonewall, *Ace in the UK*, 6.

28. Benoit, Yasmin. 2022. "The Asexual Community Has a Racism Problem. Let's Talk About It." *LGBTQ Nation*, April 5, 2022. www.lgbtqnation.com/2022/04/asexual-community-racism-problem-lets-talk.

29. Brown, *Refusing Compulsory Sexuality*, 16.

30. Daigle-Orians, Cody. 2023. "Introduction." In Madeline Dyer, ed., *Being Ace: An Anthology of Queer, Trans, Femme, and Disabled Stories of Asexual Love and Connection*. Page Street Publishing, viii–xii.

31. Przybylo, *Asexual Erotics*, 20.

32. Kirichanskaya, Michele. 2023. *Ace Notes: Tips and Tricks for Existing in an Allo World*. Jessica Kingsley.

33. Spurgas, Alyson. 2020. *Diagnosing Desire: Biopolitics and Femininity into the Twenty-First Century*. Ohio State University Press.

34. Winer, Canton, Megan Carrroll, Yuchen Yang, Katherine Linder, and Brittney Miles. 2022. "I Didn't Know Ace Was a Thing: Bisexuality and Pansexuality as Identity Pathways in Asexual Identity Formation." *Sexualities* 27 (1): 136346072210854.

35. For an excellent discussion of the exclusion of asexual people from sex-positive discourse, see Winer, Canton. 2025. "The Freedom Not to Be Sexual: Asexuality, Compulsory Sexuality, and Sex Positivity." *Journal of Positive Sexuality* 11 (1): 53–65.

36. Chen, *Ace*, 17.

37. *Intersex* is an umbrella term used to describe the bodies of people with differences in sex traits or reproductive anatomy that fall outside of the female/male binary. For an excellent account of the experiences of people with intersex traits, see Davis, Georgiann. 2015. *Contesting Intersex: The Dubious Diagnosis*. NYU Press.

38. Fausto-Sterling, Anne. 2000. *Sexing the Body: Gender Politics and the Construction of Sexuality*. Basic Books, 8.

39. Kinsey, Alfred C., Wardell B. Pomeroy, and Clyde E. Martin. 1948. *Sexual Behavior in the Human Male*. Saunders, 639.

40. Chen, *Ace*, 15.

41. Brotto, Lori A., Gail Knudson, Jess Inskip, Katherine Rhodes, and Yvonne Erskine. 2010. "Asexuality: A Mixed-Methods Approach." *Archives of Sexual Behavior* 39 (3): 599–618; Hille, Jessica J., Megan K.

Simmons, and Stephanie A. Sanders. 2020. "'Sex' and the Ace Spectrum: Definitions of Sex, Behavioral Histories, and Future Interest for Individuals Who Identify as Asexual, Graysexual, or Demisexual." *Journal of Sex Research* 57 (7): 813–23.

42. Winer, Canton. 2025. "Splitting Attraction: Differentiating Romantic and Sexual Orientations Among Asexual Individuals." *Social Currents* 12 (3). https://doi.org/10.1177/23294965241305170.

43. Smith, Jesús Gregorio Smith, and Gabriel Amaro. 2021. "'No Fats, No Femmes, and No Blacks or Asians': The Role of Body-Type, Sex Position, and Race on Condom Use Online." *AIDS Behavior* 25: 2166–76.

44. Robinson, Brandon Andrew. 2015. "'Personal Preference' as the New Racism: Gay Desire and Racial Cleansing in Cyberspace." *Sociology of Race and Ethnicity* 1 (2): 317–30.

45. Tessler, Hannah. 2023. "Aromanticism, Asexuality, and Relationship (Non-)Formation: How A-Spec Singles Challenge Romantic Norms and Reimagine Family Life." *Sexualities* 28 (1–2): 514–35.

46. Hermann, L., A. Baba, D. Montagner, et al. 2022. *2020 Ace Community Survey Summary Report.* https://acecommunitysurvey.org.

47. In BDSM communities, a slave is a submissive who surrenders all their power to a dominant. In this book, especially in Chapter 6, you'll meet many women like Lorena, who are called Doms, mistresses, or masters. Not all BDSM practitioners use the terms *master* and *slave* due to their connections to the transatlantic trade in human beings.

48. Benoit, Yasmin. 2020. "What Is Asexuality: Myths and Truths About Being Asexual." *Teen Vogue*, October 27, 2020. www.teenvogue.com/story/what-is-asexuality.

49. Benoit, Yasmin. 2021. "'A Romantic Partner Won't Complete Me, Because I Was Born Complete': How Identifying as Asexual and Aromantic Brought Me True Freedom and Happiness." *British Vogue*, February 14, 2021. www.vogue.co.uk/arts-and-lifestyle/article/asexuality-and-aromanticism.

50. Winer, Canton. 2023. "Asexual Joy." *The Sociologist Speaks.* September 6, 2023. https://cantonwiner.substack.com/p/asexual-joy.

51. Burgess, Rebecca. 2020. *How to Be Ace: A Memoir of Growing Up Asexual.* Jessica Kingsley.

52. Songbird, Tyger. 2022. "My Asexual Joy Story." *Medium*, September 8, 2022. https://medium.com/prismnpen/my-asexual-joy-story-175150a77d01.

53. Daigle-Orians, Cody. 2023. *I Am Ace: Advice on Living Your Best Asexual Life.* Jessica Kingsley.

Chapter 3. Behavior

1. Gore-Gorszewska, Gabriela. 2021. "'What Do You Mean by Sex?' A Qualitative Analysis of Traditional Versus Evolved Meanings of Sexual Activity Among Older Women and Men." *Journal of Sex Research* 58 (8): 1035–49.

2. Maines, Rachel P. 1999. *The Technology of Orgasm: Hysteria, the Vibrator, and Women's Satisfaction.* Johns Hopkins University Press.

3. Frederick, David A., H. Kate St. John, Justin R. Garcia, and Elisabeth A. Lloyd. 2018. "Differences in Orgasm Frequency Among Gay, Lesbian, Bisexual, and Heterosexual Men and Women in a U.S. National Sample." *Archives of Sexual Behavior* 47: 273–88.

4. Andrejek, Nicole, and Tina Fetner. 2019. "The Gender Gap in Orgasms: Survey Data from a Mid-Sized Canadian City." *International Journal of Sexual Health* 31 (1): 26–35.

5. Hans, Jason D., Martie Gillen, and Katrina Akande. 2010. "Sex Redefined: The Reclassification of Oral-Genital Contact." *Perspectives on Sexual and Reproductive Health* 42 (2): 74–78. Note: This study was conducted in 2007 and published in 2010.

6. Sewell, Kelsey K., Larissa A. McGarrity, and Donald S. Strassberg. 2017. "Sexual Behavior, Definitions of Sex, and the Role of Self-Partner Context Among Lesbian, Gay, and Bisexual Adults." *Journal of Sex Research* 54 (7): 825–31.

7. Peterson, Zoe D., and Charlene L. Muehlenhard. 2007. "What Is Sex and Why Does It Matter? A Motivational Approach to Exploring Individuals' Definitions of Sex." *Journal of Sex Research* 44 (3): 256–68.

8. Bowling, Jessamyn, Donna Blekfeld-Sztraky, Megan Simmons, et al. 2020. "Definitions of Sex and Intimacy Among Gender and Sexual Minoritised Groups in Urban India." *Culture, Health & Sexuality* 22 (5): 520–34.

9. For an excellent set of (and my personal favorite) books on the history of sex toys, see Lieberman, Hallie. 2017. *Buzz: A Stimulating History of the Sex Toy Industry.* Pegasus Books; Comella, Lynn. 2017. *Vibrator Nation: How Feminist Sex-Toy Stores Changed the Business of Pleasure.* Duke University Press.

10. Brown, Mark. 2023. "It's Not a Darning Tool, It's a Very Naughty Toy: Roman Dildo Found." *The Guardian*, February 19, 2023. www.theguardian

.com/science/2023/feb/20/its-not-a-darning-tool-its-a-very-naughty-toy-roman-dildo-found.

11. For an exhaustive history, see Maines, *Technology of Orgasm.*

12. Comella, *Vibrator Nation*, 8.

13. Ibid., 13.

14. Ruberg, Bo. 2022. *Sex Dolls at Sea: Imagined Histories of Sexual Technologies.* MIT Press.

15. To learn more about the first cyber brothel opened in Berlin, see https://cybrothel.com/en.

16. Black, Deon. "Sex Toys Statistics 2025: Surveys, Studies and Random Facts." Let's Talk Sex, updated April 9, 2025. https://letstalksex.net/sex-toys-statistics.

17. Straights Research. "Europe Sex Toys Market Size Is Projected to Reach USD 15.34 Billion by 2030, Growing at a CAGR of 7.2%: Straits Research." August 23, 2022.

18. BedBible Research Center. 2024. "The State of Sex Toys." Updated September 19, 2024. https://bedbible.com/state-of-sex-toys-industry-statistics.

19. "Sex Information." Come as You Are. www.comeasyouare.com/blogs/sex-information.

20. Butler, Gavin. 2019. "You Can Now Buy Sex Toys from Vending Machines in Japan." *Vice*, August 14, 2019, www.vice.com/en/article/43kdgp/you-can-now-buy-sex-toys-from-vending-machines-in-japan.

21. Stransky, Caroline. "You Can Now Buy Sex Toys from Vending Machines at Berlin's New Airport." Future of Sex. Last updated November 9, 2021. https://futureofsex.net/sex-tech/berlins-new-airport-debuts-sex-toys-vending-machines.

22. Herbenick, Debra, Michael Reece, Stephanie Sanders, et al. 2009. "Prevalence and Characteristics of Vibrator Use by Women in the United States: Results from a Nationally Representative Study." *Journal of Sexual Medicine* 6 (7): 1857–66.

23. BedBible Research Center, "The State of Sex Toys."

24. Allyn, David. 2000. *Make Love, Not War. The Sexual Revolution: An Unfettered History.* Routledge, 294.

25. Kaudo, Negesti. "34 Sex Toys and Accessories Loved by Trans, Enby and GNC Reviewers." Buzzfeed Shopping. February 11, 2022. www.buzzfeed.com/negestikaudo/sex-toys-and-accessories-beloved-by-trans-enby-and-gnc.

26. As everyone reviews their use of generative AI, I encourage people to consider several key factors related to AI. There is ample evidence that

the use of AI tools facilitates labor exploitation, especially of workers in the Global South. The pervasive use of AI comes with deleterious environmental impacts. It can contribute to skills and critical-thinking deficiencies. Many generative AI platforms rely on the stolen intellectual labor of artists and authors, and some platforms are regularly used to engage in violent sexual harassment and sexual exploitation. Furthermore, in many cases, these generative AI bots provide incorrect, unreliable, and incoherent information and citations due to a lack of access to academic databases and coding/training errors.

27. Hanson, Kenneth R. 2022. "Sex: Click Here to Upgrade." *Contexts* 21 (4): 24–9, 29.

28. The sex wars refer to feminist debates over pornography (Duggan and Hunter, *Sex Wars*). On one side, radical feminists focused only on the exploitative characteristics of sex work, particularly misogyny in pornography, and argued porn was representative of patriarchal violence (e.g., Dworkin, *Pornography*; Dworkin and MacKinnon, *Pornography and Civil Rights*). Pro-sex feminists focused primarily on the agency of sex workers and the empowerment found in sex work (e.g., Willis, "Feminism, Moralism, and Pornography"; Willis, "Lust Horizons"; Rubin, "Thinking Sex").

29. Richardson, Kathleen. 2016. "Sex Robot Matters: Slavery, the Prostituted, and the Rights of Machines." *IEEE Technology and Society Magazine* 35 (2): 46–53.

30. Levy, David. 2007. *Love and Sex with Robots.* HarperCollins, 22.

31. See also McArthur, Neil. 2017. "The Case for Sexbots." In John Danaher and Neil McArthur, eds. *Robot Sex: Social and Ethical Implications.* MIT Press.

32. Hanson, "Sex: Click Here," 29.

33. Hanson, Kenneth, and Chloé Locatelli. 2022. "From Sex Dolls to Sex Robots and Beyond: A Narrative Review of Theoretical and Empirical Research on Human-like and Personified Sex Tech." *Current Sexual Health Reports* 14 (7): 1–12.

34. Hanson and Locatelli, "Sex Dolls," 2.

35. Hanson, "Sex: Click Here," 29.

36. Hanson, Kenneth. 2022. "What Does the Personification of Love and Sex Dolls Explain About Doll Owners?" *Deviant Behavior* 44 (8); Hanson, Kenneth. 2021. "The Silicone Self: Examining Sexual Selfhood and Stigma Within the Love and Sex Doll Community." *Symbolic Interaction* 45 (569).

37. Hanson, "Personification of Love," 2.

38. Cassidy, Veronica. 2016. "For the Love of Doll(s): A Patriarchal Nightmare of Cyborg Couplings." *ECS: English Studies Canada* 41 (1–2): 203–15; Prayag Ray. 2016. "Synthetik Love Lasts Forever: Sex Dolls and the (Post?) Human Condition." In D. Banerki and M. Paranjape, eds. *Critical Posthumanism and Planetary Futures*. Springer, 91–112.

39. Zhou, Yanyan, and Bryant Paul. 2016. "Lotus Blossom or Dragon Lady: A Content Analysis of 'Asian Women' Online Pornography." *Sexuality & Culture* 20 (4): 1083–1100.

40. Vidal-Ortiz, Salvador. 2014. "Whiteness." *Transgender Studies Quarterly* 1 (1–2): 264–66.

41. McMillan Cottom, Tressie. 2019. *Thick: And Other Essays*. New Press, 44–45.

42. Curington, Celeste Vaughan, Jennifer Hickes Lundquist, and Ken-Hou Lin. 2021. *The Dating Divide: Race and Desire in the Era of Online Romance*. University of California Press.

43. For a review of research, see Döring, Nicola, et al. 2020. "Design, Use, and Effects of Sex Dolls and Sex Robots: Scoping Review." *Journal of Medical Internet Research* 22 (7): e18551.

44. Attwood, Feona. 2018. *Sex Media*. Polity, 119.

45. Jecker, Nancy. 2021. "Nothing to Be Ashamed Of: Sex Robots for Older Adults with Disabilities." *Journal of Medical Ethics* 47 (1): 26–32.

46. Peschka, Lasse, and Marius Raab. 2022. "A Thing Like a Human? A Mixed Methods Study on Sex Doll Usage." *International Journal of Sexual Health* 34 (4): 728–46.

47. Ibid., 736.

48. Gay, Roxane. 2014. *Bad Feminist: Essays*. Harper Perennial.

49. Hanson, "The Silicone Self," 15–6.

50. Brotto, Lori A., Gail Knudson, Jess Inskip, et al. 2010. "Asexuality: A Mixed-Methods Approach." *Archives of Sexual Behavior* 39 (3): 599–618; Jessica J. Hille, Megan K. Simmons, and Stephanie A. Sanders. 2020 "'Sex' and the Ace Spectrum: Definitions of Sex, Behavioral Histories, and Future Interest for Individuals Who Identify as Asexual, Graysexual, or Demisexual." *Journal of Sex Research* 57 (7): 813–23.

51. Lee, Lorelei. 2019. "Cash/Consent: The War on Sex Work." *N+1* 35: 1–31.

52. Owens, Emily. 2023. *Consent in the Presence of Force: Sexual Violence and Black Women's Survival in Antebellum New Orleans*. University of North Carolina Press.

53. Page, Cara, and Erica Woodland. 2023. *Healing Justice Lineages: Dreaming at the Crossroads of Liberation, Collective Care, and Safety.* North Atlantic Books, 8–9.

54. Haines, Staci K. 2019. *The Politics of Trauma: Somatics, Healing, and Social Justice.* North Atlantic Books, 80–81.

55. Kolysh, Simone. 2021. *Everyday Violence: The Public Harassment of Women and LGBTQ People.* Rutgers University Press.

56. Barton, Bernadette. 2021. *The Pornification of America: How Raunch Culture Is Ruining Our Society.* NYU Press.

57. Orenstein, Peggy. 2016. *Girls & Sex: Navigating the Complicated New Landscape.* HarperCollins, 13.

58. McMillan Cottom, *Thick*, 178.

59. Valenti, Jessica. 2017. *Sex Object: A Memoir.* Dey Street Books. For another extraordinary account of girls' and women's socialization under heteropatriarchy, see Melissa Febos's memoir, *Girlhood.*

Chapter 4. Identities

1. I am not the first scholar to use the kaleidoscope metaphor to describe our intersectional identities. For excellent book-length academic examples, see Messerschmidt, James W., and Tristan Bridges. 2022. *A Kaleidoscope of Identities: Reflexivity, Routine, and the Fluidity of Sex, Gender, and Sexuality.* Rowman and Littlefield; Rodríguez, Juana María. 2003. *Queer Latinidad: Identity Practices, Discursive Spaces.* NYU Press.

2. shuster, stef, and Laurel Westbrook. 2024. "Reducing the Joy Deficit in Sociology: A Study of Transgender Joy." *Social Problems* 71 (3): 791–809.

3. Beauvoir, Simone de. 2011 [1949]. *The Second Sex*, trans. Constance Borde and Sheila Malovany-Chevallier. Vintage Books, 283.

4. Butler, Judith. 2006. *Gender Trouble: Feminism and the Subversion of Identity.* Routledge.

5. Crenshaw, Kimberlé. 1989. "Demarginalizing the Intersection of Race and Sex: A Black Feminist Critique of Antidiscrimination Doctrine, Feminist Theory and Antiracist Politics." *University of Chicago Legal Forum* 140: 139–67; Crenshaw, Kimberlé. 1991. "Mapping the Margins: Intersectionality, Identity Politics, and Violence Against Women of Color." *Stanford Law Review* 43 (6): 1241–99.

6. Nash, Jennifer C. 2019. *Black Feminism Reimagined: After Intersectionality.* Duke University Press.

7. Hartman, Saidiya. 2022 [1997]. *Scenes of Subjection: Terror, Slavery, and Self-Making in the Nineteenth Century.* W. W. Norton, 94.

8. Orne, Jay. 2011. "'You Will Always Have to "Out" Yourself': Reconsidering Coming Out Through Strategic Outness." *Sexualities* 14 (6): 681–703.

9. For excellent statistical data on wealth and income inequality in the United States, see Schaeffer, Katherine. "6 Facts About Economic Inequality in the U.S." Pew Research Center. February 7, 2020. www.pewresearch.org/short-read/2020/02/07/6-facts-about-economic-inequality-in-the-u-s.

10. For excellent work on social class and sexual life, see Lancaster, Roger N. 2023. *The Struggle to Be Gay: In Mexico, for Example.* University of California Press.

11. Frank, Katherine. 2013. *Plays Well in Groups: A Journey Through the World of Group Sex.* Rowman and Littlefield.

12. Tsui, Pamela. 2024. "Erotic Capabilities: A Feminist Analysis of Sexual Justice and Pleasure in Heterosexual Sex Partying." *Sexualities* 27 (4): 918–38.

13. Bowen, Sesali. 2021. *Bad Fat Black Girl: Notes from a Trap Feminist.* Amistad, 39.

14. Edging generally refers to a sexual practice involving orgasm denial and intentionally getting close to climax but then stopping activity to prevent it from happening. This process helps to build desire and often contributes to powerful orgasms.

15. Jones, Angela. "Rethinking the Orgasm Gap: Compulsory Orgasmic Cultures and Orgasmic Pressure." Sex Chronicle, March 1, 2025. https://sexchronicle.com/the-blog/f/rethinking-the-orgasm-gap?blogcategory=Research.

16. Kimberly, Claire. 2016. "Permission to Cheat: Ethnography of a Swingers' Convention." *Sexuality and Culture* 20: 56–68.

17. Gurba, Myriam. 2023. *Creep: Accusations and Confessions.* Avid Reader Press.

18. Bentzen, Anne-Sofie, and Bente Traeen. 2014. "Swinging in Norway in the Context of Sexual Health." *Sexuality & Culture* 18 (1): 132–48.

19. Viwatpanich, Kanvee. 2010. "Swinging: Extramarital Sexuality in Thai Society." *Anthropological Notebooks* 16: 289–311.

20. Gang, Fang. *Swingers in Red China: A Study of Intimate Relationships.* Self-published.

21. Serina, Allison T., Molly Hall, Desire Ciambrone, and Voon Chin Phua. 2013. "Swinging Around Stigma: Gendered Marketing of Swingers' Websites." *Sexuality and Culture* 17 (2): 348–59.

22. Bergstrand, Curtis R., and Jennifer Blevins Sinski. 2010. *Swinging in America: Love, Sex, and Marriage in the 21st Century.* ABC-CLIO.

23. Bergstrand and Sinski, *Swinging in America*; Kimberly, Claire, and Robert McGinley. 2019. "Changes in the Swinging Lifestyle: A US National and Historical Comparison." *Culture, Health & Sexuality* 21 (2): 219–32.

24. Kimberly and McGinley, "Changes."

25. Rodriguez, Cecilia. 2016. "Naughty Travel: How 'Libertine Tourism' Is Becoming a Growing Industry." *Forbes*, December 10, 2016.

26. Serina et al., "Swinging Around Stigma."

27. Bentzen and Traeen, "Swinging in Norway."

28. For example, bars and nightclubs in Boystown, the gay enclave in Chicago, Illinois, have been criticized for catering to white affluent gay men and intentionally excluding people of color, trans people, and lesbians. For academic accounts, see Orne, Jay. 2017. *Boystown: Sex and Community in Chicago.* University of Chicago Press. For mainstream press accounts, see Rhodes, Adam M. 2020. "'We're Not Asking for Any More than What We Are Already Deserved.'" *Chicago Reader*, November 25, 2020.

29. Haywood, Chris. 2022. *Sex Clubs: Recreational Sex, Fantasies, and Cultures of Desire.* Palgrave Macmillan, 97.

30. Jones, Angela. 2019. "The Pleasures of Fetishization: BBW Erotic Webcam Performers, Empowerment, and Pleasure." *Fat Studies. An Interdisciplinary Journal of Body Weight and Society* 8 (3): 279–98.

31. Miller-Young, Mireille. 2014. *A Taste for Brown Sugar: Black Women in Pornography.* Duke University Press, 27.

32. Nash, Jennifer C. 2014. *The Black Body in Ecstasy: Reading Race, Reading Pornography.* Duke University Press, 3.

33. Vaynman, Margaret J., and J. Thomas Harviainen. 2023. "Speaking with Swingers in Spain and France: Strategies from the Swinger World." *Sexuality & Culture* 27 (1): 131–47.

34. See all of the work of Alan Santinele Martino, who runs the Sexuality and Disability Lab at the University of Calgary in Canada (www.alanmartino.com); Erickson, Loree. 2015. "Why I Love Hickies and Queer Crip Porn." In Jiz Lee, ed., *Coming Out Like a Porn Star: Essays on Pornography, Protection, and Privacy.* ThreeL Media, 224–8; McRuer, Robert, and Anna Mollow. 2012. *Sex and Disability.* Duke University

Press; Gill, Michael. 2015. *Already Doing It: Intellectual Disability and Sexual Agency.* University of Minnesota Press; Albertz, Megan, and Cynthia Lewiecki-Wilson. 2008. "Let's Talk About Sex . . . and Disability Baby!" *Disability Studies Quarterly* 28 (4); Clare, Eli. 1999. *Exile and Pride: Disability, Queerness and Liberation.* South End Press.

35. Jones, "The Pleasures of Fetishization"; Stacey, Lawrence, and TehQuin D. Forbes. 2021. "Feeling Like a Fetish: Racialized Feelings, Fetishization, and the Contours of Sexual Racism on Gay Dating Apps." *Journal of Sex Research* 59 (3): 372–84; Anzani, Annalisa, et al. 2021. "'Being Talked to Like I Was a Sex Toy, Like Being Transgender Was Simply for the Enjoyment of Someone Else': Fetishization and Sexualization of Transgender and Nonbinary Individuals." *Archive Sex Behavior* 50: 897–911.

36. Stacey and Forbes, "Feeling Like a Fetish."

37. Acker, Joan. 1990. "Hierarchies, Jobs, Bodies: A Theory of Gendered Organizations." *Gender & Society* 4 (2): 139–58; Acker, Joan. 2006. "Inequality Regimes: Gender, Class, and Race in Organizations." *Gender & Society* 20 (4): 441–64; Ray, Victor. 2019. "A Theory of Racialized Organizations." *American Sociological Review* 84 (1): 26–53; Yavorsky, Jill E. 2016. "Cisgendered Organizations: Trans Women and Inequality in the Workplace." *Sociological Forum* 31 (4): 948–69; Jones, Angela. 2025. "Cisgendered Workspaces: Outright and Categorical Exclusion in Cisgendered Organizations." *Social Problems* 72 (1): 294–314.

38. Kim, Anna. "Why You Should Visit Toronto, the World's Most Diverse City." AFAR, November 28, 2023. www.afar.com/magazine/why-you-should-travel-to-toronto-canada#:~:text=More%20than%20half%20its%20population,color%20to%20hold%20the%20post.

39. Piepzna-Samarasinha, Leah Lakshmi. 2018. *Care Work: Dreaming of Disability Justice.* Arsenal Pulp Press; O'Brian, M. E. 2024. *Family Abolition: Capitalism and the Communizing of Care.* Pluto Press.

40. Ward, Jane. 2010. "Gender Labor: Transmen, Femmes, and the Collective Work of Transgression." In Eileen Boris and Rhacel Salazar Parreñas, eds. *Intimate Labors: Cultures, Technologies, and the Politics of Care.* Stanford University Press, 78–93.

41. Taylor, Sonya Renee. 2018. *The Body Is Not an Apology: The Power of Radical Self-Love.* Berrett-Koehler Publishers, 13.

42. shuster, stef, and Laurel Westbrook. 2022 [reprinted 2024]. "Reducing the Joy Deficit in Sociology: A Study of Transgender Joy." *Social Problems* 71 (3): 791–809; Westbrook, Laurel, and stef shuster. 2023.

"Transgender Joy: Flipping the Script of Marginality." *Contexts* 22 (4): 16–21.

43. Mattson, Greggor. 2023. *Who Needs Gay Bars?: Bar-Hopping Through America's Endangered LGBTQ+ Places.* Redwood Press.

44. Hammers, Corie. 2009. "An Examination of Lesbian/Queer Bathhouse Culture and the Social Organization of (Im)Personal Sex." *Journal of Contemporary Ethnography* 38 (3): 308–35, 329.

45. Alexander, M. Jacqui. 2005. *Pedagogies of Crossing: Meditations on Feminism, Sexual Politics, Memory, and the Sacred.* Duke University Press.

46. Hammers, Corie. 2009. "Space, Agency, and the Transfiguring of Lesbian/Queer Desire." *Journal of Homosexuality* 56 (6): 757–85, 782.

47. Lorde, Audre. 1984. "Uses of the Erotic," in *Sister Outsider: Essays and Speeches by Audre Lorde.* Crossing Press, 57.

Chapter 5. Relationships

1. Brake, Elizabeth. 2012. *Minimizing Marriage: Marriage, Morality, and the Law.* Oxford University Press.

2. Schippers, Mimi. 2016. *Beyond Monogamy: Polyamory and the Future of Polyqueer Sexualities.* NYU Press.

3. Lehmiller, Justin J. 2020. "Fantasies About Consensual Nonmonogamy Among Persons in Monogamous Romantic Relationships." *Archives of Sexual Behavior* 49 (8): 2799–812.

4. Clardy, Justin L. 2023. *Why It's OK to Not Be Monogamous.* Routledge.

5. Gahran, Amy. "Riding the Relationship Escalator (or Not)." Solo Poly. November 29, 2012. https://solopoly.net/2012/11/29/riding-the-relationship-escalator-or-not.

6. De las Heras Gómez, Roma. 2019. "Thinking Relationship Anarchy from a Queer Feminist Approach." *Sociological Research Online* 24 (4): 644–60.

7. Kevin Patterson, MEd, is a Black straight cisgender polyamorous man. He is a writer and an educator and has been practicing ethical nonmonogamy since August 2002. Kevin is an active member of the Philadelphia polyamory community in the United States. He's also a well-known polyamorous educator and is a regular podcast guest. Through Poly Role Models, an interview series on Tumblr he created in 2013, his groundbreaking 2018 book, *Love's Not Color Blind: Race and Representation in Polyamorous and Other Alternative Communities*, and his For Hire

superhero series focusing on the adventures of queer, polyamorous Black women, Kevin became a leading voice in the polyamory community.

8. Wekker, Gloria. 2006. *The Politics of Passion: Women's Sexual Culture in the Afro-Surinamese Diaspora*. Columbia University Press, 173.

9. Ryan, Christopher, and Cacilda Jethá. 2010. *Sex at Dawn: The Prehistoric Origins of Modern Sexuality*. Harper Perennial.

10. Carter, Sarah. 2008. *The Importance of Being Monogamous: Marriage and Nation Building in Western Canada to 1915*. University of Alberta Press.

11. Morgensen, Scott Lauria. 2010. "Settler Homonationalism: Theorizing Settler Colonialism within Queer Modernities." *GLQ* 16 (1–2): 105–31; Morgensen, Scott Lauria. 2011. *Spaces Between Us: Queer Settler Colonialism and Indigenous Decolonization*. University of Minnesota Press.

12. Cott, Nancy F. 2000. *Public Vows: A History of Marriage and the Nation*. Harvard University Press.

13. Clardy, Justin L. 2025. "Polyamory in Black: A Companion Justification for Minimal Marriage." *Journal of Applied Philosophy* 42 (3): 777–94.

14. Sociologists Michael Omi and Howard Winant argued that societies actively create racialized meanings and that how they define and describe race shapes every facet of the social world. Racial projects or competing ideas, campaigns, and representations in media and culture all shape and reshape people's behavior and understanding of race.

15. Heath, Melanie. 2023. *Forbidden Intimacies: Polygamies at the Limits of Western Tolerance*. Stanford University Press.

16. Human Rights Committee. 2000. "General Comment 28, Equality of Rights Between Men and Women (article 3)." U.N. Doc. CCPR/C/21/Rev.1/Add.10.

17. Krantz, Rachel. 2022. *Open: An Uncensored Memoir of Love, Liberation, and Non-Monogamy*. Harmony.

18. Willey, Angela. 2016. *Undoing Monogamy: The Politics of Science and the Possibilities of Biology*. Duke University Press.

19. Ferrer, Jorge N. 2018. "Mononormativity, Polypride, and the 'Mono–Poly Wars.'" *Sexuality & Culture* 22, 817–36.

20. Halberstam, Jack. 2011. *The Queer Art of Failure*. Duke University Press.

21. Perel, Esther. 2007. *Mating in Captivity: Unlocking Erotic Intelligence*. Harper Perennial.

22. Nordgren, Andie. "The Short Instructional Manifesto for Relationship Anarchy." Andie's Log. July 5, 2012. https://log.andie.se/post/26652940513/the-short-instructional-manifesto-for-relationship.

23. Carillo, Héctor. 2017. *Pathways of Desire: The Sexual Migration of Mexican Gay Men*. University of Chicago Press.

24. Evita "Lavitaloca" Sawyers is a Black cisgender queer polyamorous educator, speaker, coach, advocate, and writer. She is also a proud parent to three beautiful children and has been nonmonogamous for well over a decade. She wrote the 2023 book *A Polyamory Devotional: 365 Daily Reflections for the Consensually Nonmonogamous.* It provides critical and thoughtful daily prompts to help readers on their journeys in nonmonogamy, no matter how long they have been participating. Evita is the creator of the Instagram series "Today's Polyamory Reminder" and was at the center of the 2016 documentary *Poly Love.*

25. Haritaworn, Jin, Chin-ju Lin, and Christian Klesse. 2006. "Poly/logue: A Critical Introduction to Polyamory." *Sexualities* 9 (5): 515–29.

26. van Eeden-Moorefield, Brad, Kevin Malloy, and Kristen Benson. 2016. "Gay Men's (Non)Monogamy Ideals and Lived Experience." *Sex Roles* 75: 43–55.

27. Barker, Meg-John, and Darren Langdridge, eds. 2010. *Understanding Non-Monogamies.* Routledge.

28. Johnson, Sarah M., Traci A. Giuliano, Jordan R. Herselman, and Kevin T. Hutzler. 2015. "Development of a Brief Measure of Attitudes Towards Polyamory." *Psychology & Sexuality* 6 (4): 325–39.

29. Grigoropoulos, Iraklis, Konstantinos-Christos Daoultzis, and Panos Kordoutis. 2023. "Identifying Context-Related Socio-Cultural Predictors of Negative Attitudes Toward Polyamory." *Sexuality & Culture* 27: 1264–87.

30. Sheff, Elisabeth, and Corie Hammers. 2011. "The Privilege of Perversities: Race, Class and Education Among Polyamorists and Kinksters." *Psychology & Sexuality* 2 (3): 198–223.

31. Landry, Samantha, Erika Arseneau, and Elizabeth K. Darling. 2021. "'It's a Little Bit Tricky': Results from the POLYamorous Childbearing and Birth Experiences Study (POLYBABES)." *Archives of Sexual Behavior* 50 (4): 1479–90.

32. Pérez Navarro, Pablo. 2017. "Beyond Inclusion: Non-monogamies and the Borders of Citizenship." *Sexuality & Culture* 21 (2), 441–58.

33. Burleigh, Tyler J., Alicia N. Rubel, and Daniel V. Meegan. 2017. "Wanting 'the Whole Loaf': Zero-Sum Thinking About Love Is Associated

with Prejudice Against Consensual Non-Monogamists." *Psychology & Sexuality* 8 (1–2): 24–40.

34. Conley, Teri D., et al. 2013. "The Fewer the Merrier?: Assessing Stigma Surrounding Consensually Non-Monogamous Romantic Relationships." *Analyses of Social Issues and Public Policy (ASAP)* 13 (1): 1–30.

35. Sheff, Elisabeth. 2014. *The Polyamorists Next Door: Inside Multiple-Partner Relationships and Families.* Rowman and Littlefield.

36. Sandbakken, Ella Marie, Anita Skrautvol, and Ole Jacob Madsen. 2022. "'It's My Definition of a Relationship, Even Though It Doesn't Fit Yours': Living in Polyamorous Relationships in a Mononormative Culture." *Psychology & Sexuality* 13 (4): 1054–67.

37. Balzarini, Rhonda N., et al. 2017. "Perceptions of Primary and Secondary Relationships in Polyamory." *PLoS One* 12 (5): e0177841.

38. Wood, Jessica, et al. 2021. "Motivations for Engaging in Consensually Non-Monogamous Relationships." *Archives of Sexual Behavior* 50 (4): 1253–72.

39. Rodríguez-Castro, Yolanda, et al. "Analysis of the Experiences of Polyamorists in Spain." *Sexuality & Culture* 26, 1659–83.

40. Cox, Derrell W., James R. Fleckenstein, and Lori R. Sims-Cox. 2021. "Comparing the Self-Reported Health, Happiness, and Marital Happiness of a Multinational Sample of Consensually Non-Monogamous Adults with Those of the U.S. General Population: Additional Comparisons by Gender, Number of Sexual Partners, Frequency of Sex, and Marital Status." *Archives of Sexual Behavior* 50 (4): 1287–1309.

41. Chaneé Jackson Kendall is a Black cisgender queer polyamorous educator from the city of Atlanta in the United States. She is a proud mama, coparenting with her partners, and has openly identified as non-monogamous and kinky for over a decade. Chaneé is also the founder and facilitator of the Intentional Polyamory cohort workshops. She has appeared on countless podcasts and is a prominent voice across public and social media platforms. Chaneé uses her voice, knowledge, and activism to help normalize polyamory as both a relationship orientation and a valid relational choice.

42. Badiee, Manijeh, and Evita Sawyers. 2024. "Black Queer Femme and Non-Binary Individuals' Polyamory: An Act of Liberation." *Sexualities* 28 (4): 11–12.

43. Horn, Tina. 2024. *Why Are People into That? A Cultural Investigation of Kink.* Hachette.

44. Steele, Catherine Knight. 2021. *Digital Black Feminism.* NYU Press; Bailey, Moya. 2021. *Misogynoir Transformed: Black Women's Digital Resistance.* NYU Press.

Chapter 6. Communities

1. See, for example, Beemyn, Brett. 1997. *Creating a Place For Ourselves: Lesbian, Gay, and Bisexual Community Histories.* Routledge; Ghaziani, Amin. 2014. *There Goes the Gayborhood?* Princeton University Press; Orne, Jason. 2017. *Boystown: Sex and Community in Chicago.* University of Chicago Press; Greene, Theodore. 2024. *Not in My Gayborhood: Gay Neighborhoods and the Rise of the Vicarious Citizen.* Columbia University Press.

2. Newton, Esther. 2014. *Cherry Grove, Fire Island: Sixty Years in America's First Gay and Lesbian Town.* Duke University Press.

3. Hunter, Albert. 1974. *Symbolic Communities: The Persistence and Change of Chicago's Local Communities.* University of Chicago Press; Hunter, Albert. 2006. "Contemporary Conceptions of Community." In Ram A. Cnaan and Carl Milofsky, eds., *Handbook of Community Movements and Local Organization.* Blackwell, 20–33.

4. Baldwin said this in an interview with poet Nikki Giovanni in 1971.

5. For an excellent account of the real-world experiences of a professional dominatrix, see Febos, Melissa. *Whip Smart: A Memoir.* Thomas Dunne Books. For academic studies, see Kassandra Sparks's 2025 exceptional dissertation, *Theaters of Perversity: The BDSM Sex Economy in New York City.* PhD diss. University of California–Berkeley, www.proquest.com/LegacyDocView/DISSNUM/32172329; and Lindemann, Danielle. 2012. *Dominatrix: Gender, Eroticism, and Control in the Dungeon.* University of Chicago Press.

6. Newmahr, Staci. 2011. *Playing on the Edge: Sadomasochism, Risk, and Intimacy.* Indiana University Press.

7. See the chapters by Karen Holt ("Survivors of Sexual Victimization and the Negotiation of BDSM Play") and Valerie Rubinsky, Angela Cooke-Jackson, and Alejandre Rodriquez ("From Pain to Healing: Kink and Communication in Sexual Assault Recovery") in Simula, Brandy L., Robin Bauer, and Liam Wignall, eds. 2023. *The Power of BDSM: Play, Communities, and Consent in the 21st Century.* Oxford University Press, 240–60, 261–83.

8. Cruz, Ariane. 2016. *The Color of Kink: Black Women, BDSM, and Pornography.* NYU Press.

9. Cowart, Leigh. 2021. *Hurts So Good: The Science and Culture of Pain on Purpose.* PublicAffairs.

10. Musser, Amber Jamilla. 2014. *Sensational Flesh: Race, Power, and Masochism.* NYU Press, 1.

11. For a fantastic account of how gender, race, and sexuality shape experiences, see Bauer, Robin. 2008. "Transgressive and Transformative Gendered Sexual Practices and White Privileges: The Case of the Dyke/Trans BDSM Communities." *WSQ: Women's Studies Quarterly* 36 (3): 233–53. For an excellent overview of academic empirical research on people's experiences, see Simula, Brandy L. 2019. "Pleasure, Power, and Pain: A Review of the Literature on the Experiences of BDSM Participants." *Sociology Compass* 13 (3): 1–24. For fantastic first-person-driven accounts of kinky people's experiences from across the spectrums of gender, race, abilities, ages, and other categories of difference, see Bannon, Race, et al., eds. 2024. *Kink Is.* Unbound Edition Press.

12. Scott, Gini Graham. 2014. *Erotic Power: Exploring the World of BDSM.* Skyhorse Publishing; Faccio, Elena, Davide Sarigu, and Antonio Iudici. 2020. "What Is It Like to Be a BDSM Player? The Role of Sexuality and Erotization of Power in the BDSM Experience." *Sexuality & Culture: An Interdisciplinary Quarterly* 24 (5): 1641–52.

13. Fennell, Julie. 2018. "'It's All About the Journey': Skepticism and Spirituality in the BDSM Subculture." *Sociological Forum* 33: 1045–67.

14. Sisson, Kathy. 2007. "The Cultural Formation of S/M: History and Analysis." In Darren Langdridge and Meg Baker, eds. *Safe, Sane, and Consensual: Contemporary Perspectives on Sadomasochism.* Palgrave, 10–34; Weiss, Margot. 2015. "BDSM." In Patricia Whelehan and Anne Bolin, eds. *The International Encyclopedia of Human Sexuality.* John Wiley & Sons, 1–6.

15. Stein, Stephen K. 2021. *Sadomasochism and the BDSM Community in the United States.* Routledge.

16. Thompson, Mark. 2004 [1991]. *Leatherfolk: Radical Sex, People, Politics, and Practice.* Daedalus Publishing.

17. Landridge, Darren, and Meg Barker, eds. 2007. *Safe, Sane, and Consensual: Contemporary Perspectives on Sadomasochism.* Palgrave.

18. Carlström, Charlotta. 2017. "Gender Equal BDSM Practice—a Swedish Paradox?" *Psychology & Sexuality* 8 (4): 268–79.

19. Drdová, Lucie, and Steven Saxonberg. 2022. "Generations of BDSM Czech Style: The Elimination of Roles in Role-Playing?" *Sexualities* 25 (7): 944–61.

20. Weiss, Margot. 2011. *Techniques of Pleasure: BDSM and the Circuits of Sexuality.* Duke University Press.

21. Erickson, Jennifer M., et al. 2022. "Challenge at the Intersection of Race and Kink: Racial Discrimination, Fetishization, and Inclusivity Within the BDSM (Bondage-Discipline, Dominance-Submission, and Sadism-Masochism) Community." *Archives of Sexual Behavior* 51 (2): 1063–74.

22. Graham, Benjamin C., et al. 2016. "Member Perspectives on the Role of BDSM Communities." *Journal of Sex Research* 53 (8): 895–909.

23. Thompson, *Leatherfolk.*

24. SAMOIS. 1987. *Coming to Power: Writings and Graphics on Lesbian S/M*, third ed. Alyson Publications.

25. Count Boogie. *Perverted Podcast*, episode 123. "John Baku from Fetlife." October 10, 2017. https://soundcloud.com/perverted-podcast/123-john-baku-from-fetlife.

26. Morris, David Z. "How Kink's Largest Social-Networking Site Fails Its Users." *Atlantic*, March 3, 2015. www.theatlantic.com/health/archive/2015/03/how-kinks-largest-social-networking-site-fails-its-users/385586.

27. Smith, Jordan Michael. "He Developed a Devoted BDSM Following Online. Then He Was Accused of Rape." HuffPost, March 2, 2020. www.huffpost.com/entry/fetlife-bdsm_n_5e569604c5b6fc7a9e38d065.

28. Snow, Olivia. "The Internet's Most Popular Fetish Site Is Flagging People as Sex Workers: FetLife Has Never Been Super Friendly Towards Sex Workers." *Vice*, August 11, 2022. www.vice.com/en/article/the-internets-most-popular-fetish-site-is-flagging-people-as-sex-workers.

29. Feast, Fancy. "Users on a Site for Kinky People Say the Racism Has Become Unsustainable." *Buzzfeed*, October 16, 2020. www.buzzfeednews.com/article/fancyfeast/fetlife-racism-kink-alt-right-anti-semitism.

30. Holt, Karen. 2016. "Blacklisted: Boundaries, Violations, and Retaliatory Behavior in the BDSM Community." *Deviant Behavior* 37 (8): 917–30.

31. Galilee-Belfer, Mika. 2020. "BDSM, Kink, and Consent: What the Law Can Learn from Consent-Driven Communities." *Arizona Law Review* 62 (2): 507–38.

32. Beachy, Robert. 2014. *Gay Berlin: Birthplace of a Modern Identity.* Vintage Books.

33. Lugosi, Mistress Bella. "The End of an Era: Some Words on the Closure of Studio Avalon." December 3, 2020. www.mistressbella

lugosi.com/2020/12/03/end-of-an-era-some-words-on-the-closure-of-studio-avalon.

34. Webster, Craig, and Molly Klaserner. 2019. "Fifty Shades of Socializing: Slosh and Munch Events in the BDSM Community." *Event Management* 23 (1): 135–47.

35. Robinson, Brandon Andrew. 2025. "'I Feel the Most Pleasure When I Don't Have to Worry': On Sexual Comfort, t4t, and Trans Pleasure." *Sex & Sexualities* 1 (1): 22.

36. The archive revealed a lapse from the summer of 1988 until January 1989. A 1989 newsletter said the group fell into disarray and "collapsed" in the summer of 1988 over "political squabbles," but they reorganized by January 1989.

37. Box 16, Dorothy Allison Papers, David M. Rubenstein Rare Book & Manuscript Library, Duke University.

38. Patel, Samir S. "How the Leatherdykes Helped Change Feminism." *Atlas Obscura*, May 1, 2017. www.atlasobscura.com/articles/leather-feminism-lesbian-leatherdyke-bdsm.

39. Heying, Sarah. 2023. "'How Not to Get Killed': Feminist Aftercare in the Dorothy Allison Papers." *Signs: Journal of Women in Culture and Society* 48 (4): 897–921, 905.

40. Allison, Dorothy. "Voices of Feminism Oral History Project," interview by Kelly Anderson, November 18 and 19, 2007. Smith College, 58.

41. Dorothy Allison Papers, Box 16.

42. Box 35, correspondence folders, 1984, Winter/Spring Newsletter, Dorothy Allison Papers, David M. Rubenstein Rare Book & Manuscript Library, Duke University.

43. Allison, "Voices of Feminism."

44. Box 19, Dorothy Allison Papers, David M. Rubenstein Rare Book & Manuscript Library, Duke University.

45. Box 33, correspondence folders, February 9, 1982. Dorothy Allison Papers, David M. Rubenstein Rare Book & Manuscript Library, Duke University.

46. Dorothy Allison Papers, Box 16.

47. The LSM's relationship with GMSMA became incredibly strained in 1988 after GMSMA revoked Dorothy Allison and Pat Califia's honorary memberships. The leadership of the GMSMA believed that Allison and Califia had publicly defamed and impugned the organization's reputation when they disagreed with several of GMSMA's positions at a community conference in Dallas. In response, GMSMA issued public announcements

and sent mass communications to many community members outside of GMSMA, thus also defaming Allison and Califia within the broader community.

Conclusion

1. Perel, Esther. 2007. *Mating in Captivity: Unlocking Erotic Intelligence.* Harper Perennial.

2. Page, Cara, and Erica Woodland. 2023. *Healing Justice Lineages: Dreaming at the Crossroads of Liberation, Collective Care, and Safety.* North Atlantic Books.

3. Barnett, Jerry. 2016. *Porn Panic!: Sex and Censorship in the UK.* Zer0 Books.

4. Rothman, Emily F. 2021. *Pornography and Public Health.* Oxford University Press.

5. Fahs, Breanne. 2014. "'Freedom to' and 'Freedom from': A New Vision for Sex-Positive Politics." *Sexualities* 17 (3): 267–90.

6. Taylor, Sonya Renee. 2021. *The Body Is Not an Apology: The Power of Radical Self-Love*, second ed., Berrett-Koehler Publishers, 12.

7. Taormino, Tristan, et al., eds. 2013. *The Feminist Porn Book: The Politics of Producing Pleasure.* Feminist Press.

8. Davis, Angela. 1981. *Women, Race, and Class.* Vintage Books.

9. Meyer, Doug. 2022. *Violent Differences: The Importance of Race in Sexual Assault Against Queer Men.* University of California Press.

10. Patterson, Jennifer, ed. 2016. *Queering Sexual Violence—Radical Voices from Within the Anti-Violence Movement.* Riverdale Avenue Books.

11. For excellent work on moral sex panics, see Herdt, Gilbert, ed. 2009. *Moral Panics, Sex Panics: Fear and the Fight Over Sexual Rights.* NYU Press; Lancaster, Roger N. 2011. *Sex Panic and the Punitive State.* University of California Press.

12. Edelman, Lee. 2004. *No Future: Queer Theory and the Death Drive.* Duke University Press.

13. Muñoz, José Esteban. 2009. *Cruising Utopia: The Then and There of Queer Futurity.* NYU Press, 95.

14. SAMOIS. 1987. *Coming to Power: Writings and Graphics on Lesbian S/M*, 3rd ed. Alyson Publications.

15. Berkowitz, Eric. 2015. *The Boundaries of Desire: A Century of Bad Laws, Good Sex, and Changing Identities.* Counterpoint.

INDEX

Sara Miller Photography

Angela Jones is a professor of women, gender, and sexuality studies at Stony Brook University. Their work focuses on African American political thought and protest, feminist theory, gender, race, sexuality, and sex work. Jones has written or edited ten books, including *Sex Work Today*, *Black Lives Matter*, and *Camming*. They live in New York.